## Praise for *The Republic of Imagination*

"Do novels still matter in a world where real-life stories are so dramatic? Azar Nafisi's captivating *Republic of the Imagination* answers this question with a resounding yes. Animated by an electrifying intelligence and a generosity that is nothing short of uplifting, this blend of memoir, biography, and a deep reading of three quintessentially American literary texts makes a successful case for the importance of fiction. Nafisi links the freedom of imagination that unites all readers to the founding ideals of our country and the personal values we claim as Americans. . . . Her prose is breezy and conversational. The reading experience is like having coffee with your favorite brilliant professor, hanging on her every word about a beloved book." —*The Boston Globe*

"Nafisi is a master essayist who sinuously weaves together elements of memoir, criticism, biography, and history; you don't realize how completely these topics interpenetrate each other until you come to the end of a chapter or section, often (at least in my case) with eyes stung by tears. No one writes better or more stirringly about the way books shape a reader's identity, and about the way that talking books with good friends becomes integral to how we understand the books, our friends, and ourselves. . . . She argues: Great fiction actually shows us how to overcome the divisions of race, creed, gender, class, and national origin by guiding us to a fuller understanding of our shared humanity. When you look at it in that light, it's not only American literature that has the power to make a nation out of a miscellaneous conglomeration of outcasts, oddballs, exiles, and vagabonds. Literature itself, by its very nature, unites us. Nothing could be more American than reading it, and nothing more dangerous than forgetting its power." —Laura Miller, *Salon*

"Nafisi presents a passionate and compelling case for the return of the imagination to our nation's esteem. At a time when the liberal arts are increasingly devalued (art and music are cut from school curricula; politicians call for an end to liberal arts funding at public universities; the Common Core suggests that seventy percent of what school kids read be 'informational texts'), Nafisi sounds this warning: A society that dismisses its literature is a society that risks losing its freedom. . . . As a teacher, she often hears the question posed to all English teachers: Why do we have to read this? This book is a thoughtful and brilliant answer to that question."  —*Minneapolis Star-Tribune*

"In works by Mark Twain, Sinclair Lewis, and Carson McCullers, Nafisi finds the essence of the American experience, filtered through narratives not about exceptionalism or fabulous success, but alienation, solitude, and landscape. Her argument is compelling, but more than that, her pleasure in these works is contagious. . . . Will Americans be as willing to take to heart a book that puts us on the spot and asks of us the same serious questions that Nafisi asked of the regime in Tehran? We are more spread out than Iranians, more thoughtless, more susceptible to the marketing of ignorance, perhaps—especially in an election season. But read it. It will do you good."

—Jane Smiley, *The Washington Post*

"Nafisi delves into what it means to be an American through three key books and laces their examination with numerous references to other novels and writers. This book is a priceless gift to readers who revel in literary fiction."  —*Chicago Tribune*

"Nafisi is back, this time exploring novels that speak to her about America (now her home). . . . She reminds us that immigrants bring many things to America, starting with a fresh set of eyes."

—*Vanity Fair*

"Nafisi reflects on her lifelong love for Western literature through an exhilarating exploration of three American classics."

—*O, the Oprah Magazine*

"A stirring book that's part memoir, part literary guide . . . Nafisi makes the passionate case that we need to read as if our quality of life depended on it."

—*More*

"*The Republic of Imagination* is disarming and provocative defense of the grand themes of literature, particularly as they are found in three very American novels. It's designed as a tonic and inspiration for those concerned about the cultural drift away from literature in particular, and a broad education in the humanities in general, in the age of the tweet, the YouTube video, and the Reddit meme. . . . A blend of memoir and polemic sure to arouse the inner English professor in most readers."

—*Santa Cruz Sentinel*

"Literature—no, the world—needs more people like Azar Nafisi. . . . What makes *The Republic of Imagination* so wonderful is Nafisi's irrepressible conviction in the power of fiction to show us who we are. But it's more than that, too. Underneath her literary analysis and her personal reflections, Nafisi's book carries an implicit argument about American values. For her, an American not by birth but by choice, the country she loves was both formed and created by its literature, the myths that both reflect us and instruct us. That's where we belong, she says. And that's what we should look to for guidance and difficult truths." —*The Millions*

"Nafisi ardently elucidates characters, settings and themes, and links each book to larger questions. She also weaves in lively memoirs of friendships crucial to her as a reader, grounding her literary observations in the personal."

—*The Cleveland Plain Dealer*

"In elegant, insightful prose, she blends literary criticism, personal history, and social commentary to create an enticing invitation to inhabit the Republic of Imagination."                    —*Shelf Awareness*

"In *The Republic of Imagination*, the mirror-image of her first book, Nafisi explores the influence fiction has had on life in America, where literature, while not outlawed, is endangered. . . . Her opening tribute to the power of literature segues into revelatory close readings of the three novels she selected, after much deliberation, as salient expressions of the American spirit, specifically our restlessness, 'unending questioning,' and perpetual sense of outsiderness. . . . As a deeply engaged envoy from that republic, Nafisi urges us to read widely and inquisitively."
                    —*Booklist* (starred review)

"A passionate argument for returning to key American novels in order to foster creativity and engagement. . . . Literature, writes Nafisi, is deliciously subversive because it fires the imagination and challenges the status quo. . . . Her literary exegesis lightly moves through her own experiences as a student, teacher, friend, and new citizen. Touching on myriad literary examples, from L. Frank Baum to James Baldwin, her work is both poignant and informative."                    —*Kirkus Reviews*

"We are all citizens of Azar Nafisi's Republic of Imagination. Without imagination there are no dreams, without dreams there is no art, and without art there is nothing. Her words are essential."                    —Marjane Satrapi

"A lovely book: sharp in observation and wholly readable."
                    —Larry McMurtry

PENGUIN BOOKS

# THE REPUBLIC OF IMAGINATION

Azar Nafisi is the author of *Reading Lolita in Tehran,* a long-running #1 *New York Times* bestseller that was embraced by book groups and published in thirty-two languages, and *Things I've Been Silent About: Memories of a Prodigal Daughter*, also a widely translated *New York Times* bestseller. *Reading Lolita* received many awards, including the Nonfiction Book of the Year Award from BookSense, and was a finalist for the PEN/Martha Albrand Award for Memoir. She received the Franklin Creativity Laureate award for *The Republic of Imagination*.

A fellow at Johns Hopkins University's School of Advanced International Studies, Nafisi taught English and American literature for eighteen years in Iran and has now been teaching for fifteen years in America. She appears regularly on radio and TV and speaks to audiences around the world about the vital role of fiction as an antidote to ideology and how the simple act of reading can help us build more meaningful lives. She lives in Washington, D.C., and is now an American citizen.

# The REPUBLIC of IMAGINATION

## A LIFE IN BOOKS

### AZAR NAFISI

Illustrations by Peter Sís

PENGUIN BOOKS

PENGUIN BOOKS
An imprint of Penguin Random House LLC
375 Hudson Street
New York, New York 10014
penguin.com

First published in the United States of America by Viking Penguin,
a member of Penguin Group (USA) LLC, 2014
Published in Penguin Books 2015

Copyright © 2014 by Azar Nafisi
Penguin supports copyright. Copyright fuels creativity, encourages diverse voices, promotes free speech, and creates a vibrant culture. Thank you for buying an authorized edition of this book and for complying with copyright laws by not reproducing, scanning, or distributing any part of it in any form without permission. You are supporting writers and allowing Penguin to continue to publish books for every reader.

Illustrations by Peter Sís. Copyright © 2014 by Peter Sís.

Grateful acknowledgment is made for permission to reprint the following copyrighted works:
"next to of course god america i" Copyright 1926, 1954, © 1991 by the Trustees for the E. E. Cummings Trust. Copyright © 1985 by George James Firmage. From *Complete Poems: 1904–1962* by E. E. Cummings, edited by George J. Firmage. Used by permission of Liveright Publishing Corporation.
Excerpt from "Let America Be America Again" from *The Collected Poems of Langston Hughes*, edited by Arnold Rampersad with David Roessel, Associate Editor. Copyright © 1994 by the Estate of Langston Hughes. Used by permission of Alfred A. Knopf, an imprint of the Knopf Doubleday Publishing Group, a division of Random House LLC and Harold Ober Associates Incorporated. All rights reserved.

THE LIBRARY OF CONGRESS HAS CATALOGED THE HARDCOVER EDITION AS FOLLOWS:
Nafisi, Azar.
The republic of imagination : America in three books / Azar Nafisi.
pages cm
ISBN 978-0-670-02606-7 (hc.)
ISBN 978-0-14-312778-9 (pbk.)
1. Nafisi, Azar. 2. English teachers—United States—Biography. 3. Iranian American women—Biography. 4. American fiction—Appreciation—United States.
5. Books and reading—United States. 6. National characteristics in literature.
7. Twain, Mark, 1835–1910. Adventures of Huckleberry Finn. 8. Lewis, Sinclair, 1885–1951. Babbitt. 9. McCullers, Carson, 1917–1967. Heart is a lonely hunter. I. Title. II. Title: America in three books.
PE64.N34A3 2014
813.009—dc23
2014022287

Printed in the United States of America
1  3  5  7  9  10  8  6  4  2

Designed by Nancy Resnick

Penguin is committed to publishing works of quality and integrity. In that spirit, we are proud to offer this book to our readers; however, the story, the experiences, and the words are the author's alone.

To my family, Bijan, Negar and Dara Naderi
And in memory of my friend Farah Ebrahimi

Let America be America again,
Let it be the dream it used to be.
Let it be the pioneer on the plain
Seeking a home where he himself is free.

. . .

O, yes,
I say it plain,
America was never America to me,
And yet I swear this oath—
America will be!

—Langston Hughes, "Let America Be America Again"

# Contents

# Introduction

A few years ago I was in Seattle signing books at a marvelous independent bookstore called Elliott Bay when I noticed a young man standing by the table, watching me. When the line had dwindled, he finally addressed me. He said he was passing through Seattle, visiting a friend, and he wanted me to know he had lived in Iran until recently. "It's useless," he said, "your talk about books. These people are different from us—they're from another world. They don't care about books and such things. It's not like Iran, where we were crazy enough to xerox hundreds of pages of books like *Madame Bovary* and *A Farewell to Arms*."

Before I had time to think of a response, he went on to tell me about the first time he had been arrested, late at night during one of the usual random car searches by the revolutionary militia. He had been taken into custody with his two friends, more for their insolence than for the contraband tapes found in the car. They were kept for forty-eight hours and then released without explanation, after being fined and flogged. There was no denying that a normal day in the life of a young Iranian is very different from that of most young Americans.

I had heard such stories many times before, but there was something unusual about this young man. He spoke in a casual tone that made what he said all the more poignant, as if he were trying to negate the event by describing it in a nonchalant manner. He said that during the floggings, it was not just the pain but the humiliation that had made him feel for a few moments as if he were leaving his body and becoming a ghost, watching himself being flogged from a distance. "It made it easier," he added, "as a ghost."

"I know what you mean," I said. "It was a good survival technique."

"It still is," he said, with his knowing smile.

By now there was a line again, patiently and politely waiting, and I made a silly remark to the effect that perhaps America was a land of ghosts anyway. He did not react to that. Instead he handed me a Post-it note and said, "I don't have a book. This is for a friend."

I signed my name on that orange Post-it and gingerly handed him my card. "Let's be in touch," I said. He took both the Post-it and the card and of course he never did get in touch. But I never lost track of him completely, because that young man, with his serene smile and his words, revisits me in strange places and seemingly unrelated encounters. He has stayed with me partly because I felt then, as I do now, that I had disappointed him—something was expected of me that was not fulfilled. When I realized he was going to haunt me for the foreseeable future, I decided to give him a name: Ramin, in honor of another young man I had known in Iran who told me about a similar experience. All these ghosts—how do we fulfill our responsibilities toward them?

Thinking over what Ramin had said, I found it intriguing that he had suggested not that Americans did not understand *our* books but that they didn't understand their own. In an oblique way, he had made it seem as if Western literature belonged more to the hankering souls of the Islamic Republic of Iran than to the inhabitants of the land that had given birth to them. How could this be? And yet it is true that people who brave censorship, jail and torture to gain access to books or music or movies or works of art tend to hold the whole enterprise in an entirely different light.

"These people," he had said with his inscrutable smile, "are different from us. They don't care about books and such things." Every once in a while, after a talk, during a book signing or over coffee with an old friend, this point will come up, usually as a question: "Don't you think that literature and books were so important in Iran because there was so much repression there? And don't you think that in a democracy there is no such urgent need for them?"

My impulse now, as then, is to disagree. The majority of people in this country who haunt bookstores, go to readings and book festivals or simply read in the privacy of their homes are not traumatized exiles. Many have seldom left their home-town or state, but does this mean that they do not dream, that they have no fears, that they don't feel pain and anguish and yearn for a life of meaning? Stories are not mere flights of fantasy or instruments of political power and control. They link us to our past, provide us with critical insight into the present and enable us to envision our lives not just as they are but as they should be or might become. Imaginative knowledge is not something you have today and discard tomorrow. It is a way of perceiving the world and relating to it. Primo Levi once said, "I write in order to rejoin the community of mankind." Reading is a private act, but it joins us across continents and time.

But perhaps there is another, more personal reason for my

disagreement with Ramin: I cannot imagine myself feeling at home in a place that is indifferent to what has become my true home, a land with no borders and few restrictions, which I have taken to calling "the Republic of Imagination." I think of it as Nabokov's "somehow, somewhere" or Alice's backyard, a world that runs parallel to the real one, whose occupants need no passport or documentation. The only requirements for entry are an open mind, a restless desire to know and an indefinable urge to escape the mundane.

Long before I made America my home, I inhabited its fiction, its poetry, its music and films. My first fictional journey to America took place when I was about seven, when my English tutor in Tehran introduced me to *The Wonderful Wizard of Oz*. Our main text was a book with simple stories about a pair of American siblings, predictably a girl and a boy. One peculiar feature of these two fiercely clean and well-groomed urchins was that no matter what happened to them, their expressions were fixed in a perpetual smile. I knew their names (was it Jack and Jill? Dick and Jane?), their last names (the Smiths? the Joneses? the Partridges?), where they lived, their daily routine, their school. None of these small and essential details have stayed with me. There was little in their world that made me want to know these smiling, immaculately groomed children any better. The only thing I remember about that book, the one thing that was slightly interesting, was its cover: gritty to the touch, with an image of the two siblings foregrounded on a dark green background.

Near the end of each session, my tutor would close our

exercise book and make her way to the kitchen, from which she would emerge with a glass of cherry sherbet and a worn copy of *The Wonderful Wizard of Oz*. She read only a few pages each time, keeping me in suspense, impatient for our next meeting. Sometimes she would tell me stories from the book or have me read a short passage. I was mesmerized by the orphan Dorothy, who lived in the middle of a flat gray landscape somewhere in the middle of nowhere with her dour and hardworking aunt and uncle and whose only cheerful companion was her dog, Toto. What would happen to her when a cyclone lifted her up with her house, with Toto trapped inside, and landed them in a magical place called Oz? Like millions of children, I impatiently followed Dorothy and her growing group of friends in search of the mighty Wizard of Oz, the only person who could give the Scarecrow a mind, the Tin Man a heart and the Lion courage, and make possible Dorothy's journey home.

Had I been able to formulate my first impressions of the United States, I might have said that there was a place in America called Kansas, where people could find a magic land at the heart of a cyclone. Because that was the first time I had heard the word "cyclone," I can honestly say that *The Wonderful Wizard of Oz* taught me both its real and imagined meanings. Kansas and Omaha were soon followed by a river called Mississippi and many more cities, rivers, forests, lakes and people—the orderly suburban households of Nancy Drew, the frontier towns of *Little House on the Prairie* and stormy plantations of *Gone with the Wind,* the Kentucky farm of *Uncle Tom's Cabin* and the dusty, sultry southern streets of *To Kill a Mockingbird,* where justice was as embattled a notion as it would soon be in Tehran. Later, these were joined by Faulkner's Mississippi, Fitzgerald's St. Paul, Edith Wharton's New York and then Richard Wright's and Ralph Ellison's very different New York, Raymond Chandler's Los Angeles and the southern towns of Flannery O'Connor, Eudora Welty and Carson McCullers. Even now I feel there are so many geographical and fictional terrains left to discover. Perhaps this was the main reason why I could not agree with Ramin: America, to my mind, cannot be separated from its fiction.

When they were young my parents were not wealthy, but all through their lives the one thing they never hesitated to give my brother and me was books. They would entrust friends who traveled abroad with long lists of titles they couldn't find for us in Tehran. As I grew up and wanted the things my friends had, my father would tell me time and again in different ways that I should not focus on things. Possessions, he would say, can't be relied on—they're easier to lose than to obtain. You should value what you can carry with you until the day you die.

One of the first books my father brought home for me to read in English was *Tom and Jerry*. I still remember when he gave me *The Little Prince* and *Charlotte's Web*, which taught me that something as fragile and forgettable as a spider's web could offer up a hidden universe. When I first read *The Adventures of Tom Sawyer*, I was intrigued by Tom's seductive charm but did not really like him—maybe his bag was too full of tricks. In time, books and the world of the imagination they unlocked would become the portable possessions my father had hoped I would always carry with me.

Every Thursday evening, he would take me to a movie house in the fun part of town and I looked forward to our private time together all week. I remember walking hand in hand with him down Naderi Avenue, itself like a scene in an impressionist movie, with its chaotic shops selling nuts, spices, coffee, pirashki and ice cream. Alongside Iranian films, we saw ones starring Ismail Yasin, Fernandel, Norman Wisdom and Vittorio De Sica and the romantic dramas of the Indian superstars Raj Kapoor and Nargis. And, of course, we saw American films: *Spartacus* and *Ivanhoe,* *Mogambo,* Laurel and Hardy, *South Pacific* and one of my favorites, Danny Kaye's *Hans Christian Andersen.* I was not sure what to make of American musicals, where characters suddenly started gyrating in the middle of a meal or while walking down the street, as if overtaken by a mischievous genie, bursting into song only to calm down the next minute and resume eating or talking or kissing. Ever since, I have thought of America as a land of song and dance. From an early age I nurtured an idea of America that I believed in even if I knew that its reality, like any reality, was certain to fall short in some way and disappoint.

My father translated the tales of La Fontaine for my brother and me, doing all of the drawings himself, and wrote simplified versions of the classic Persian poets Ferdowsi and Nezami. More than anything when I think of him, this is what I remember: his sharing of his time and pleasure with me, as if I were his equal, his companion and co-conspirator. There was no moral lesson to be drawn; it was an act of love, but also of respect and trust.

Eleven years have now passed since I met Ramin at that bookstore in Seattle, and since then I have traveled thousands of miles over thirty-two states, conversing mainly about the subject he and I talked about that day. And he did have a point. Between my first book tour, in 2003, and the next one, in 2009, many of the places I visited had undergone a significant transformation or vanished: Cody's in Berkeley, seven branch libraries in Philadelphia, twelve of the fourteen bookstores in Harvard Square, Harry W. Schwartz in Milwaukee and, in my own hometown of Washington, D.C., Olsson's and Chapters. At first it was the independent bookstores, then came the bigger chains: Borders (I wrote *Reading Lolita in Tehran* at the Borders on Eighteenth and L, now a Nordstrom Rack) and, more recently, the Barnes & Noble in Georgetown, replaced by a cavernous Nike store—and the list goes on.

It is not just bookstores and libraries that are disappearing but museums, theaters, performing arts centers, art and music schools—all those places where I felt at home have joined the list of endangered species. *The San Francisco Chronicle,* the *Los Angeles Times,* the *Boston Globe* and my own hometown paper, *The Washington Post,* have all closed their weekend book review sections, leaving books orphaned and stranded, poor cousins to television and the movies. In a sign of the times, the Bloomberg News website recently transferred its book coverage to the Luxury section, alongside yachts, sports clubs and wine, as if to signal that books are an idle indulgence of the super-rich. But if there is one thing that should not be denied to anyone rich or poor it is the opportunity to dream.

Long before that extremely cold, sunny morning in December 2008 when I took a loyalty oath at an Immigration Services office in Fairfax, Virginia, and finally became an American citizen, I had often asked myself, What transforms a country from a place you simply live in or use as a refuge into a home? At what point do "they" become "us?" When you choose to call a place home, you no longer treat it with the episodic curiosity of a guest or a visitor. You are concerned with the good and the bad. Its shortcomings are no longer merely topics of conversation. You wonder, Why are things this way and not another? You want to improve the place, to change it, to make your complaints known. And I had done enough complaining by then to know it was time I became an American citizen.

When the founding fathers conceived of this new nation, they understood that the education of its citizens would be essential to the health of their democratic enterprise. Knowledge was not just a luxury; it was essential. In those days, men who worked for a living were not thought to be fit for public life and a liberal arts education was essential for anyone aspiring to join the political class of the new republic. Over time, politics became a more contentious enterprise, and a new political class was born that had little time for cultivated gentleman farmers who read Cicero and Tacitus for pleasure. Of course, the founding fathers' hope was that one day all Americans, regardless of their wealth or station, would have an opportunity to read Tacitus and Cicero. The point of their new democracy was not just to vote but to make accessible to most citizens what had until then been enjoyed by only a few. Museums, libraries and schools were built to further this democratic ideal. Jefferson, who spent his life collecting books, many of which he donated to the Library of Congress, boasted that America was the only country whose farmers read Homer. "A native of America who cannot read or write," said John Adams, "is as rare an appearance . . . as a Comet or an Earthquake."

I have often wondered whether there is a correlation between the growing lack of respect for ideas and the imagination and the increasing gap between rich and poor in America, reflected not just in the gulf between the salaries of CEOs and their employees but also in the high cost of education, the incredible divide between private and public schools that makes all of the fine speeches by our policy makers—most of whom send their children to private schools anyway, just as they enjoy the benefits and perks of their jobs as servants of the people—all the more insidious and insincere. Those who can afford private schooling need not worry about their children being deprived of art, music and literature in the classroom: they are more sheltered, for now, from the doctrine of efficiency that has been radically refashioning the public school curriculum.

American students, we are told, are falling behind in reading and math; on test after test, they score below most European students (at the level of Lithuania), and the solution, rather than seeking to engage their curiosity, has been testing and more testing—a dry and brittle method that produces lackluster results. And so resources are pulled from the "soft" fields that are not being tested. Music teachers are being fired or not replaced; art classes are quietly dropped from the curriculum; history is simplified and moralized, with little expectation that any facts will be learned or retained; and instead of reading short stories, poems and novels, students are invited to read train schedules and EPA reports whose jargon could put even the most committed environmentalist to sleep.

The crisis besetting America is not just an economic or political crisis; something deeper is wreaking havoc across the land,

use or relevance and should thus be subservient to other, more "useful" fields. In fact, imaginative knowledge *is* pragmatic: it helps shape our attitude to the world and our place in it and influences our capacity to make decisions. Politicians, educators, businessmen—we are all affected by this vision or its lack. If it is true that in a democracy, imagination and ideas are secondary, a sort of luxury, then what is the purpose of life in such a society? What will make its citizens loyal or concerned about their country's well-being, and not just their own selfish pursuits? I would argue that imaginative knowledge is, in a very practical sense, indispensable to the formation of a democratic society, its vision of itself and its future, playing an important role in the preservation of the democratic ideal. At some point this state of affairs became an obsession with me, and I began to think that there must be some connection between the demise of the idealistic or moral aspects of the American dream and its material side. I started collecting newspaper accounts and statistics on the state of the humanities, alongside articles on education, health care, social mobility and all the other component parts of the material aspect of the American dream. Parallel to works of poetry and fiction, biography and history, my office and my home gradually became filled with cuttings from newspapers and magazines and printouts of Internet articles. I began reading blogs on education and books about the Internet or the state of the economy, surprising my friends with references to Joseph Stiglitz and Jaron Lanier. In my notebooks I copied down statements by policy makers and media pundits. My husband routinely complained about the many programs I had taped—PBS, *60 Minutes,* Jon Stewart, Stephen Colbert—leaving little room for him to record his soccer games. Words that I had never paid attention to now made frequent appearances in my notes, alongside phrases like "income inequality" and "upward mobility." After the fashion of my student days, I pasted a few sentences on a piece of paper and wrote underneath, in red ink, "The American dream?" Later, I added: "The way we view fiction is a reflection of how we define ourselves as a nation. Works of the imagination are canaries in the coal mine, the measure by which we can evaluate the health of the rest of society."

And yet I was not unaware that the current state of affairs was partly due to the fact that many of our dreams had been fulfilled. America is far more inclusive now than it was even four decades ago, when I was a student at the University of Oklahoma. Technology has opened many different vistas; it has connected us to the rest of the world in unimaginable ways and created possibilities for education and knowledge on a vast scale. In Iran, it has allowed students and people of all ages who are opposed to theocratic rulers and their oppressive ways to find a voice that cannot be censored, to form a community of people sharing the same ideals and passions.

The current crisis is in some respects the outcome of an inherent contradiction at the heart of American democracy, one that Tocqueville so brilliantly anticipated. America's desire for newness and its complete rejection of ties and traditions lead both to great innovations—a necessary precondition for equality and wealth—and to conformity and complacency, a materialism that invites a complete withdrawal from public and civic spheres and disdain for thought and reflection. This makes it all the more urgent, in this time of transition, to ask new questions, to define not just who we are but who we want to be.

For Ramin, "freedom" and "individual rights" were not mere words. He had experienced their deprivation in concrete terms and had been forced to read books, listen to music, dance and hold hands with his girlfriend in secret, like a criminal, and like a criminal he had been punished—over here we can safely say tortured—when his transgression was discovered. How could he comprehend the careless attitude he found toward ideas and imagination in the country that had produced Emily Dickinson and Ralph Ellison? For him, as for millions of others who have lost a country and a life coming to this land in search of the fugitive freedom they were denied back home, imagination and ideas are not accessories; they are essential to the preservation of identity, to what makes us human beings with a right to life, liberty and the pursuit of happiness. And so while all of these future or would-be citizens will celebrate the generosity of America, its gift of choice and freedom, they are often more anxious than those born here about the potential of squandering what is now so frequently taken for granted.

I could have told Ramin that in many ways totalitarian and democratic societies are one another's distorted mirrors, each reflecting and predicting the other's potentials and pitfalls. In countries such as Iran, imagination is threatened by a regime that desires total control over the lives of its citizens, for whom resistance against the state is not just a political act but an existential one. But what of democracies, where that naked tyranny does not exist? In a totalitarian country, brutality and repression are present in their most blatant forms: torture, arbitrary laws, executions. Ironically, within such societies, the value of imagination, its threat to the existence of the state as well as its importance to the lives of citizens, is quite obvious—which is one reason why people in repressive societies tend to take great risks to read banned books, watch banned films and listen to banned music. For them literature is not simply a path toward literacy or a necessary step in their education. It is a basic need, a way to reclaim an identity confiscated by the state.

Although literacy is the first and essential step toward the kind of engaged citizenry necessary for a thriving democracy, it is not enough, for it is only the means to an end. What we learn and how we learn it is just as important. Regardless of their ideological inclinations, autocracies like those wreaking havoc in Iran, China, Zimbabwe, Saudi Arabia and North Korea are afraid, and justifiably so, of the aftermath of literacy—namely, knowledge, the bite of the forbidden fruit, with its promise of a different kind of power and freedom. That is why the Taliban destroys schools and wishes to murder young teenage girls like Malala who are brave enough to publicly articulate their passionate desire for education and freedom.

The Russian poet Joseph Brodsky memorably quipped that Lenin, Stalin and Mao were all literate people—Stalin was an editor, and Mao wrote "some verse," as he put it. The problem was "their hit list was longer than their reading list." It is not for no reason that totalitarian states view the so-called liberal arts as dangerous and subversive and seek to eliminate them at all costs. They know the dangers of genuine free inquiry. Their fear of democratic societies and their hostility toward them are less a function of military might than of culture, and all the trouble that can bring. And so it is that they ironically appreciate what we increasingly dismiss and devalue.

In a democracy, the arts tend not to threaten the state or to exert such a sense of urgency. You can be seduced into a paralysis of consciousness, a state of intellectual indolence. "The real danger for a writer is not so much the possibility (and often the certainty) of persecution on the part of the state, as it is the possibility of finding oneself mesmerized by the state's features, which, whether monstrous or undergoing changes for the better, are always temporary." Again, Brodsky! This is true of both democracies and totalitarian societies. Every state, including a totalitarian one, has its lures and seductions. The price we pay for succumbing is conformity, a surrender of one's self to the dictates of the group. Fiction is an antidote, a reminder of the power of individual choice. Every novel has at its core a choice by at least one of its protagonists, reminding the reader that she can choose to be her own person, to go against what her parents or society or the state tell her to do and follow the faint but essential beat of her own heart.

What made Brodsky, Nabokov, Czeslaw Milosz and Hannah Arendt—all of whom took refuge in America (Einstein too, for that matter)—resist the totalitarian states of their home countries and reject the empty temptations of Western democracies was essentially one and the same thing: they knew that to negate and betray that inner self was not just a surrender to the tyrant's will but a sort of self-inflicted death. You become a cog in a vast and invisible wheel over which you have no control—Charlie Chaplin's *Modern Times,* only without the comedy.

That inner self is what makes it possible for private individuals to become responsible citizens of their country and of the world, linking their own good to that of their society, becoming active and informed participants. For this they need to know, to pause, to think, to question. It is this quality that we find in so many of America's fictional heroes, from Huckleberry Finn to Mick Kelly in *The Heart Is a Lonely Hunter.* How can we protect ourselves from a culture of manipulation, where tastes and flavors are re-created chemically in laboratories and given to us as natural food, where religion is packaged, televised and tweeted and commercials influence us to such an extent that they dictate not only what we eat, wear, read and want but what and how we dream. We need the pristine beauty of truth as revealed to us in fiction, poetry, music and the arts: we need to retrieve the third eye of the imagination.

If my students in Iran and millions of other brave souls like Malala and Ramin risked their lives in order to preserve their individual integrity, their access to free thought and education, what will we risk to preserve our access to this Republic of Imagination? To say that only repressive regimes require art and imagination is to belittle life itself. It is not pain and brutality that engender the need to write or the desire to read. If we believe in the first three words of the Constitution, "We the People," then we know that the task of defending the right to imagination and free thought is the responsibility not just of writers and publishers but of readers, too. I am reminded of Nabokov's statement that "readers are born free and ought to remain free." We have learned to protest when writers are imprisoned, or when their books are censored and banned. But what about readers? Who will protect us? What if a writer publishes a book and no one is there to read it?

"Until I feared I would lose it, I never loved to read. One does not love breathing." So says Scout in *To Kill a Mockingbird*, expressing the feelings of millions. We must read, and we must continue to read the great subversive books, our own and others'. That right can be guaranteed only by the active participation of every one of us, citizen readers.

As a child, I was too mesmerized by the Land of Oz to pay much attention to that other place where Dorothy lived, her home in Kansas. It is described in some detail: The house is really one large room where Dorothy, Aunt Em, Uncle Henry and Dorothy's dog, Toto, all live. "When Dorothy stood in the doorway and looked around, she could see nothing but the great gray prairie on every side. Not a tree nor a house broke the broad sweep of flat country that reached to the edge of the sky in all directions. The sun had baked the plowed land into a gray mass, with little cracks running through it. Even the grass was not green, for the sun had burned the tops of the long blades until they were the same gray color to be seen everywhere. Once the house had been painted, but the sun blistered the paint and the rains washed it away, and now the house was as dull and gray as everything else."

Dorothy's relatives, the only human beings she comes into contact with, are not merely dull but stern and uncommunicative. Aunt Em, we are told, used to be pretty, but "the sun and wind had changed her, too. They had taken the sparkle from her eyes and left them a sober gray; they had taken the red from her cheeks and lips, and they were gray also." She never smiles. There is a rather frightening description of poor Aunt Em's reaction to Dorothy when she first arrives after her mother and father have died: "Aunt Em had been so startled by the child's laughter that she would scream and press her hand upon her heart whenever Dorothy's merry voice reached her ears; and she still looked at the little girl with wonder that she could find anything to laugh at." Uncle Henry, "stern and solemn" is also gray and never laughs. He works from morning to night and "did not know what joy was."

Only Toto, the merry little black dog, "saved her from growing as gray as her other surroundings." And yet Dorothy never complains. She never wants to leave that dull farm in Kansas. Dorothy is no Alice, running after a white rabbit or its magical equivalent. She is not bored with her seemingly boring life. She is no Little Prince roaming the earth and acquiring wisdom—nor is she the mischievous wooden doll Pinocchio, who has to climb into the jaws of a whale in order to become human. She is a little girl thrown into the magic world of Oz by accident, because that cyclone uprooted her as she was going about her business, like any other girl her age.

Dorothy has an unwavering determination to return home. Nothing is more important to her than Kansas and her stern relatives' lonely house in the middle of nowhere. When the Scarecrow says to her, "I cannot understand why you should wish to leave this beautiful country and go back to the dry, gray place you call Kansas," she responds, "That is because you have no brains." And then she goes on to explain, "No matter how dreary and gray our homes are, we people of flesh and blood would rather live there than in any other country, be it ever so beautiful. There is no place like home."

There have been many interpretations of this story offered up over the years. Some have described it as an allegory of the political and economic circumstances of its times (it was published in 1900) or a reflection of its author's support of the Populist Party and of his ideas on monetary reform. The yellow brick road leading to Oz has been compared with the gold standard, and the Emerald City to the land of greenbacks and fake ideals, while Dorothy's silver slippers (ruby red in the film) represent the Populists' support for the use of free silver instead of gold. The famous Metro-Goldwyn-Mayer Technicolor talkie, made in the thirties, has likewise been interpreted in light of its times (in this case the Great Depression). All of this is interesting, and some of it does ring true—as with many stories, one of the pleasures of *The Wonderful Wizard of Oz* is its many levels of allusion and meaning. But we would have forgotten it long ago if not for its magic. That magic is at the heart of the story, a minor miracle that has nothing to do with political allegories. It is not just Dorothy's miraculous uprooting and transportation to the Land of Oz; it is what greets her when she comes home. Dorothy returns to Kansas safely, but her home has changed in essential, if seemingly imperceptible ways. We can sense it in Aunt Em's transformed attitude—she has been watering the cabbages when she sees Dorothy running toward her. "'My darling child!' she cried, folding the little girl in her arms and covering her face with kisses."

Dorothy's lesson—and it is the lesson of every great story—is that the land of make-believe, that wonderland, the magical Oz, is not far away; it is, in fact, in our backyard, accessible if only we have the eyes to see it and the will to seek it. Dorothy, Alice, Hansel and Gretel all return home, but they will never be the same, because they have learned to look at the world through the alternative eyes of the imagination. That essential transformation is a change of heart. In a depersonalized and atomized environment, the heart preserves our essential humanity and makes possible our connection and communication with the rest of the world. We the readers are like Dorothy or Alice: we step into this magical world in order to return and retell the story through our own eyes, thus giving new meaning to the story as well as to our lives. This is the reason we need readers—not just in our academies but everywhere, in every town, in every walk of life. We need readers to give a new spin to the experience we call life.

It is interesting that Dorothy's time in the Land of Oz is not presented as a dream—the reader is left to draw her own conclusions as to whether these things really happened. Perhaps this blurring of the lines between everyday reality and dreams is in fact the true magic of Dorothy's story: the fact that for her, the most enchanted place is her humble home in all its bare simplicity.

I first discovered Dorothy's story many decades ago in Tehran, in a home that no longer exists, and I have returned to it in my new home of Washington, D.C. My physical homes have changed, but the story remains, and so does its magic. What would life be like without that wonderland in our backyard? Like most children, I had my own desire for elsewhere, for a secret hiding place that would take me to a parallel world. And, like most children, I differentiated between my real and imagined worlds—instinctively I knew that at some point I would have to return to real life, and that was okay, so long as I had my portable world of the imagination with me. Somehow the stories, the travels to Oz and to Wonderland, with Pinocchio into the stomach of the whale, and later to that remote planet where the Little Prince watered that one flower—his self-centered rose—made me more willing to go through the routines of life. At times I feel as if the Land of Oz, along with Alice's Wonderland and Scheherazade's room, is fading and receding the way light recedes into darkness. We all know how easy it is to lose our real homes. What will we do in the absence of this most enduring of all homes, this Republic of Imagination?

Life after a totalitarian revolution is not unlike a day after a cyclone. The air may be crisp and brilliant, but there is plenty of debris around to remind us of what is missing. You have to ask yourself, Where should I start to pick up the pieces? In a country as ancient as Iran, telling stories has been a time-tested way of resisting political, social and cultural invasion. Our stories and myths became our home, creating a sense of continuity with a past that had been so consistently plundered and obliterated. For many of us, lighting out was the only way to survive; it was not always possible or desirable in a physical sense, but we could escape through the realm of imagination and ideas.

Home! How deceptive and fragile that enticing concept can be. For an immigrant, any new country is always conceived either negatively or positively in light of the country left behind. For me, my new home was always firmly rooted in its fictional landscapes. All I had left from my beloved Iran was the portable world of memories and literature that my father had taught me to appreciate. I knew when I left (and nothing has happened since to change this view) that it was the only world upon which I could safely rely.

It was in Iran that I discovered the close relationship between individual rights and the right to free expression, the indispensability of a democratic imagination. My students might have been opposed to (with some justification) or ignorant of America's policies, but they celebrated its music, its films and its literature. It seems right to me that the fiction of one country should kindle one's understanding of another—not the "other" captured and domesticated by certain academic theorists and guardians of political correctness but that living, breathing other that Atticus alludes to in *To Kill a Mockingbird* when he says, "You never really understand a person until you consider things from his point of view . . . until you climb inside of his skin and walk around in it."

Difference is always celebrated in literature, but the cult of difference can become dangerous when it is not accompanied by that shock of recognition and the realization of how alike we are—that, despite our differences, our hearts beat to the same rhythms and we are all capable of the best and the worst. It is this realization of our shared humanity that makes it possible for people to make their home in another country. Exile always entails a sense of loss. Home is not home anymore, but in time a different place offers up the potential for new memories and relationships.

When I left Iran for good and came to America with my family in 1997, I had so much to be grateful for. My husband,

Bijan, found a job working as a civil engineer, and I enrolled my children in the local public school. We bought a house, and I was offered a job teaching at the School of Advanced International Studies at Johns Hopkins University. At first I reveled in my newfound freedom: at last, I could craft my own curriculum without having to worry that the dean would call me in if my hair slipped out from underneath my headscarf, or for my unorthodox and casual behavior toward my students, or the unsavory books I taught. But nothing is as simple as that—there were new challenges and new ideologies as fiercely and rigidly defended as any in Iran. Like all ideologies, the one I now found myself confronting depended on a simplification of reality and a generalization of concepts—looking to complacent, ready-made answers and inviting little self-questioning. What had started as a serious theoretical questioning of authority had by now become an easy formula, applied to both literature and reality. From this perspective, nothing that pertained to old norm and judgments would be tolerated. Classic texts were now suspect, symbols of scorned elitist orthodoxy. Eighteen years had passed since I had finished my doctorate in America, and many of the English and American writers I had taught in Iran had not fared well in my absence. Here too they had been tried and judged and found wanting.

Living under the Islamic regime's black-and-white system, my views had become more complex and nuanced. I drew closer to the fiction I so loved, in which everyone was granted a voice, even the villain. Students who disagreed with my political views—and who, being in a place of power, could have denounced me because of my unruly habit of voicing those views—would come to my office to talk about Bellow or Nabokov, Ibsen or the Islamic Republic speaking with insight and passion about Virginia Woolf? Does that detract from her loyalty to her own culture, or does it reveal her confidence in herself and her ability to transcend the proximate circumstances of her life and upbringing?

I wrote *Reading Lolita* because I wanted people to know that Iranians, real Iranians, are not some exotic other, a product of "their culture," but that we too are people, like the rest of you. Some of my students were religious and some were not; some were orthodox Muslims and some were secular Muslims; some were Baha'i or Zoroastrian, and there were some who hated religion and some who died for that belief—while some never thought of religion at all. I wanted to show the world that the Iranian youth, the students I was in close contact with for eighteen years, when deprived of access to the world, communicated with it through its golden ambassadors, the very best it could offer: its poets and novelists, playwrights, musicians and filmmakers.

After the success of *Reading Lolita,* I was invited to speak to groups all across the United States, in red states and blue, big cities and small. At first the invitations were mostly from colleges, and then book festivals, museums and civic associations, and a wide variety of different high schools like City Honors School in Buffalo, Thomas Jefferson High School in Virginia, Spence and Choate and the Bronx Academy, where through the enthusiastic efforts of one teacher, Amy Matthusen, each year for the past three years I have held a question–and–answer session with her class. In San Antonio, a young woman told me that she was an elementary school teacher and that the art class had recently been dropped and her students shared a music teacher with another school. She herself worked as a part-time librarian to make ends meet. She said this

Dorothy simply responds, "I am Dorothy, the Small and Meek." Dorothy and her companions discover in the end that the myth of Oz's power is as much of a sham as their belief in their own weakness, and that they, led by Dorothy, can do what Oz was powerless to achieve: destroy the Wicked Witch and liberate the frightened citizens—a myth worthy of a people who had defeated a mighty empire in search of their own independence.

Dorothy is one in a long line of American heroines and heroes, small and meek, who somehow manage to appear greater than their mighty opponents. This quality is usually revealed once the protagonists are separated from their actual homes and surroundings. Huckleberry Finn is perhaps the most memorable of those humble citizens of the imaginary America who stand up to forces great and terrible, but Huck refuses to return home, thus foreshadowing the destinies and shaping the choices of so many other fictional American characters who either leave home, never to return, or long to do so. These homeless protagonists of American fiction become the true guardians of what is best in American individualism, never identifying happiness with wealth or power. Perhaps in no other fiction, in fact, is materialism so frowned upon, or defined as the root of so many evils—an ironic but salutary reminder for a country so blatantly devoted to the pursuit of wealth and power.

I have always been drawn to America's vagrant nature, so well portrayed and celebrated in its best works of fiction. I believe that many of those who, like my family and me, migrated to America from all over the world can feel at home in it because it allows us both to belong and to be outsiders. It somehow encourages our vagabond self—befitting a nation that started its life by deliberately choosing to become an orphan. No fictional characters are quite so suspicious of home as those wandering the landscape of American fiction. These homeless characters become disturbing and dangerous, loitering with intent on the margins of our consciousness.

All writers and poets are strangers, or pariahs, as Hannah Arendt chose to call them. They look at the world through the eyes of the outsider, but only American writers turn this attribute into a national characteristic. "All men are lonely," wrote Carson McCullers, and then she added, "But sometimes it seems to me that we Americans are the loneliest of all. Our hunger for foreign places and new ways has been with us almost like a national disease. Our literature is stamped with a quality of longing and unrest, and our writers have been great wanderers. Poe turned inward to discover an eerie and glowing world of his own. Whitman, that noblest of vagabonds, saw life as a broad open road. Henry James abandoned his own adolescent country for England and the airy decadence of nineteenth-century drawing-rooms. Melville sent out his Captain Ahab to self-destruction in the mad sailing for the great white whale. And Wolfe and Crane—they wandered for a lifetime, and I am not sure they knew themselves just what it was they sought."

McCullers wrote this piece to advise American writers to come back home, to turn inward, as she put it, but the fact is that even in turning inward, we need to reflect on this constant restlessness, this unending questioning, this battle between the desire for prosperity, status and success and the urge to walk away from it all, to be wary of complacency—in short, to perform the miracle of the small vagabond Huck, who followed his heart as he floated on a raft down the Mississippi. "This singular emotion, the nostalgia that has been so much a part of our national character, must be converted to good use," McCullers continued. "What our seekers have sought for we must find. . . . America is youthful, but it can not always be young. Like an adolescent who must part with his broken family, America feels now the shock of transition. But a new and serene maturity will come if it is worked for. We must make a new declaration of independence, a spiritual rather than a political one this time. . . . We must now be homesick for our own familiar land, this land that is worthy of our nostalgia." McCullers herself knew that this urge for wandering, for the always new, was what kept America America, what gave it vitality. Meek and small characters, orphans, outcasts—not just because of their race, class or gender but because of what Elizabeth Cady Stanton so eloquently defined as their solitariness—abound in the vast and capacious terrain of American fiction. One can argue that they represent the myth of American rebellion. There is some truth in that, but it has been a long time since America moved from the margins to the center of power, with the privileges of wealth replacing those of birth—a long time since George Washington and Benjamin Franklin refused wages because they felt they were public servants and should be immune from the temptations and corruption of money.

We need to remember that, despite the prevalent attitude today that arrogantly defines success as money, the real heroes of this nation's fictional landscape are vagrants, marginal and subversive, from Melville's Bartleby, the scrivener whose mantra is "I would prefer not to," to the heroines of Henry James and Edith Wharton, Ralph Ellison's Invisible Man, Zora Neale Hurston's Janie, Bellow's Herzog, Philip Roth's Sabbath or Omar Little of *The Wire,* who reminds us of the importance of a code of honor. All seek integrity and listen to their hearts' dictates, cautioning us against our willingness to betray the American dream when it is, as Fitzgerald put it, besmirched with the "foul dust that floats in the wake" of our dreams.

The thought of writing this book first came to me when I was finishing the last chapter of *Reading Lolita in Tehran*. At the time, I thought of calling it *Becoming an American*. I did not want my readers to believe that the books we read were meaningful simply because they were illicit and frowned upon by the moral guardians in Iran. I wanted them to know how vital they were in America, too, as the freedom that so many fictional characters lay claim to is not political but moral, a freedom to turn their back on society and what is expected of them and to forge their own lonely path. I have chosen to focus on three novels, starting with *The Adventures of Huckleberry Finn* in part because I was fascinated by the idea that Huck, who rejected the concept of roots and tradition, became a parent to so many homeless protagonists of American fiction. Why these three books? The choice was not easy. When I first presented an outline to my publisher, I struggled to slim down the list of books I would discuss to twenty-four. But before long I found Huck dominating the story, just as Lolita had before. I think of this book as the story of Huck Finn's America, and of his fictional progenies. I chose to focus on two of those—Sinclair Lewis's *Babbitt*, featuring an anti-Huck who craves status and acceptance and all of the outward signs of material success, and Carson McCullers's *The Heart Is a Lonely Hunter*, with its lonely band of listless misfits longing to connect, helpless in a world built on longing but not its fulfillment.

I could have chosen dozens more—Melville, Hemingway, Zora Neale Hurston, Dawn Powell, Nathanael West and others all clamored for their own chapters and will have to await another book. I wanted to end before the 1960s because what followed in their wake was a new era, in terms of both social and political realities and the direction of American fiction, and needed a different context. I felt that James Baldwin, as a writer and civil rights activist, was most suited to mark the termination of what I think of as the classical period of American fiction and the beginning of a new epoch. When I made the decision to devote my epilogue to Baldwin, I was not aware of the extent to which he would come to represent to me the truth of the present, its crises and my hope for its future.

Over the course of my readings, reflections and recollections I came to see associations between Baldwin and Twain, an affinity that Baldwin had never acknowledged or even hinted at, one that existed not by choice but as a testament to other affinities unknown and maybe even unwanted. Because in life and writing James Baldwin was a descendant of the "infinitely shaded and exquisite mongrel" that Twain once claimed kinship with.

From the moment Plato's philosopher king threw the poet out of his Republic, we knew that imagination was dangerous to authority and that the alternative eye of the poet would always be deviant and unpredictable, always subverting authority and captivating souls. It is with this idea in mind that I wrote this book at the dawn of a new century, which has begun with doubts and anxieties and a crisis that goes far beyond the immediate economic one. It is written not out of despair but out of hope, by which I mean not a simple giddy optimism but the belief that once you know what is right and what matters, you can get there with enough determination. My experiences in Iran gave me a definition of hope that is very different from simple optimism. What I have in mind is most closely captured by Václav Havel, who said, "Hope is a state of mind, not of the world. Hope, in this deep and powerful sense, is not the same as joy that things are going well, or willingness to invest in enterprises that are obviously heading for success, but rather an ability to work for something because it is good."

I believe all great art and literature, all great deeds of humanity, rely on this fragile and most enduring hope. One function of art is to be a witness and historian of man's endurance, to provide "conclusive evidence" that we have lived. The central theme of the play *Antigone,* written in 441 B.C., about a young woman's dilemma as she finds herself caught between the pressures of obeying the dictates of personal honor and burying her brother, who rebelled against the kingdom, or of heeding a more public notion of justice and obeying the law of the king, her uncle, by letting his corpse rot unburied, resurfaces in various guises today even in our most popular story forms, in episodes of *Boston Legal* and *White Collar.* If we need fiction today, it is not because we need to escape from reality; it is because we need to return to it with eyes that are refreshed, or, as Tolstoy would have it, "clean-washed."

Six years ago, I swore a public oath in a bland government office building, but I became an American citizen long before that, when I first began to trace my imaginary map of America, beginning with Dorothy's Kansas and the desiccated farmland of the Ingalls sisters. That America is a country of immigrants is a truism, and even now it remains the case—it is populated by people from many parts of the globe who have brought with them the restless ghosts of their original homelands, making homelessness an integral part of American identity. More than any other country, America has become a symbol of exile and displacement, of choosing a home, as opposed to being born in it.

The first immigrants and their descendants devastated the homes of this new land's original occupants, uprooting some while enslaving others. But their saving grace was the invention of a dream. There was something in that dream, in the imagination of America's founders and the humanistic spirit they embodied, that made it possible for later generations to question and subvert the conditions under which they wrote their founding documents, the Constitution and the Declaration of Independence, so that later men and women like Frederick Douglass, Abraham Lincoln, Elizabeth Cady Stanton, Susan B. Anthony, Martin Luther King Jr. and others would make those words their own, insisting on new freedoms and reminding us, as the historian Gordon Wood so eloquently put it, that "it is not suffrage that gives life to democracy, it is our democratic society that gives life to suffrage." This, for me, is the intersection where the real America meets the imaginary one. This is how I explained my view of America to my children. If you believe your country was founded on the actualization of a dream, then an obvious and essential question arises: How can you dream without imagination?

For homelessness and despair, for the injustices and suffering imposed on us by the fickleness of life and the absoluteness of death, imagination has no cure. But it finds a voice that both registers and resists such injustice, evidenced by the fact that we do not accept things as they are. So much of who we are, no matter where we live, depends on how we imagine ourselves to be. So much of the home we live in is defined by that other world in our backyard, be it Dorothy's Oz or Alice's Wonderland or Scheherazade's room, to which we have to travel in order to see ourselves and others more clearly.

Stories endure—they have been with us since the dawn of history—but they need to be refreshed and retold in every generation through the eyes and experiences of new readers sharing a common space that knows no boundaries of politics or religion, ethnicity or gender—a Republic of Imagination, that most democratic republic of all. For every writer deprived of the freedom of speech, millions of readers are also deprived of the freedom to read what they might have told us. That is why the voice of a poet who endured and resisted tyranny should be the voice of conscience, reminding us of what is essential: "Since there are no laws that can protect us from ourselves, no criminal code is capable of preventing a true crime against literature," Joseph Brodsky said in his Nobel Prize acceptance speech. "Though we can condemn the material suppression of literature—the persecution of writers, acts of censorship, the burning of books—we are powerless when it comes to its worst violation: that of not reading the books. For that crime, a person pays with his whole life; if the offender is a nation, it pays with its history."

My conversation with Ramin and subsequent conversations over the years with those who have felt homeless in their own home—those who have carried their ghosts with them while in some way believing in and relying upon that other home, the portable one—inspired the writing of this book. Later my thoughts were reshaped by conversations with other readers, those I like to call intimate strangers, the ones who create an invisible, almost conspiratorial society, bound by the books they read. This book is for them. My hope is that they will find a home in its pages.

# PART I

# *HUCK*

The books that the world calls immoral are books that show its own shame.

—Oscar Wilde, *The Picture of Dorian Gray*

I muse upon my country's ills—
The tempest bursting from the waste of Time
On the world's fairest hope linked with man's foulest crime.

—Herman Melville, "Misgivings"

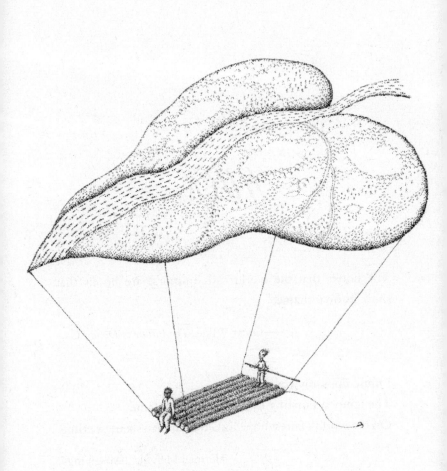

# 1

"'Huck Finn's Progenies'" is not a good subtitle for your book. 'Children' would be better, but not much. Find something easier on the ear," Farah said with finality. "And now, tell me all about it."

Farah was my best friend from childhood. She always wanted to know what I was up to, and she wouldn't stop needling me about my book. "Tell me all about it," she would say, "from start to finish." I told her it was impossible, that I seldom if ever showed my writing to anyone other than my editor. And besides, how could I tell her all about a book I had not yet written? She'd just have to wait.

"I can't afford to wait," she said with a smile. "I might not be around to read it."

I couldn't offer the usual platitudes—"Of course you'll be around. You have beaten the cancer so far; you will beat it this time, too." Because we both knew this time was different.

She kept smiling, with no trace of self-pity or pain, just pure mischief—she had me where she wanted me. It was a typical Farah gesture, letting on that she was manipulating you into doing what she wanted, making you complicit in a conspiracy against yourself. This was what made it possible for her to transcend and resist what her daughter would later call the "hurdles" in her life. Farah herself once good-naturedly complained that the gods above must have known her tolerance for hardship, because they kept "blessing" her with all manner of nightmares. She had survived a revolution and a war, had been smuggled across the border from Iran into Turkey, seven months' pregnant, her two-and-half-year-old daughter in tow while her husband was being tortured in a Tehran jail—to name just one example among many.

"I want to know," I said, "just how low you will stoop."

Ignoring me, she said, "And don't forget I am an editor. Pretend I am *your* editor."

She was a senior editor at the International Monetary Fund, not exactly the kind of editor I had in mind. But Farah and I had a long history.

We were driving back to Georgetown from Chevy Chase, where we had spent over two hours at a Borders bookstore that no longer exists with Farah's older sister, Mahnaz, jumping from heated discussions of the presidential race in America (this was 2008, and despite Obama's victory in the primaries, we were still debating the comparative merits of Obama and Clinton) to gossip, shopping, the Iranian government's machinations and my upcoming interview for U.S. citizenship. Because after eleven years in Washington, I had finally applied to become an American citizen. Farah took this as a cue to proselytize for her latest obsession, a passionate enchantment with U.S. history.

Before she became too ill to drive, the three of us would meet regularly in bookstores dotted around Georgetown and Dupont Circle, or at the Cheesecake Factory in Chevy Chase, or Leopold's in Cady's Alley, to talk and talk. We would be giddy with excitement, too impatient to let one another finish our sentences, childishly interrupting with a chaos of allusions and shortcuts understandable only to ourselves. Even at the hairdresser (because we three would meet there, too, when one of us needed a haircut or a blow-dry), we would be so raucous that soon the polite and considerate owner relegated us to a back room, serving us cappuccinos while we tried in vain to keep our voices down.

Farah and Mahnaz had both majored in English literature—rare for Iranians even now, and more so then—and our discussions were always peppered with exchanges about books. We were related, but blood alone was not responsible for this intimacy. Long before I was called into a drab office at Immigration Services to answer a few questions and take an oath as a newly minted American citizen, we shared the complicity of being citizens of two countries, straddling two such different worlds. We belonged to two languages, simultaneously reminding us of the country we had left behind and the one we had chosen to make our new home. More than anything else, it was that ready access to two languages, to their poetry and fiction, to their cultures, vague as that term might seem, that provided us with a temporary feeling of stability.

I have always believed it was that initial sense of kinship, the sharing of the same dreams and our love of literature, that sustained our friendship—that led us to take that car ride and so many others like it, when Farah and I would often get so involved in conversation that we would inevitably lose our way, miss an exit on Rockville Pike and almost always be late for our meetings with Mahnaz, who sat like patience on a monument, trying to find something funny in our schoolgirl excuses and suppressed giggles.

"You must bring more U.S. history in your new book, the

way you did with Iran in *Reading Lolita,*" Farah said, turning toward me instead of keeping her eye on the road. "How else can you write about American fiction?"

Farah was never shy about telling me what to do. I started to complain that when I once mentioned Tocqueville in a graduate seminar, one of my students had raised her hand and asked, "Who is Tocqueville?"

"Can you believe it?" I said, with mounting indignation. "At a school for international studies, for heaven's sake!" I would soon discover that most of the class did not know about the Frenchman who had written *Democracy in America.* "I bet quite a few of my students in Iran would at least have heard of him."

"All the more reason," Farah said, seemingly unperturbed, "why you should read Joseph J. Ellis's *Founding Brothers.*"

Two years later, I would accompany Mahnaz to Farah's bedroom to choose a keepsake from a pile of books randomly stacked against the wall, like a group of orphaned children waiting for a new parent. I did not hesitate in picking *Founding Brothers.* I could not think of any book that reminded me more of the intimately joyous times Farah and I spent together—any book, that is, other than *The Adventures of Huckleberry Finn.*

It so happened that Farah's prediction came true; she didn't get a chance to read my book. Five years after that conversation, I had not yet finished writing it. The main hurdle was the chapter we talked so much about, the one on Huck Finn. It took me more than two years to write it, and then I set it aside for another year because it didn't feel right—too much analysis, too little heart. Looking over my notes in frustration, I kept coming across my conversations with Farah. Then it hit me that she had left me the key to the chapter in our exchanges, when Huck became so central to our musings about becoming American, about the meaning of exile and home. Farah had made peace with what it meant to live with a divided heart.

I had not thought seriously of writing about those conversations until I received an e-mail from Farah's daughter in response to my inquiry about how a dog Farah had adopted in the last months of her life had come to be called Huck. "There was something about Huck Finn in the air in our house that last year," Neda wrote back. "Mom started talking about your project and was entranced. Imagination and the journey-quest is at the heart of every life well-lived. Sometime in the months before she died, she asked me to get a book on tape for her and download it to her iPod. I borrowed *Huck Finn* from the library and put it on her iPod and while she was listening to it with earbuds, I was listening to it at work during the long, long hours of watching Congress grind to a halt. And I still haven't been able to return the original. Yes, I am effectively a thief."

Huck came to mean more to Farah as she sorted through her memories and sought to tell herself and her daughter the story of her own journey—her "adventure," if that is the right word for all manner of bad luck. In fiction, every treachery and setback appears to serve some end: the characters learn and grow and come into their own. In life, it is not always clear that the hijacking of our plans is quite so provident or benign.

When Farah and I met in those last eighteen months of her life, we seldom talked about anything other than *Huck Finn*—like two teenage best friends in love with the same elusive boy. Our conversations took place in different parts of Washington, usually somewhere between Foggy Bottom (my home) and Georgetown (hers), at her house or in various coffee shops and restaurants, and sometimes, when she felt well, on walks around the waterfront or along the canal. In every one of these places, our conversations would take us to familiar landscapes as sudden windows opened up, framing vistas of our past lives. So many things were happening then—two wars halfheartedly and desultorily waged, the economy going from bad to worse, heated election campaigns, and new hopes forming the seeds of new disillusionment both in Iran and in the United States. Farah was elated at the prospect of Obama and gave dinners and talks that she would rope me into, mobilizing everyone she knew between bouts of chemotherapy and radiation. She was in and out of the hospital for ever more painful operations, trying new treatments, until finally there was no treatment and I would find her bicycling to the clinic to get vitamin C shots, and then she had a new dog, small and mischievous—Huck.

Throughout that dreadful year, the original Huck was our guide, our inspiration, the thorn in our side who reminded us to be true to ourselves and who goaded us when we became too complacent, too conventional in our preoccupations, whenever we seemed too comfortable with our lot. He gave us vital clues as to the kind of Americans we wanted to be. He reminded us— and this was something I kept coming back to—that at their best, American heroes are wary of being overcivilized, that they carve out their own path and look to their heart for what is right and just. How far we seemed to be, I would confide complicitly to Farah, from that America, the one we had both discovered so many years ago when we first read *Huckleberry Finn*.

structured like a story: over a period of four decades, Farah and I would meet, separate and reconnect at crucial points in our lives in Iran and America. Looking over the computer file I've named Farah, I notice how often during our talks we would move from Huck to the startling parallels in our own lives, our rediscovery of each other at different stages, moving to the beat of the political and social upheavals in our country of birth, Iran, and our adopted country—or, rather, the one that adopted us—America. It was as if we were fated to meet every decade or so and to take it from there: Tehran, Chicago, Oklahoma City, Tehran, Washington, D.C. Who knew that Tehran would someday be part of that irretrievable landscape to which Farah herself has now migrated? She once remarked that it was eerie, the way our relationship seemed to be based on a "harmless" version of Edgar Allan Poe's "William Wilson." "Only you are not my evil double," she said, "but a double." We were each other's clarifying shadows, or distorted mirrors, I thought.

Our first separation came when, at ten, she left Iran to live with her strikingly beautiful mother, Ferdows, who had divorced her handsome and wayward husband, leaving an opulent life in Iran to start a new one in the United States, with barely a cent to her name. Why did she leave? Farah, Mahnaz and I would periodically return to this question, without ever agreeing on a satisfactory answer. People talked about Ferdows when she left. "Why couldn't she tolerate a little fickleness?" they would ask. "Don't all men have a roving eye? But not all men are as kindhearted and generous as Majid Khan!" ("My father," Farah later said, "was a distant figure with whom there was little contact and no conversation. My mother moved about in beautiful robes, smelling of powder and perfume, a bundle of keys to various storage trunks and closets tinkling in her pocket.")

My mother admired Farah's mother and always spoke of her with respect tinged with envy. According to one persistent family rumor, my mother was infatuated with Ferdows's husband, but I think the real reason for her fascination was that she instinctively grasped Ferdows's audacity and courage. She had taken the kind of step my mother would have liked to and never had, leaving behind security, comfort, beloved friends. For a woman who had never worked in her life, who had always had servants and cooks to take care of the household, to begin a new life with little money, waitressing at tables in an alien country and working her way up—that was courage, something all of her children, including Farah's brother, Hamid, the beloved but unacknowledged male in the family, inherited.

The women in that family all turned out to be exceptional and audacious, each in her own headstrong and independent way. The grandmother chose to become a Baha'i, a banned sect, inviting all manner of persecution, and later Mahnaz became a women's rights activist and the first minister for women's affairs in the shah's government, and had the honor of being on the Islamic Republic's blacklist of people who were to be executed for "warring with God" and "spreading prostitution." (Later, in exile, when the rulers of the Islamic Republic tried to silence her, Mahnaz continued in the same vein, as an innovative and dedicated champion of women's rights.) Farah, the youngest, the baby of the family, never did appreciate her own courage, her stamina, in the face not just of human cruelties but of those more inevitable and immutable ones.

We shared a family and a history and lived parallel lives, but perhaps equally important we shared a passion for American literature. Farah was the first and most exalted citizen of my Republic of Imagination. While I pined and opined, she drafted our constitution, wrote its bylaws and documented its history. I knew I would be its scribe, but she goaded and prodded me to write and challenged me when I grew lazy or complacent. I knew I wanted to write about Huck, to capture what he could teach us, at a time of reality TV and phony bombastic patriotism, about a more authentic American ideal. Farah reminded me that what Huck stood for, what he embodied, was a set of values grounded in history. We still read Huck today—American students will come across him again and again—but are we really listening to what he has to say? When I asked my students in Washington to read him, some would look at me quizzically, as if to say, "Why Huck? What can he possibly have to teach us?"

# 3

Who says fantasy is not potent? All through the seventies, during our student years, Farah and I had lived mainly in an imaginary America—more Tom Sawyer than Huck, we imposed our own fantasies on Iran as well as America. Like many of my age, I participated in various political groups in a decade that saw the blossoming of the civil rights and women's movements and that ended abruptly for me in 1979 with the Islamic revolution in Iran. Passionate times tend to produce a dangerous smugness as the dizzying satisfaction of helping to put the world aright takes over the urge that motivated the protest in the first place.

In those days, I felt I was living in two different Americas: the America of the Vietnam War and the civil rights and women's rights movements, of Nixon and Watergate, and the neighboring country I had discovered through its fiction, poetry, film, art and music: John Coltrane, Miles Davis, Janis Joplin, Judy Collins, Edward Hopper, the Harlem Renaissance, the Marx Brothers, Howard Hawks, Woody Allen, Herman Melville, Flannery O'Connor, William Faulkner, Ralph Ellison, Edith Wharton, F. Scott Fitzgerald, Nathanael West, Raymond Chandler, Emily Dickinson, Elizabeth Bishop, William Carlos Williams, Sylvia Plath, E. E. Cummings. These were my heroes, the founding parents of the America I felt I knew and belonged to. Reality was confusing and polarized, while fiction was complex, paradoxical and illuminating: that whole vast continent of art and the imagination gave weight and substance to the urgent, emotional, simplified world of protests and demonstrations.

We were too young to have participated in the civil rights movement that had defined the sixties, that of Martin Luther King Jr. and James Baldwin. Ours was a different era, of the Black Panthers, Eldridge Cleaver and Stokely Carmichael: more impatient, more violent, more ideological and more fantasy-oriented. I participated in the protests—we all did—but my heart was in that other America, the one I discovered through its fiction and poetry.

I had not seen Farah for more than a decade when suddenly we were at the same convention in Chicago in 1976, having coffee and discussing the speech I was going to give. We belonged to opposing factions in the Confederation of Iranian Students, and since her group held the leadership posts, she was responsible for checking my speech, making sure I covered all the "right positions" and did not stray too far from the party line. Our meeting that day was cordial, even affectionate, although we did not talk about personal matters, about what had happened to us since we had last said goodbye in Tehran so many years ago. For Farah the Iranian student movement was her whole life; it became a home, a shelter, in a way it never was for me.

What had happened between Farah's departure for the United States, at the age of ten, and our meeting in Chicago to create this distance between us? In an account of her life based on many hours of taped interviews—which her sister, Mahnaz, published in her book *Women in Exile* in 1994—Farah mentions how lonely she was in high school in the States. "I was never quite thin enough, my hair never straight enough, my outlook never close enough to the prevailing standards, and the standards, even when they stressed nonconformity, were strictly observed." So, she says, "I played the piano, listened to classical music, read Victorian novels, and felt out of place."

Only once in all this time did she return to Iran, for a summer, and then she felt a fateful sense of belonging. "I was somehow made whole by the realization that this was home," she told Mahnaz, "and what happened here mattered to me." She would make the most important decisions in her life based on that desire for belonging. She wanted what Huck Finn appeared to be escaping from—a comfortable and predictable home.

When she returned to California after that summer, she was drawn to the Iranian student movement mainly by a desire to recapture this sense of belonging. Despite the fact that she had left Iran as a child, the Iranian activists accepted her as their own. Their gatherings felt like a "club"; for the first time, she had a network of friends around whom her life was structured. "What drew me to the Association at the beginning was more the camaraderie than the political cause," she told Mahnaz. "The passion for the cause came much later."

Farah never did anything halfway. Once she committed herself to the movement, she cast all doubts aside. She held rallies, went on long marches, and joined a forty-eight-hour vigil in front of the Iranian consulate in Chicago in the dead of winter. She even tied herself up to the Statue of Liberty once with a group of friends to protest the shah. All of these activities became more glorious, and somehow more justified, when she fell in love with Faramarz, a popular student leader, handsome and charismatic, who was a few years older than her. Those were the days when men tried to seduce you, if not with grass and mescaline, then through a discussion of Engels's *The Origin of the Family, Private Property, and the State.* Farah and I both joined the student movement not just out of a sense of justice, but because we found in it a connection to our old home. And yet Farah felt a sense of identification with the group that I never did with any political or ideological organization. Twain, James and Howells belonged to a private world; I read them late at night, in silent places.

That was a decade when all sorts of "vice" and all forms of rebellion flourished simultaneously side by side, the Maoists and Marxist–Leninists, the Trotskyites, the hippies, the feminists, the civil rights activists, the Vietnam veterans, even the Hare Krishna.

We would sing songs about Joe Hill and chant Neil Young's "Don't Let It Bring You Down," occupying administration buildings alongside the "flower children" as well as members of the Black Panthers or the Revolutionary Communist Party—one movement for peace and one for war. While some protested and marched militantly, others would streak across the lawns and occupy movie houses in small towns like Norman, Oklahoma, where I happened to be studying *Huckleberry Finn*.

My first inkling of Huck's subversive character was more the result of a literary discovery than a political one. From the great Charles Dickens's *Oliver Twist* to Frances Hodgson Burnett's syrupy *Little Lord Fauntleroy*, orphans were a fixture in nineteenth- and early-twentieth-century literature. It was and perhaps still is seductive to follow the misadventures of a lonely and poverty-stricken orphan in a cruel and ungenerous world, only to be rewarded in the end, alongside our protagonist, with a wealthy relative and a warm home. We emerge comfortable in the knowledge that, despite all the terrible things happening in this terrible world, all's well that ends well.

But here was one little orphan who not only did not find a home but was repulsed by its very idea, taking off whenever he was offered one. That, to my mind, told us a great deal about Mr. Huckleberry Finn. Yes, it is true, he wasn't an orphan, strictly speaking—his father is alive for part of the book—but the same could be said of little Cedric Errol, the velvet-clad Little Lord Fauntleroy, whose mother meekly follows him to England. And yet both were most decidedly creatures of the orphan novel.

When I first mentioned this concept to Professor Elconin,

he seemed intrigued by it and encouraged me to write a paper on the subject, but, like so many other projects, that paper and my enthusiasm were soon forgotten in favor of seemingly more urgent matters. Yet I never quite forgot the orphan Huck and the knowledge that both the reward and the punishment for his straying from the fold was a permanent state of homelessness.

Perhaps there was a connection between my activism and love of literature. I was drawn to the songs and to the emotional high of participating in an illicit movement. Farah, however, was dead serious—at heart she was far less quirky than me, far more pragmatic. She fulfilled her revolutionary goals with the discipline of a hardworking student, bringing to the task the same meticulous practicality that she would later put into finding a job to support herself and her two young children. She asked fewer questions than I did and was loyal to her group and to her beloved, Faramarz.

She would describe her relationship with Faramarz as one of "comradeship, love and respect." But in our stolen moments, what she talked about was passion—he had taught her how to love; with him she had seen herself anew, and, perhaps for the first time, she approved of what she saw. Even when the time came to question and doubt and finally to distance herself from the movement, she was one of those rare individuals who broke her ideological ties and remained personally loyal, refusing to betray those who had first given her a sense of belonging.

This loyalty had its costs, and sometimes manifested itself in absurd situations. Mahnaz described with laughter how once she had gone to New York to participate in a meeting at the UN and left Farah, who had come to visit, in her car during the meeting. On her return, Mahnaz found Farah trying to convert her limo driver to the revolutionary cause. "I kept telling her, when we were working on her CV," Mahnaz told me much later, "that tying yourself to the Statue of Liberty is not the best recommendation for a job."

Two decades later, all three of us were refugees in Washington, D.C., laughing at our own follies. We used to reflect on how ironic it was that I, the restless one, the loner, the crazy "literature person," had a more stable life than Farah, the pragmatic if occasionally impulsive problem solver, ever had. Every time she managed to create a space that she might call home, fate, politics or her own hidden impulses would take that safe haven away from her.

Pragmatists are sometimes more prone to illusion than dreamers; when they fall for something, they fall hard, not knowing how to protect themselves, while we dreamers are more practiced in surviving the disillusionment that follows when we wake up from our dreams. It turned out that Farah's illusions and fantasies about America were nothing compared with the ones she harbored about Iran, and no place would be more dangerous for her than the one she had originally called home.

# 4

Farah called me late at night. I was watching *Masterpiece Mystery! Inspector Morse*. "Hello, Azi-joon," she said. "Had it not been you, I would not have answered the phone," I said. "I'm watching something important."

Ignoring me, she went on. "I've found a great quote for you. . . ."

She proceeded to read a long passage by Arthur Miller about Twain. She had found it in *The Illustrated Mark Twain,* which for some reason she was reading: "'He wrote as though there had been no literature before him . . . as though he had discovered the art of telling a story about these folks that inhabit this continent. . . . And that there was no other continent—it's like something that rose up out of the sea and had no history. And he was just telling what he ran into.'"

I had to admit it was a great quote.

"See you tomorrow," she said mischievously. "I don't want to keep you from something important." And with that she hung up.

I wanted to continue watching Inspector Morse, but I couldn't focus anymore, so instead I picked up Joseph Ellis's biography of Washington from the shelf and started looking through the parts I had underlined.

When I called Farah the next afternoon, I caught her trying to take a nap.

"I've been busy," I told her. "I want to read you a line from George Washington's final speech as commander in chief— I found it in your book by Joseph Ellis."

She mumbled a bit about needing to sleep, but then she said, "Okay, fine, what is it?"

I cleared my throat and did my best George Washington impersonation: "'At this auspicious period, the United States came into existence as a Nation, and if their Citizens should not be completely free and happy, the fault will be entirely their own.'"

Washington believed it was essential that America, having won her freedom, should not squander it on petty squabbles. He wrote his open letter to the governors of the newly independent states in large measure to warn them to resist factional disputes that might pit one state against another. "The foundation of our Empire was not laid in the gloomy age of Ignorance and Suspicion," he wrote, "but an Epoch when the rights of mankind were better understood and more clearly defined, than at any former period." He understood that a certain habit of mind and disposition of character was and would remain the key to America's greatness.

Farah said, "I told you—you had to use U.S. history. See you tomorrow?"

"Yes."

# 5

Two decades before Hemingway's proclamation that Huck Finn was "the best book we've had," Twain's friend William Dean Howells wrote, "Emerson, Longfellow, Lowell, Holmes— I knew them all and all the rest of our sages, poets, seers, critics, humorists, they were like one another and like any other literary men; but Clemens was sole, incomparable, the Lincoln of our literature."

When I told Farah about that quote, one of my favorites, she shrugged as if to say, "So what?" Then she turned away and said in a matter-of-fact way, "You might as well say the Jefferson of our literature."

She meant it facetiously, but maybe she was right, because if there was any figure in the history of American fiction who, through his writing, created a literary declaration of independence, it was Mark Twain. He was the first to deliberately cut himself off from the prevailing traditions of the mother tongue. With *Huck Finn* he helped forge a new national myth, giving us a hero who looked and spoke like one of the tramp protagonists of the European novel, but whose values and principles were more akin to those of the great epic heroes.

Huck was a mongrel, an outcast, uneducated and unmoored, and since his creation countless Americans have recast themselves in his image. He was suspicious of the smothery ways of conventional society, but in his ideals, his moral courage, his determination to open himself up to the lessons of nature and the vagaries of experience, he was as much a product of the Enlightenment as were George Washington and Benjamin Franklin, or so I came to think when I followed Farah's advice and began reading more American history.

In some respect, Mark Twain started with the same basic premise as the founding fathers: he saw himself participating in a wholly new enterprise, trying to actualize the ideals of democracy culled from Greece and Rome. In doing so, like Adam, he could not help but commit the ultimate sin against his creators: declaring independence. There are wonderful stories about Twain's disdain for Europe, its aristocracy and vanity. He compared Venice to Arkansas and mocked Europe's preoccupation with its cultural heritage, but if, unlike his more established peers Henry James, William Dean Howells and James Fenimore Cooper, he did not fawn on Europe, he had far more knowledge and appreciation for the land of his ancestors than he let on. Nor was he ignorant of European culture: he appreciated Shakespeare, Dickens, Balzac and Tocqueville; his favorite character was Joan of Arc, and he passionately hated some of Europe's most popular novelists, like Sir Walter Scott and (alas) Jane Austen.

Twain himself was much appreciated in Europe. He traveled extensively around the Continent and even lived in Italy for ten years. He was feted by European royalty and by his peers, including a young Rudyard Kipling, but he never sought to compete with European writers on their own terms. The question that seemed to animate him was how to articulate the new reality back home, the distinct new American identity—how to give America its own voice. He could be critical of the affectations of his fellow countrymen, as he was in *The Innocents Abroad* of the ignorant but arrogant type he came across at a restaurant in Marseille, loudly telling everyone how great it was to drink wine with dinner while boasting that he was a "free-born sovereign, sir, and American, sir, and I want everybody to know it!" (That person, whose arrogance stems from his ignorance, is alive and well in America today, still ranting and raving against "old Europe.")

I had decided to teach a new class on American fiction the following semester. I wanted to start with Huck and to ask my students to consider what it means to write a great American novel. Can one really speak of *American* fiction? I had become obsessed with Eudora Welty's claim that art "is never the voice of a country; it is an even more precious thing, the voice of the individual, doing its best to speak, not comfort of any sort, indeed, but truth. And the art that speaks it most unmistakably, most directly, most variously, most fully, is fiction; in particular, the novel."

# 6

It is easy to talk about the break with Europe; that aspect is obvious. America, among Britain's colonies, would become the black sheep of the family, rebellious and unruly. When it chose to cut away from its parents, it had to negate everything about them, but then it was also a direct heir to the traditions and culture of the "old country." How could one remain true to those traditions and at the same time radically subvert them? One can see this tension in the works of Twain's giant elder brothers, Hawthorne, Melville, and even Poe. But that is really not Huck's concern. In creating *Huckleberry Finn,* Twain distanced himself not only from Europe but from those who founded America, the Pilgrims. He started from scratch and conjured a character as yet unborn, one whose language had been alien to fiction until then.

This was the main thrust of the lecture I was preparing on that gray, gloomy day, when, sitting on the couch with my notes on my knees, a cigar that I never smoked dangling from my lips to assuage a nervous tension I had whenever I wrote, pen in one hand and phone in the other, Farah called me on her cell. She was at the clinic around the corner from my house, one of those healing centers that offers alternative remedies when more conventional doctors no longer know what to do.

She wanted to talk during the long hour she spent taking her vitamin C cure.

"Huck Finn predicted America," I told her. "He predicted— or at least laid the groundwork for—the two of us talking and arguing simultaneously in two languages in this city called Washington, D.C."

Farah would have none of it. Ever the pragmatist, she pointed out that Huck wouldn't have been much interested in the musings of two middle-aged Iranian women in Washington, D.C. But I wouldn't be so easily dissuaded. I decided, since she wanted to talk, that I would give her a preview of the first lecture of my new class. For some time now, she had been my most committed student, though I often felt that she had more to teach me than vice versa.

I wanted to begin with something that would jolt the class from its usual docile torpor. For a while I entertained the idea of having them all read an outrageous, dazzlingly confected speech that Twain delivered in 1881 to the New England Society of Philadelphia on the anniversary of the Pilgrims' landing on Plymouth Rock. Here, as in most of his essays and speeches, he sallies forth with humor, but underneath the pretense of comedy is a message that is dead serious.

Speaking to descendants of the *Mayflower,* he begins by asking his audience why they would wish to celebrate "those ancestors of yours of 1620—the *Mayflower* tribe," whom he describes as a "hard lot" who "took good care of themselves, but they abolished everybody else's ancestors." Twain differentiates himself from his hosts, telling them, "I am a border ruffian from the state of Missouri. I am a Connecticut Yankee by adoption. I have the morals of Missouri and the culture of Connecticut, and that's the combination that makes the perfect man." Then he goes on to say, "But where are my ancestors? Whom shall I celebrate? Where shall I celebrate? Where shall I find the raw material?"

Identifying with those "abolished" ancestors, he assumes the identity of America's persecuted underdogs and says his first American ancestor was "an early Indian." "Your ancestors skinned him alive, and I am an orphan. Not one drop of my blood flows in that Indian's veins today. I stand here, lone and forlorn, without an ancestor." Next he calls himself a Quaker. "Your tribe," he says, "chased them out of the country for their religion's sake. . . . [They] broke forever the chains of political slavery, and gave the vote to every man in this wide land, excluding none!— none except those who did not belong to the orthodox church." Then he invokes the Salem witches and, finally, the most persecuted and marginalized of all, the black slave: "The first slave brought into New England out of Africa by your progenitors was an ancestor of mine—for I am of a mixed breed, an infinitely shaded and exquisite Mongrel. I am not one of your sham meerschaums that you can color in a week."

It was his recognition of this mongrel quality in the American identity—earlier expressed by Whitman in *Leaves of Grass* when he says, "Do I contradict myself? / Very well then I contradict myself, / (I am large, I contain multitudes)"—that enabled Twain to create an epic of the first American rogue. Many great writers of literature challenge and tackle conformity, but he made it a national characteristic to be always new, to start as if there had been no precedent. He found a verbal equivalent to the language of jazz, that other very American, exquisitely mongrel form of imaginative expression.

After Twain, it becomes difficult to talk about America without acknowledging those absent ancestors, conveniently airbrushed out of the preferred mythology of America's glorious origins. Twain's heresy in *Huckleberry Finn* was no longer against the original fatherland, Britain—or, in a larger context, Europe—but against this new and in a sense more menacing "father," the "*Mayflower* tribe." He became the epic narrator of this challenge, a theme that from then on was picked up and articulated in many different forms in the great works of American fiction.

"Hear your true friend—your only true friend—listen to his voice." Tongue in cheek but also dead serious, he tells the *Mayflower* grandees in Philadelphia: "Disband these societies, hotbeds of vice, of moral decay—perpetuators of ancestral superstition. . . . I beseech you, I implore you, in the name of your anxious friends, in the name of your suffering families, in the name of your impending widows and orphans, stop ere it be too late. Disband these New England societies, renounce these soul-blistering saturnalia, cease from varnishing the rusty reputations of your long-vanished ancestors, the super-high-moral old ironclads of Cape Cod, the pious buccaneers of Plymouth Rock—go home, and try to learn to behave!"

Twain's most effective act of heresy was a literary declaration of independence from all previous forms of fiction, even those he revered. In most of his work, but most perfectly in *Huckleberry Finn,* he set out to give shape and voice to this mongrel, who was not just on the margins of society but without a space within its literary orbit. This is what fates Huck to be seemingly unable to fully articulate his own story, and why others, in fact far less articulate, constantly try to impose their own stories on him, reforming Huck and enslaving Jim. Unlike our modern-day "rogues" who are such masters of self-promotion, Huck and Jim are representative of their nation exactly because they are the least represented.

## 7

I was impatiently waiting for Farah at the coffee shop of the Phillips Collection, one of my hidden lairs, where I worked and rewarded myself by wandering around the museum at intervals and gazing at my favorite paintings. I had underlined a quote from Twain's journal, knowing that this was to be the focus not just of my chapter on Twain but of the whole book. I was living in the deceptively liberating period after finishing a book and handing the galleys to the publisher. I had already started thinking and talking about the main themes for my new book, as well as planning the course for next term, which was to start with *Huck Finn*. I kept feeling that I was on the verge of a new discovery, but not quite there. I hoped talking to Farah would help clarify things for me.

When Farah arrived, after we bought our drinks and settled on a table situated under a portrait of Duncan Phillips and his wife, I pushed toward her my summary of my *Huck* chapter: "Reading his story, we slowly discover three things: (1) Huck's adventures, like Edward Hopper's paintings, are variations on the theme of aloneness. (2) These adventures, although filled with great humor, are not that of a young, restless boy searching for fun and diversion, or a nineteenth-century version of Holden Caulfield rebelling against the shoddy grown-up world, but that of a lonesome boy running for his life. (3) The whole story is shaped around one central theme, best articulated by Mark Twain in a notebook entry of 1895, in which he describes *Huck Finn* as 'a book of mine where a sound heart & a deformed conscience come into collision & conscience suffers defeat.'"

I was excited like a child and almost felt like saying, "How cool is that?!"

I felt I had found the secret, the source of Huck's rebellion, his individuality, his morality. One of Twain's greatest contributions was to transform the seat of morality from conscience to the heart, from public mores and dictums to individual experience and choice. I inevitably suggested to Farah "Between a Sound Heart and a Deformed Conscience" as the subtitle for my book. For Twain, as for any great novelist, reality was the clay waiting to be shaped. There was a collusion, not a collision, between fiction and reality, and that collusion functioned as antidote to the lies, illusions and fantasies that our monitoring conscience imposes on us. To me, this was the best argument against those who consider fiction irrelevant.

Farah was intrigued by the idea and against the subtitle. "Too academic," she said. "By which I mean too abstract." Which was basically the same reaction I got from my real editor.

Afterwards, I took Farah to a room where mainly the pictures by African American painters were housed. I wanted her to see the series painted by Jacob Lawrence on the migration of African Americans from the rural South to the urban North between the

First and Second World Wars. Lawrence had said, "To me, migration means movement. There was conflict and struggle. But out of the struggle came a kind of power and even beauty."

# 8

*Huckleberry Finn* was the first book I taught when I went back to Iran in 1979 and accepted a position in the Department of English Language and Literature at the University of Tehran. So at a time when our leaders were denouncing America to charmed throngs as an imperialist Satan, I found myself struggling to define America, with its complexities and paradoxes, for my restless students through the eyes of its fiction. I had come to believe that American fiction was at once its moral guardian and its best critic. In Iran in those days, as the revolution raged all over the city and on campus, it was easy to feel orphaned in your own home, and most of my students immediately connected to the two homeless refugees, Huck and Jim. The first thing a totalitarian mind-set does is strip its citizens of their sense of identity, rewriting their past to suit its goals, and rewriting history to serve its ends. Already my students understood that Huck's defiance took courage, that it was not always easy to turn your back on what everyone else was doing, however morally repugnant it might seem. The course, simply called "Research," its description as vague as its title, was a huge undergraduate class designed to help students do just that: research. I was told that I should teach the different stages of writing a research paper. "Why don't you choose a typical American novel," the head of the English department recommended. "Americans are in such vogue these days." He himself was a Hemingway man, an extremely popular teacher who was also in vogue—for all the wrong reasons, of course, seeing how almost every day there was some call or demonstration against American imperialists and their domestic lackeys. Just three months after that conversation, no one but a few eccentrics like he and I would think of America in terms of Hemingway or Twain. The Americans everyone was talking about were the hostages held in the embassy, which happened to be situated not far from the university.

How was it that in America I had been demonstrating in front of the White House, running away from tear gas and shouting political slogans, and now in Tehran, in the midst of a real revolution, under the threat of real bullets, I found myself in my bedroom, poring over Mark Twain into the early hours of morning and wondering how to teach the idea of beauty? Perhaps it was the very intensity of life during revolutionary times, its extreme and violent intrusions into each and every aspect of our being, that made us more sensitive to questions that just a year or two earlier might have seemed purely academic. My dilemma that evening was how to share with my students what I had so often experienced myself when reading a poem, a play, a novel: that immense sense of gratitude and joy, that spark of recognition that Vladimir Nabokov called the "tingle in the spine."

Research. From the beginning of their freshman year, my students would have been taught how to use the library, how to find articles and background information, to cite quotations and structure footnotes. I did not want to ask for more of the same.

I thought it would be more exciting, and perhaps more fruitful, to treat literary research the way one would a treasure hunt, following a web of clues until one could piece together the genesis of the story, or the motive, or the crime. Parallel to all the mechanical aspects of writing a paper, and before using outside sources, I wanted the class to do another kind of research, to trace the book through its process of formation.

"Just remember," I told them, "the word 'civilization' is transformed on the very first page by Huck into 'sivilization.' That is a clue to the whole book—that slight change in spelling subverts the word's meaning and implications. The key words in this novel—like 'respectable,' 'conscience,' 'heart,' 'white' and 'nigger'—none of them have their conventional meanings. Remember the word 'topsy-turvy,' which we discussed last week? It applies to *Alice in Wonderland* and, in a different context, to *Huck Finn*." I wanted them to feel the subversiveness of the text, to experience it as Twain's first readers might have.

Nima, one of my students who now lives in the United States, reminded me recently of the hue and cry I made, in one of the last classes I taught in Iran, over the mistranslation of the word "sivilization." One day a student brought in the Persian translation of *Huck Finn* and showed me how the well-meaning translator had simplified matters for his readers by rendering "sivilization" in its correct Farsi spelling. This had led to a long discussion in class about the issue of integrity and the fact that in every novel, including this one—indeed, perhaps especially this one—words were flesh, blood and bones, as well as soul and spirit. You have a right to interpret them however you wish, but no right—*no* right—to mutilate them or to perform plastic surgery on the text for your own comfort and pleasure.

I would be reminded of this exchange two decades later in Washington, D.C., when another well-meaning publisher took it upon himself to expunge another word, more inflammatory by far, from the text, arguing that he saw no reason to offend sensitive modern readers. So he decided to excise the word "nigger"—a word used 219 times over the course of the book—from his edition. He was not the first to express concern. In 1957 the NAACP called *Huck Finn* racially offensive, and since 1976 the charge has resurfaced in one form or another every decade or so. Toni Morrison beautifully weighed in on the subject, arguing that "the narrow notion of how to handle the offense Mark Twain's use of the term 'nigger' would occasion for black students and the corrosive effect it would have on white ones" was "a purist yet elementary kind of censorship designed to appease adults rather than educate children. Amputate the problem, band-aid the solution." So the publisher was in good company, but no one up until now had actually dared to tamper with the text.

I watched the latest iteration of the controversy play out in horror, glued to the *60 Minutes* piece on the subject and furiously mumbling to myself and jotting down notes. I was reminded of how professors and publishers in Iran, like the walrus and the carpenter tearfully eating the oysters in *Through the Looking-Glass,* would provide elaborate and self-serving justifications for their decision to delete words like "wine" and "lovemaking" from works of fiction. Of course, there was a difference—as the publisher of NewSouth Books dutifully explained, his change had not been mandated by the government, and people had the right to voice their objections, as well as to read the uncensored version, which was still available. In Iran, most publishers and teachers agreed to censor texts because severe repercussions could be expected for failing to do so. In this instance, censorship was rooted in a sense of righteous indignation, as the publisher explained how he, a native of Alabama, had witnessed Dr. King's and other civil rights leaders' struggles and been transformed by them, and how in altering the book now, he only wanted to do the right thing.

In a democratic society, we do not practice the savage methods of an autocratic regime, but we find new and pernicious ways of expressing our prejudices. Education's goal is to impart knowledge, and knowledge is not only heretical but unpredictable and often uncomfortable. One has to pause and imagine what it would mean to censor all that is uncomfortable from our textbooks. How, if you cannot face the past as it was, can you ever hope to teach history?

"Delicacy—a sad, sad false delicacy," Twain wrote to his friend William Dean Howells, "robs literature of the two best things among its belongings: Family-circle narratives & obscene stories." He wanted to shock us, to make us uncomfortable, to arouse us from our indolent acquiescence. And he wanted us to feel. "Don't say the old lady screamed," he advised. "Bring her on and let her scream." What disturbs us about *Huck Finn* is that we hear the scream only too well, and that, perhaps, is not what we bargained for when we set out to read the adventures of a small boy drifting down the Mississippi.

Twain's use of the word "nigger" demonstrates more than anything else how deeply and perniciously justifications for slavery were ingrained in the minds of Americans. Each time the word is used, it is simultaneously questioned, subverted, destabilized and discredited—in the same manner that terms like "respectable" or "white" are transformed and undermined. When Huck tells Aunt Sally that no one but a "nigger" was killed and she expresses her joy at no one's being killed, this, as the saying goes, speaks volumes—not about the inhumanity of slaves but about the utter blindness of a good-hearted, God-fearing woman.

My students in Iran offered up a few innovative papers; they had not yet succumbed to the revolutionary mind-set that would soon grip campus. I remember two quite excellent ones from unlikely admirers of Huck, one of whom was the president of the newly formed Islamic students' association. Some addressed the myth of American innocence à la Leslie Fiedler, and one girl had gone to the trouble of tracing the roots of the name Huckleberry. I don't remember now what definition she came up with, but recently I checked a dictionary out of curiosity and came up with:

1. Fruit: the edible dark-blue fruit of a bush related to the blueberry.
2. Plant like blueberry: a bush that bears huckleberries. Native to: North America. Genus: Gaylussacia.

Her reasoning went something like this: the huckleberry, a wild and rare berry belonging to North America, symbolized Huckleberry, the wild and rare boy, so typically American. Of course, the plant's name was as deceptive as the boy himself, because a huckleberry resembles a blueberry but is not one. Was Huck the wild fruit to Tom Sawyer's tamer blueberry? I confess, the tame blueberry is my own contribution; now that I had been transformed from student to teacher, I could afford to abuse literary theory's potentials for endless cat-and-mouse games with the text.

I remember one essay in particular, by a girl who objected to my choice of *Huck* on the grounds that it was too sad. Perhaps I remember this girl so well because she did not even pretend to write a research paper. Life was too overwhelming for her to make any attempt at objectivity. Her paper included few, if any, references or footnotes, and its language, following the curves and contours of her feelings, was for the most part barren and formal, but every few lines it veered into a poetic sentence or two. Her central point was more of a complaint than an argument: Why should students be made to read about this homeless and "unhappy" little boy and the fugitive slave who accompanied him at a time when they themselves felt so insecure? During one of her many digressions, she had questioned how representative this book was of America, wondering whether Americans really were this restless and lonely, because the America she had read and heard about was a happy and carefree place, so full of color: just look at the movies!

A year or so later, I too would dream of taking refuge in that other America, a Hollywood confection, only from the start I knew it was as true—or as false, for that matter—as the idea of Iran I had nurtured during my student years. Soon universities, always at the forefront of protest and dissent, would be shut down in a long and bloody confrontation as students and faculty united in protest against the government's so-called Cultural Revolution, another name for the Islamization of the universities, which three decades later the Islamic regime has not yet succeeded in accomplishing, or at least not completely. Friends and relatives were on the run, sometimes making a quick stop at our place, their final destination unknown. Within the next few years, many among them were jailed or executed or fled the country. That girl and her classmates, the free way we had talked and debated, would soon belong to a past as distant and unreachable as America itself. Who would have time now to worry about the nomads of American fiction?

As the reality of the Islamic Republic insinuated itself into our lives and Tehran lost its colors and sounds, America was transformed in my imagination into a lush, green, teasingly colorful and desirable land. The more alien and menacing Tehran became, the more we had to withdraw from its public spaces, the more vibrant America's fictional landscape appeared in my imagination. Yet it was obvious to me even then that the America I yearned for was more an invention of life in the Islamic Republic than the country I had known as a student. So I clung to that fictional other country, whose vagrant and at times unhappy citizens were the ones who helped me keep things in perspective when daily life began to feel more and more like a very bad dream.

# 9

Until I started teaching *The Adventures of Huckleberry Finn*, I thought that Huck and Jim's main obstacles to freedom were members of "respectable" society, like Miss Watson, but the more I delved into the book, the more I realized that it was far more subtle than that. Miss Watson and her Sunday-school mentality were the most obvious "villains" in the story, but no society is shaped mainly by its elites, and a Sunday-school mentality appears in different forms throughout the novel, in people vastly different from one another; for example, Pap, the other side of the coin to Miss Watson, her uncouth and unwashed mock-up in more ways than one, and—wait for it—Tom. Yes, Tom! In fact, I would go so far as to say that Tom is the real villain of this story.

My students, both in Iran and in the States, had little trouble accepting this notion, but the first time I suggested it to Farah, she shook her head and said, "I think you are getting carried away. Tom is just a kid—he doesn't have Miss Watson's power."

"Exactly because he is a kid," I said, "he is even more dangerous. Because no one takes him and what he represents seriously—except for Huck and Jim." Then I added, "Don't you worry, Tom is respectable, all right. That's the root of the problem. He has no heart."

We had several arguments about this, and she even threatened to attend my class, which she never did, but I would like to believe that I finally convinced her. All one had to do was follow Tom, who appears only at the beginning and the end of the book, each segment mirroring the other: in one he plays a seemingly harmless game, and in the other his game is not so funny anymore, as it has potentially fatal consequences.

*The Adventures of Huckleberry Finn* is a reaction and response to *The Adventures of Tom Sawyer*. That story, in fact, ends more with Huck than with Tom. When, at the end of their adventures, the two friends find gold and return home as heroes, Tom goes back to the fold, where Judge Thatcher has grand plans for his future, but Huck disappears, escaping the pious Widow Douglas, who wants to adopt and educate him. The wide search for Huck is fruitless until Tom Sawyer discovers his old friend among some "empty hogsheads," having just breakfasted "upon some stolen odds and ends of food and was lying off, now, in comfort, with his pipe."

Tom's pleas for Huck to return fall on deaf ears. Huck asks his friend to take possession of his share of gold, and every once in a while to give him a few cents. He informs him that in the widow's house "everything's so awful reg'lar a body can't stand it." When Tom lamely tells him that is how everybody lives, Huck says, "I ain't everybody, and I can't STAND it." Then he heretically philosophizes that "being rich ain't what it's cracked up to be. It's just worry and worry, and sweat and sweat, and a-wishing you was dead all the time." He has no desire to be rich and live in those "smothery houses."

Huck is softened only when Tom slyly tells him that he can't be a part of his gang of robbers if he refuses to become a respectable member of the community. Tom reasons that robbers are more high class than pirates: in most countries they are "awful high up in nobility—dukes and such." If Tom accepts Huck as he is, then "what would people say?" They will say that these robbers are "pretty low characters." The book ends with Huck promising to return and to stay for a month with the Widow Douglas.

Most of the occupants of the smothery houses in *Tom Sawyer* can be found in *Huckleberry Finn*. Only in *Tom Sawyer* the houses are brighter—they impose discipline but also allow space for mischief, young love and light adventures leading to the discovery of gold treasures. There is deviance and rebellion, but the rebels and the conformists come to some form of peaceful coexistence. Boys will be boys—they play pranks—but all will be well, and in the end they will grow up to become judges and lawyers and respectable citizens.

In *Huckleberry Finn,* from the very first page the reader feels that something is not quite right in those prim and proper homes, that there lurks an unspeakable menace in their hidden nooks and crannies. We gradually realize that Huck's use of the word "smothery" is not merely a figure of speech. For him, life in his native town leads to "a-wishing you was dead all the time." Rejecting the kind of respectability that inevitably accompanies stability and security, Huck sets out on his own in pursuit of another American dream: freedom.

In the second paragraph of *The Adventures of Huckleberry Finn,* Huck informs us that the Widow Douglas had decided to take him up and "sivilize" him. But, he writes, "it was rough living in the house all the time, considering how dismal regular and decent the widow was in all her ways; and so when I couldn't stand it no longer, I lit out." The story ends not with his return or his discovery of the pleasures of a new home, but in a circular way, with another escape when another pious and well-meaning woman, Aunt Sally, offers, as he puts it, to "adopt me and sivilize me, and I can't stand it. I been there before." So, he declares, "I reckon I got to light out for the Territory ahead of the rest." The two leave-takings, at the start and end of the book, mirror each other just as the first eight chapters reflect the last ten. "Sivilize" is the operative word. Twain will make it his own, subverting not just the respectable view of the world, but his readers' expectations, following John Locke's maxim that all authority is error.

The first chapter begins innocently enough with the same complaints that Huck expressed in *Tom Sawyer* about living with the pious Widow Douglas. But unlike *Tom Sawyer,* this story is no longer about the kinds of restrictions that any "healthy" boy would try to escape from: waking up on time, going to school, brushing his teeth, saying his prayers before each meal or attending the obligatory Sunday school. Unlike the cheery atmosphere of *Tom Sawyer,* a dark mood pervades this quite ordinary world that is far more sinister and menacing than the uncertain wilderness in which Huck will take refuge.

Huck describes a hilarious conversation with the stern Miss Watson, Widow Douglas's sister. When Miss Watson preaches about the rewards of going to heaven (where she is headed) and the punishments of hell (Tom Sawyer's future abode), Huck informs her that he wouldn't want to go to heaven without Tom Sawyer. He then goes on to tell us that "Miss Watson kept pecking at me, and it got tiresome and lonesome," until finally they all went to bed.

So far we have a humorous scene, but then the trapdoor opens beneath our feet as Huck goes on to describe how he sat in a chair in his room and "tried to think of something cheerful, but it warn't no use. I felt so lonesome I most wished I was dead. The stars were shining, and the leaves rustled in the woods ever so mournful; and I heard an owl, away off, who-whooing about somebody that was dead, and a whippowill and a dog crying about somebody that was going to die; and the wind was trying to whisper something to me, and I couldn't make out what it was, and so it made the cold shivers run over me. . . . I got so down-hearted and scared I did wish I had some company." All of this happens in the second page of the first chapter, where the words "dead" and "die" occur three times in one paragraph that also mentions a ghost feeling restless in its grave.

While preparing for my class, I got into the habit of reading the relevant passages aloud, almost acting them out, an exercise that I carried over to the class itself, where, during our discussions, I would ask my students to volunteer reading certain passages from the book. It was amazing how the varying moods and emotions leaped off the pages and took on a life of their own. When H. L. Mencken compared Twain to Shakespeare and Cervantes, he did have a point—in *Huck Finn* Twain created a new language from scratch and, along with it, a new world.

In that opening scene, nature, the leaves, the stars, the whip-poor-will, the dog and the wind all are mournful and fearsome, unlike the wilderness Huck will later take refuge in, where even danger is a "healthy" part of life. For Tom Sawyer, living in a "dismal regular" house might be a nuisance, but it is the other side of the coin to his wild fantasies and imaginary adventures. Whereas for Huck to be "regular," to submit to someone else's rules, was literally akin to death.

When I read those passages to Farah, she said they made her feel as if that boy were living in a coffin. "It's enough to make you wish you were a-dying," she said. "We forget Huck was just a small, lonely boy."

In the second chapter, Huck and Tom, on their way to their secret game of "robbers," run across the Widow Douglas's slave, Jim. Against Huck's protests, Tom plays a trick on Jim: while he is sleeping, Tom takes off his hat and hangs it from a branch, a foreshadowing of a far crueler trick he will engineer at the end of the story, with more serious consequences.

Tom and Huck meet up with other boys, members of Tom's band of robbers, and pretend to loot and murder people, committing all these acts in "style," like highwaymen, and as it's done "in the books." Their victims must be killed because, as Tom explains, "some authorities think different, but mostly it's considered best to kill them." From the start, the reader can see that Tom is Huck's best friend only superficially. His language is a variant of the language used by the "respectable" Miss Watson. Like her, he goes by the book, regardless of the cost to real people. We know to which world Tom really belongs, thanks to his choice of language. When one of the boys objects to his plans, Tom says, "Now, Ben Rogers, do you want to do things regular, or don't you?" Then he goes on to say, "Don't you reckon that the people that made the books knows what's the correct thing to do? Do you reckon *you* can learn 'em anything? . . . No, sir, we'll just go on and ransom them in the regular way." Language is the key to character. All the words that frighten Huck and drive him away from the widow's smothery home are used by Tom: "regular," "it's considered best," "the correct thing to do."

Tom's language is what Huck instinctively finds wrong with him when, after a month, he resigns from the gang of robbers. Tom Sawyer, Huck tells us, "called the hogs 'ingots,' and he called the turnips and stuff 'julery,'" while a blazing stick was a "slogan." When Huck objects to Tom's foolish pranks, he is called ignorant. But unlike Tom and Miss Watson, Huck is a thinking person. He thinks over Tom's claims for three days. It is only then that he decides that it was "only just one of Tom Sawyer's lies," and at the end of the chapter he declares, "I reckoned he believed in the A-rabs and the elephants, but as for me I think different. It had all the marks of a Sunday-school." What the "marks of a Sunday-school" look like in real life we will discover at the end of the book.

As Huck tries to adjust to life at the Widow Douglas's home, his tramp of a father appears on the scene. Greedy for the gold Huck found, he steals his own son, beats him to the point of death and locks him in a shed. Pap is perhaps the most repulsively portrayed character in the story, and it is not incidental that the quality most emphasized is his whiteness. "There warn't no color in his face, where his face showed; it was white . . . a white to make a body's flesh crawl—a tree-toad white, a fish-belly white." Pap's physical repulsiveness matches his character, reflected in his rant against the government for doing nothing to rein in the free black man from Ohio he sees in town, who has the "whitest shirt," the "shiniest hat," a "gold watch and chain, and a silver-headed cane" and is also a "p'fessor in a college, and could talk all kinds of languages, and knowed everything"—and, worst of all, he could vote in his own state. This makes Pap furious. He threatens to never vote again, asking, "What is the country a-coming to?" It's a comment reminiscent of more recent rants by pundits and politicians.

As with the Widow Douglas, Huck tries to adjust to his situation with Pap. But there is something restless in him, an urge to question authority. The questioning leads to solitary reflections—"long thinks," he calls them—that precede all the momentous decisions he makes throughout the story. Huck begins to get used to his routine with his Pap, until something jolts him and makes him run: his Pap tells him that the judge is trying to get him back to the Widow Douglas's, where Huck envisions himself again becoming "so cramped up and sivilized." Pap tells him that if the judge decides in her favor, he will hide Huck somewhere no one can find him, leading to Huck's decision to go so far away that neither "the old man nor the widow couldn't ever find me any more."

"The secret source of Humor itself is not joy but sorrow," Twain wrote in his journal. This constant interplay of humor and sorrow becomes a structural part of the novel, shaping its characters, scenes and, most important, its language. When Huck is sent by Sophia, the lovelorn girl in the Grangerford household, to return to church and fetch her "Testament," which she's left behind, Huck finds that no one is in the church, except "maybe a hog or two," who might have gotten in because there was no lock on the door and in summer, hogs like cool places. Then he adds, "If you notice, most folks don't go to church only when they've got to; but a hog is different." This casual comment is as effectively comic as another understated statement is tragic: when Huck witnesses, from up in a tree, as two warring clans, the Shepherdsons and the Grangerfords, massacre one another and he says, "I ain't a-going to tell *all* that happened—it would make me sick again if I was to do that. I wished I hadn't ever come ashore that night to see such things. I ain't ever going to get shut of them—lots of times I dream about them."

## 10

It was a beautiful day, and I was walking toward the West End Library to check out a book. There was some shouting behind me, and I turned around to see Farah, in her bicycle helmet and gear, calling me "kiddo" and laughing. She wanted to join me later to have coffee and talk about Huck. At this point, I was thinking of subtitling my book "*Huck Finn's Mongrels.*"

It was what she called one of her "good days," and she was in a feisty mood when she joined me an hour later at the Soho coffee shop, on P Street and Twenty-second, one of the few independently owned coffee places in town. I wanted Farah to see it: I told her it reminded me of the coffee shops we'd frequented in Berkeley during our student days—shabby and colorful furniture and cushions, the ponytailed proprietor always present behind the counter. Good coffee, real mugs.

We got my cappuccino, her green tea and a scone to share and moved to a table at the farthest corner of the room.

"What's up?" she said.

"What's up with *you*?" I said back.

She smiled and told me her friend Bahram had said she should do two things for him: "Dye your hair and don't die." "So," Farah said with her most inscrutable smile, "I dyed my hair!" She said it had been difficult for him to articulate his feelings, and the way he had done so had touched her a lot. And then she said again, "So what's up?"

I told her I had started reading a biography of Mark Twain.

Our exchanges over the previous few months had diverted me toward a whole pile of books that I probably shouldn't have been reading. The more I read about Twain's life, the more amazed I was by his almost instinctive hatred of slavery.

"The next time I teach *Huck Finn,* I will assign more auto-biographical material," I said. I had become obsessed by Virginia Woolf's assertion that "fiction is like a spider's web, attached ever so slightly perhaps, but still attached to life at all four corners." I had always been intrigued by this magical interaction, the curious and constant interplay of fiction and reality, their affinities and rivalries.

"In my schoolboy days I had no aversion to slavery," Twain reminisced late in life. "I was not aware that there was anything wrong about it. No one arraigned it in my hearing; the local papers said nothing against it; the local pulpit taught us that God approved it, that it was a holy thing, and that the doubter need only look in the Bible if he wished to settle his mind—and then the texts were read aloud to us to make the matter sure; if the slaves themselves had an aversion to slavery they were wise and said nothing."

His childhood memories left such a mark on him that slavery became to his mind a universal symbol of man's cruelty, stupidity and depravity. In 1904, years after the publication of *Huck Finn,* he wrote in his notebook, "The skin of every human being contains a slave." The impact of his childhood experiences grew as he himself grew older and took up other causes: defending the Jews, women, the people of the Congo, workers and all of the oppressed; claiming to be a revolutionary; already predicting the ideological wars to come when he declared not

"My country right or wrong" but "My country—when it is right."

Witnessing the mistreatment by a German hotel manager of an Indian servant who accepted his punishment without protest, Twain writes that the incident "carried me instantly back to my boyhood and flashed upon me the forgotten fact that this was the *usual way* of explaining one's desire to a slave." He remembered his own father's regular cuffing of their slave boy and the accidental murder of a slave by his master, confessing that as a child he had accepted such treatment as natural, although he also felt "sorry for the victim and ashamed for the punisher."

Twain felt it was not enough to condemn slavery; he felt he had to investigate as a writer its effects on the lives of individuals. In Notebook 35, he wrote: "In those old slave-holding days the whole community was agreed as to one thing—the awful sacredness of slave property. To help steal a horse or a cow was a low crime, but to help a hunted slave, or feed him or shelter him, or hide him, or comfort him, in his troubles, his terrors, his despair, or hesitate to promptly betray him to the slave-catcher when opportunity offered was a much baser crime, & carried with it a stain, a moral smirch which nothing could wipe away. That this sentiment should exist among slave-owners is comprehensible—there were good commercial reasons for it—but that it should exist & did exist among the paupers, the loafers the tag-rag & bobtail of the community, & in a passionate & uncompromising form, is not in our remote day realizable. It seemed natural enough to me then; natural enough that Huck & his father the worthless loafer should feel it & approve it, though it seems now absurd. It shows that that strange thing, the conscience—that unerring monitor—can be trained to approve any wild thing you *want* it to approve if you begin its education early & stick to it."

*Huckleberry Finn* is in this respect a bitter indictment of our social conscience, "the unerring monitor," as he called it. It looks at how ordinary and decent people, or outcasts like Huck and Pap, could abandon their hearts and take the easy road, embracing ugly thoughts and prejudices when they are sanctioned by society. Could such horrors as slavery or the Holocaust happen without the complicity and voluntary blindness of decent, ordinary people, those who go to church and volunteer for good works and yet can easily turn, as they do in *Huck Finn,* into a murderous mob? It might have been this question that gave *Huck* such a dramatic sense of urgency when I taught it in those violent revolutionary days in Iran.

Twain remembered his own mother, who, like the Widow Douglas or Aunt Sally, was "kind-hearted and compassionate" but "was not conscious that slavery was a bald, grotesque, and unwarrantable usurpation." When acting on her instincts, she impulsively took the victim's side, seemingly unaware of the contradictory nature of her actions and feelings. In his *Autobiography,* Twain mentions a small slave boy, Sandy, who came from Maryland and had no friends or family. As a young boy, he was bothered by Sandy's incessant singing and complained about it to his mother. "Poor thing," she told him, "when he sings, it shows that he is not remembering, and that comforts me; but when he is still, I am afraid he is thinking, and I cannot bear it. He will never see his mother again; if he can sing, I must not hinder it, but be thankful for it." Twain remarks, "It was a simple speech . . .

but it went home, and Sandy's noise was not a trouble to me any more."

As a child, Twain recalls, "all the negroes were friends of ours, and with those of our own age we were in effect comrades. . . . We were comrades, and yet not comrades; color and condition interposed a subtle line which both parties were conscious of, and which rendered complete fusion impossible." From one of the slaves on the farm where he grew up, he learned the language and the mesmerizing power of stories. The best on that farm was "Uncle Dan'l," "whose sympathies were wide and warm and whose heart was honest and simple and knew no guile." He explains, "He has served me well, these many, many years. I have not seen him for more than half a century, and yet spiritually I have had his welcome company a good part of that time, and have staged him in books under his own name and as 'Jim,' and carted him all around—to Hannibal, down the Mississippi on a raft, and even across the Desert of Sahara in a balloon—and he has endured it all with the patience and friendliness and loyalty which were his birthright. It was on the farm that I got my strong liking for his race and my appreciation of certain of its fine qualities."

In real life, Samuel Clemens befriended Frederick Douglass and Booker T. Washington and paid for the tuition of Warner McGuinn, who was among the first black students to study law at Yale. "The shame is ours, not theirs," he wrote in his letter to the dean of the Yale Law School in 1885, "& we should pay for it."

# 11

There were many ways of fighting slavery, from attempting to change the laws to preaching to shaming the slave owners to taking up arms. One way was to write from a silenced and traumatized perspective, which in itself was an act of insubordination and great daring. Memoirs by former slaves, both biographies and fictional accounts, are heartbreaking, reclaiming as they do mutilated and confiscated lives. But the monstrous reality weighed too heavily on their fictional narratives. Their language, often sentimental and formal, cannot adequately give voice to characters, or express their individual burdens. Decades would pass before slave narratives developed the language and the form necessary to escape from the strictures of an authority that not only dominated their reality but also interfered with their imagination. (Notwithstanding the occasional hidden gem, like an astonishing book discovered by Henry Louis Gates Jr., called *Our Nig,* by Harriet E. Wilson, that in some ways could be considered a companion to *Huck Finn.*)

And then, of course, there was *Uncle Tom's Cabin,* published in 1852. Despite its defects as a novel, *Uncle Tom* touched the hearts of millions of readers. Henry James said it was as if "a fish, a wonderful, leaping fish, had simply flown through the air." It was so effective in stirring up emotion that more than a century later, in the Islamic Republic of Iran, my daughter, after finishing the book, woke up every morning for a whole week crying for the death of Uncle Tom and his little friend Eva.

Unlike *Huck Finn,* which challenges all authority, perhaps especially that of religion, most of the fictional slave narratives were "Christian" in tone and message. In one sense, of course, they offered up an alternative view of Christianity, challenging slave owners and their preachers to defend and justify slavery. In this sense, *Uncle Tom's Cabin* and novels by African Americans such as *Iola Leroy* claim Christianity and make it their own. As Edmund Wilson writes in *Patriotic Gore,* which Paul Berman described to me as "wrong analysis, great portraits," Uncle Tom himself is a true example of Christian charity, turning the other cheek. His triumph lies in his refusal to become vengeful like his white masters.

It is interesting that the two protagonists in *Uncle Tom's Cabin* are also a slave and a young child, as if only a child not yet tainted by "conscience" or trained to hate by society can truly empathize with a slave. Eva, unlike Huck, is not a vagrant but the beautiful daughter of Tom's new master, whom he loved "as something frail and earthly, yet almost worshipped her as something heavenly and divine." We are told he "half believed," when he first saw her, "that he saw one of the angels stepped out of his New Testament." Tom meets Eva St. Clare on a riverboat headed down the Mississippi River, and the bond between them is based on their good hearts and love of the Bible. Eva's kindness and friendship make Tom's separation from his family seem easier. Unlike Huck, Eva does not change much over the course of the story: she is pure and constantly questions the condition of slaves. On her deathbed, she requests that her father free all the family slaves.

As powerful as *Uncle Tom* is, it was written for a political and social purpose, and it shows. Rather than let the characters do the work, Harriet Beecher Stowe intervenes and desperately at times tries to persuade the reader of the heinous nature of slavery. And while she portrays many characters forcefully, she cannot resist giving "white attributes" to her black characters. Little Eva, the most important character in the novel after Tom, is also the weakest. She never quite wholly acquires flesh and blood and is a little irritating, reminding us of just how earthy and real Huck Finn is. He does not play on our sentiments, but stirs our hearts in ways we had never imagined possible.

Stowe was quick to say that she was seduced by ideas; stories were for her a vehicle through which to present those ideas to incite action. Twain was attracted to ideas when he could turn them into stories. She wanted to change the world, while he challenged the world by creating an alternative reality. After touring St. Paul's Cathedral during a trip to London in 1872, Twain wrote in his notebook: "Expression—expression is the thing—in art. I do not care what it expresses, and I cannot tell, generally, but expression is what I worship, it is what I glory in, with all my impetuous nature."

Although from the moment they meet, Jim depends on Huck for his life and freedom, in more ways than one Huck's own freedom and life depend on Jim. This is not only because Jim looks after Huck and helps him find food and shelter but also because he is the first person to see Huck after his staged death, and so in one sense he resurrects him. Like the rest of us, Huck needs to be seen in order to exist. Later, he discovers that he needs to feel, to empathize with others, in order to become more fully himself. All through their adventures, Huck finds his own moral compass with the help of Jim. As soon as they meet under new circumstances, Jim is transformed from Miss Watson's "nigger" to his best mate as they go from "he and I" to "we."

With his resurrection, Huck's hitherto hidden qualities come to the surface as he gradually transforms from Tom Sawyer's second-in-command and Miss Watson's reform project into a responsible individual, one who knows how to face danger, how to take care of himself and his mate. Their relationship proves the truth of Twain's maxim that "Lincoln's proclamation . . . not only set the black slaves free, but set the white man free also."

Jim is the most orphaned character in the story, as his whole race has been abducted from its home and subjected to a permanent state of orphanhood—a fact that adds poignancy to his escape in search of the family he has been torn from. While living as Miss Watson's slave, Jim has no identity of his own. He and Huck need to leave the territory ruled by oppressive conventions in order to become real to each other and true to themselves. In this new territory, for the first time Jim becomes a whole human being, a father and a husband, an individual with a heart and a past. Until he and Huck discovered each other, no white person had ever acknowledged that. Just as Jim resurrects Huck, Huck resurrects Jim.

In all respects, Jim is different from the white people Huck has left behind. He questions the system of beliefs sanctioned by religious and social authorities, and he is the only individual with whom Huck has genuine exchanges. Despite their lack of articulateness, their fresh, unconventional and unsophisticated views reveal far more than we can glean from any other character in the book.

Some critics and academics in America have questioned Twain's presentation of Jim, especially his superstition, which they feel is insulting. It is true that Jim is deeply superstitious: to him, both the animate and inanimate worlds are full of magical signs and symbols, encrypted messages from on high. For those of us who have lost our power to perceive the world magically, this might appear to be a negative point, a sign of his inferiority. And yet Jim's superstition is not like Miss Watson's religion—a rigid dogma, a set of rituals used as bargaining chips to secure a future place in heaven. His magical thinking is a key to his survival in a terrible world over which he has no control. Jim's magic is designed not to harm others but to protect them, just as it protects him.

Between Tom's manipulative fakeries, Pap's rants and raves, the duke and the dauphin's molestations of language to cheat decent people out of their livelihoods, and the pious Miss Watson's stories about heaven and hell, everyone in this book is in the business of making up stories, but is there anyone among them who is more genuine and true to his heart than Jim? It turns out that this uneducated man is far more learned when it comes to matters of the heart than the educated guardians of morality and has far more common sense. Ignorance of the heart, in this book, is the greatest sin.

Huck's relationship with Jim provides his wandering with a legitimate meaning and purpose. In fact, by choosing the most dangerous company possible, that of a runaway slave, Huck goes not just against the values of the small town he has left behind but against his own better judgment. With Jim, the real adventures of Huckleberry Finn begin. Away from the authority of the white masters, away from the house that enslaves Jim and oppresses Huck, they create a world with their own rules.

As they navigate, observing the "lonesomeness of the river," they are constantly threatened by the danger and violence that emanate like poisonous fumes from the land and its "smothery houses": the feuding between the seemingly civilized and church-going Grangerfords and Shepherdsons, the cold-blooded and open killing of a helpless drunk, seething mob anger, the tarring and feathering of the duke and the dauphin. Charlatans, murderers and decent, God-fearing people will all hunt down runaway slaves. These events gather to create a symphony of savagery and fear, variations on human cruelty and brutality, inviting us to agree with Huck that "it was enough to make a body ashamed of the human race."

From its first to its last page, *Huck Finn* shows us that everything that is accepted as the norm, as respectable, is in essence not normal or respectable. It is a book in which "educated" people are the most ignorant, stealing is "borrowing," people with "upbringings" are scoundrels, goodness is heartless, respectability stands for cruelty, and danger lurks, most especially at home. It is a book in which being "white" is not a badge of honor and you will go to hell if you do the right thing. In fact, apart from Huck himself and the three orphan sisters whose inheritance he tries to preserve, there is hardly a white character in the book who does not do something either despicable or idiotic. Each time Huck wonders how someone like Jim can be so "white," he is denying that the values of humanity and decency are in fact "white" and suggesting that perhaps their rightful owner is a slave named Jim.

While there is a great deal of violence in the book, not once does Twain show us a physical act of violence against a slave. Perhaps this is because it would take away from the deeper violence, the humiliation and annihilation of a person that results from refusing to acknowledge him as a human being, the desire to generalize him out of existence, to deny him human feelings and emotions. Within the confines of this upside-down world, the only way for Huck and Jim to survive is to be dead, which is why, all through their journey, they conceal their real identities and take on various disguises. Yet the book is not about the search for identity; it is about the necessity of hiding one's true self.

This flight and violence and obfuscation presented us, in Tehran, with a startling similarity to our own lives. Farah and I knew something about this, because in those post-revolutionary days we all went underground and learned to hide our true selves. When you live in an authoritarian state, to remain alive you have to pass yourself off as someone else. Jim and Huck break every possible rule by lying, cheating and stealing. But we believe them to be good and true. So they force us to question and reexamine what we would consider to be basic, unchanging moral principles: Under what conditions might it be right to lie, to break the law, to cheat, to blaspheme?

## 12

It is intriguing how memory hangs on to small details, saving the scraps of experience for the time when those insignificant details will shape the tone and texture of that lost time. I was reminded recently of the two times I saw Farah after her return to Tehran. The first time, I was still teaching at the University of Tehran; it must have been 1980, because the veil had not yet become mandatory. I saw her sitting on the steps of the Faculty of Literature and Foreign Languages, talking to a friend. Farah was an adjunct, teaching English in the same department where I had a full-time position. The other time, my husband and I saw her standing by a Coca-Cola kiosk, a bottle of Coke in one hand, deep in conversation with a woman I did not know. Both times, we greeted each other briefly but did not stay to talk or exchange contact information. And both times, she gave me a very particular smile.

Farah conveyed a great deal through her smiles. Sometimes I felt she used them instead of words, challenging you to try to catch their meaning: there was the conspiratorial smile, and the manipulative or appeasing one, the knowing smile, the secretive smile and then the one that signified distance. That was the smile she had offered me on those two brief encounters in Tehran. While acknowledging me, she wanted to go no further than that chance meeting.

In those days, I was used to furtive looks—I can still picture my student Razieh in the street by the university after one of the regime's massacres, coming toward me from the opposite direction, or a former student activist at Berkeley silently catching my eye. Even my own cousins Saiid and Fahimeh could not be acknowledged in public. This made them all so close and yet so distant, as if they already belonged to another world, predicting the ghosts they would soon become.

The next time I saw Farah was in the United States in 1990, eight years after she had left Iran. I was there for only three days, for a conference. She came to pick me up in her car, looking buoyant; I remember she wore a cap that made her look like a young boy. We had lots of fun, giggling and laughing like teenagers, and talked about everything but the thing that had divided us: the movement and politics in Iran. It was a sign of the changes we had both undergone since we last sat opposite each other in Chicago that we wanted to reconnect based on what had first brought us together: our family ties and our friendship.

I hesitated to ask her about her time in Iran, uncertain what wounds I would reopen. By then her escape from Iran had become history, and thus a story, with carefully worn contours. In my memory of those two times I saw her in Tehran, we both appeared nonchalant and carefree, but in reality they were dark days, filled with so much anxiety and fear about the war with Iraq and the constant violence. It had become customary to hear about relatives, friends and students who had been arrested, tortured and killed. A lucky few managed to flee the country, but I had my share of cousins hiding out or killed, friends on the run, students executed. Farah's was one story among many. That was the time my nightmares began, and to this day they are with me.

For a long time, Farah was reticent to talk about those days. It was years before she finally agreed to divulge something of her story, when her sister persuaded her to sit for long hours for an interview that Mahnaz later transformed into a more fluid narrative and published in her book *Women in Exile*. At the time, Farah did not want to reveal her own identity, partly for security reasons and because she still hoped to go back to Iran. So in the book she refers to her husband as Hormoz and to herself as Azar.

Farah had returned to Tehran in jubilant exultation in February of 1979, a week after the revolution. One can only imagine her emotion when, for only the second time since she had left Iran at the age of ten, she found herself diving down through the mountains into the Tehran airport. All of the borders were closed in the first days of the revolution, and her group had been stranded in Germany. "So we did what we knew best," she explained. "We protested. And it worked." A plane was sent for them, and all of those who had supported the revolution from afar returned together in triumph. On landing in Tehran, the religious students left the plane chanting, "Long live the Islamic revolution," while Farah and her comrades walked out shouting, "Long live freedom and liberty." The airport was controlled by the Revolutionary Guards and closed to commercial air traffic. There was no doubt from the start that the guards were firmly on the side of the Muslim students. "Within four years of that day," Farah said, "all but one of my friends who came with me on that plane were dead."

In Tehran, Farah didn't call her father or her husband's parents. "The revolution," she said, "took priority over all ties and relationships." She found a job teaching English, but as in the United States, she devoted herself mainly to her revolutionary activities.

Faramarz arrived shortly afterwards—he had stayed behind to rally together more student supporters. By then the divisions had become more violent. I remember how one moment we were all dancing in the streets and kissing one another—communists, Islamists, and bazaaris—and the next those same streets were barricaded by violent protests and the songs gave way to the sound of bullets. It started with the persecution of secular leftists, then the nationalists, and finally the Islamists who disagreed with Ayatollah Khomeini and his followers.

The leftist groups who were very active before and during the revolution did not have much popular support in Tehran. Farah describes how, after a large workers' demonstration, she and a few others from her group stayed behind to talk to the workers. "They listened politely, but as we turned to leave, one of them called to us, waving his hand. 'Bye-bye!' he said in English, grinning with amusement. Nothing seemed to express more clearly the foreignness of our contingent to those workers whom we had thought our natural allies."

By then Farah had lost her faith in Marxism. She felt vulnerable, and, like so many members of partisan and ideological groups, she was afraid to be branded a traitor by people who had become like a family to her or of appearing, as she put it, "passive, afraid, bourgeois." Faramarz found it more difficult to part with either his group or his ideology. He was, by Farah's account, not so much a believer as "a prisoner of the mind-set he had helped to create. He was one of the leaders who had helped radicalize the group. He had motivated others to become 'revolutionaries,' unbending, unafraid, and unchanging. And now he had to stand up to the young radicals and face their contempt. He knew they would interpret the change in him as loss of courage, as choosing the personal above the cause. They would consider him a cop-out. He had taught them to think this way, and so he wavered and waited, not willing to save himself alone, not able to save the others, his mind in terrible turmoil."

It is heartbreaking how Farah used to talk of those moments of tranquillity when, despite the ominous signs surrounding them, she and Faramarz came close to having a "normal" home life. She once told me how surprised she was by this newfound sense of happiness amid the uncertainty and violence of the revolution. She was trying to establish a language school, and Faramarz was rediscovering his family and his talent for crafts and carpentry. "Our daughter was now an energetic two years old. I was pregnant with my second child. . . . We read and talked and listened to music and watched the latest American films on video, which, strangely enough, were regularly smuggled into Iran. We took very little security precaution for a group fast becoming one of the priority targets for the regime. Some evenings, when there was no video to watch, we would get together with friends and each act out a whole film for the others. We laughed mindlessly at someone's depiction of *Manhattan;* we were excited and frightened by a rendering of *Psycho*.

"I was very happy with my life, but also constantly afraid," Farah said. "At the end of each day, I would breathe easier and say to myself, *Another day and no disaster.* At the beginning of each day, the thought crossed my mind that this may be the last day of peace and safety."

Then, after the ouster of the first Iranian president, Bani-Sadr, one faction in their group decided on armed insurrection against the regime. I cannot imagine how, even then, they could have believed that they would ever garner enough support to destroy the new Islamic state. But these were giddy times, when toppling governments seemed like child's play for a band of passionate revolutionaries. The place they chose for their insurrection was Amol, a beautiful small town near the Caspian Sea. After months of discussion among themselves, Faramarz and Farah openly declared their opposition to the plan, earning the contempt of the radical faction within their group. "Faramarz was called a coward and an opportunist by the very people who once circled around him to speak." The insults and intimidation served only to strengthen his resolve. Farah couldn't remember whether he resigned or was pushed aside from his leadership position in the group, but still he did not quit.

In politics, the world is divided into good and bad, and obviously we are on the side of the good. We know we will not go through the pain of investigating, doubting and being doubted. Questions of ethics and principle shift from individual choice to that of the group. Only in this instance, Farah blinked. The group was going too far, and she had the strength to do what few of us can: assert her own private sense of right and wrong and distance herself from the group. It is what Huck did when he broke from Tom and his band of robbers.

By January 1982 the group had moved weapons, tents and food supplies to the forests near Amol. Their attack was planned for January 25. That morning, nearly a hundred men and women attacked the headquarters of the police and guards in Amol.

They fought for fifteen hours. Many were killed and many more captured. As Farah told Mahnaz, "The leaders had planned for victory but not for retreat."

The regime at first kept the news of the attack quiet. Farah and Faramarz heard about it by word of mouth. They should have left then. There were people being tortured in prison who sooner or later would reveal their names and whereabouts. Faramarz and a few others who had opposed the plan but remained loyal to the group thought they should not abandon their friends in hard times like these and just went on with life. "Like a sparrow confronting a cobra, we were paralyzed," Farah said. It is important to understand how far they had moved ideologically and emotionally from the time when Farah had sought friendship and support—"a home," as she called it—in the movement.

Farah and Faramarz celebrated the Iranian New Year, Nowrooz, on March 21, as usual. They lived perhaps with more intensity than before but "with no conscious recognition of impending disaster." They made fun of the mullahs on television. "We laughed at their vulgarity, their crassness and stupidity," Farah said. "But even though we were looking at them from the vantage point of our Western upbringing, which made them appear even more ludicrous, we thought of them as ours to deal with, our problem. This feeling of belonging to a society, identifying with it in spite of its faults, is something I have never felt before or after this period. I have never again been a participant in the life of a nation."

Finally, six months after the Amol attack, Faramarz asked Farah to contact a relative to find out how her brother had been smuggled out of the country. Faramarz had to go to another meeting, and she was to meet him at his mother's house for lunch. In Mahnaz's account, she describes how, as Farah walked to his mother's house, she went over all the things she had to tell him, for she always ended the day by telling Faramarz everything. More students had registered for her school, and she felt they were close to making a decision about their future. It was a hot summer day, and she was seven months' pregnant. "But I felt light and happy, walking briskly, smiling at my own shadow."

He didn't show up for lunch. At six o'clock that evening, she went back to their apartment. She sat on the floor and stared at the carpet and waited. She went to the nearest phone booth at eight.

How do you write about such things? It is as if, by recounting them, you are participating in inflicting pain. When Huck tells us about the clan warfare between the Shepherdsons and the Grangerfords, his non-description makes the horror of the atrocities he witnessed all the more real. "I ain't a-going to tell *all* that happened—it would make me sick again if I was to do that. I wished I hadn't ever come ashore that night to see such things. I ain't ever going to get shut of them—lots of times I dream about them."

Every time I review Farah's story and others like it, I am reminded of what an acquaintance told me at the start of the revolution: "I cannot believe we welcomed our own murderers into town with festivities and joy, carrying them on our shoulders." We all seemed to be playing a role onstage, only suddenly the knives were real.

Farah was lucky to find a temporary shelter at a good friend's house with a gorgeous garden, close to the dreaded Evin prison, where her husband and his comrades were kept. "It was strange to be in that beautiful garden with its ancient oak trees and the stream passing through the peaceful landscape," she told Mahnaz. The garden was close enough to the prison compound that she could hear, at dawn, the loudspeakers sounding out the call to morning prayer. She said that the sound shook the house. "Every morning at dawn I walked to the wall at the bottom of the garden to listen to the chants of the prisoners. I thought if I listened carefully I would be able to distinguish [his] voice among all the others'. I thought if I concentrated enough he would feel my presence nearby. I refused to think of torture. I refused to think that [he] would probably not be among those prisoners."

# 13

During her last years, but especially that final year, a circle formed around Farah, consisting of her family and friends. Her second husband, Habib, was both a witness and a participant in the comings and goings within this increasingly private world. Each one of us was honored with a special role in Farah's life, and everyone was more than his or her assigned role: Mahnaz was more than a sister, Neda more than a daughter, Nema more than a son, Hamid more than a brother, Jaleh more than a former comrade and best friend, Roshanak more than a former sister-in-law, Bahram more than an intellectual companion, and within that exclusive list I was left with the role of more than a childhood friend. We all knew and talked about the fact that no matter what happened in the future, our small group would always be bound by our love for Farah, by the privilege of having shared the secret sorrows and joys of those moments we spent together because we had spent them with her.

I remember one lunch in particular, at Leopold's, when Farah wanted to talk about Huck. I was having a hard time with my chapter and wanted to talk about something else. She was eating an arugula-and-fig salad, and I had a coffee and a fruit tart. I was gazing at a girl who'd just walked in carrying an Hermès bag. She was holding the bag on a bent elbow, a little distant from her body. Trying to divert Farah from her single-minded focus, I said, "Look at the way that girl is holding her bag, in order to fore-ground it and make people admire the bag, and by extension its owner. But," I added, "it makes me feel as if she is holding a dead rat a little distance away from her body to avoid further contact."

Farah was playing with her salad and did not respond—by then she had lost her appetite.

"It reminds me of some of our so-called intellectuals," I continued. "The academics especially, who carry their ideolo-gies, which they call 'theory,' like an Hermès bag, basking in its light, making others wow and bow."

Farah was too obstinate to be so easily sidetracked. "Don't you mean Mark Twain's progenies, instead of Huck's?" she asked.

I had meant Huck Finn's. Twain had his own distinguished literary brood, but I was interested in Huck's children, his de-scendants. I shared Hemingway's theory—she had heard me many times on the subject—that all, or at least many, of the dis-tinctive characteristics and preoccupations of American fiction could be traced back to *Huckleberry Finn*. I had even come to believe that America owed its most sacred foundational myth—that of restless individualism—to that orphan boy who'd left home to escape being "sivilized" by his aunt. This question of America's founding myths had become a more urgent preoccupation to me, as all around us there seemed to be a contest going on to define who was more or less American.

I had received a few weeks earlier a notice from the Citizenship and Immigration Services office in Virginia, informing me that I should present myself early in the morning in a few weeks' time for my citizenship interview. If accepted, I would then be invited to swear an oath of allegiance, after which I would be an American citizen. What does it mean to be American? Is it a descriptive fact or a whole set of ideas and values that one can choose to believe in? Farah and I felt that if we did not define what it meant for us, then someone else would do it for us, and in so doing they would define us. We hadn't come this far to let that happen again.

My husband, Bijan, would watch the news obsessively when he got home from work, as he still does every night, and follow the news from Iran on the Web, which at that time was quite alarming. I paced around the kitchen in despair, talking back to the creeps on television lecturing us about the heroic, patriotic need to curtail civil liberties for the sake of "security." I started to keep a little book of political euphemisms, just like the one I had kept in Iran. "Patriots" were those who don't question the government's new laws, "homeland" something that needed to be defended, and everywhere, even at school, we were being reminded of the need for "security." "Have a safe day." Safe? When did that enter into the equation?

The Islamic revolution forever changed the meaning of words like "spirituality," "religion," "virtuous," "decadent," "alien." These words became orphans associated with fear, danger, corruption and the state, in the same way that in the Soviet Union words like "proletariat," "dictatorship," "equality," "freedom" and "revolution" had lost their original meaning. In democratic societies, words do not kill, but they are effective at numbing our hearts and minds, to the point that we become tolerant of things that go against our principles and values. The wealthy are "job creators" and the poor are "parasites," unemployed teachers and firefighters should make "sacrifices," members of Congress are "protecting our future," candidates "package" and "repackage" themselves, and almost every public personality or "celebrity" has a "brand" or is in the process of "rebranding." "Diversity" is an unimpeachable mandate, and everything is done and justified in the name of "the American people."

Why is it that American politicians feel they have a right to speak for the republic? Writers are left with the burden of reclaiming America, snatching it back from their grasp. While some shrug it off, others, like Philip Roth and David Foster Wallace, will seek to be the voice of conscience, or the voice of the heart, as Twain might have put it. I found myself digging through the books Farah had recommended to me (my homework, she called it) for different views of what it means to be American. One need only read the letters exchanged by John Adams and Thomas Jefferson in the latter part of their lives to know that most of our public debates today are parodies of what once constituted the American political discourse.

"Why not go back to the original myth?" I asked Farah, warming up. She was still feverishly reading American history, and I, as always, was searching for answers in fiction, so we made a perfect team. We joked that together we would come up with a new declaration of independence. We would save the idea of America from its more noxious defenders.

That was when I dramatically announced to my close circle of friends that once I'd started watching more *Law & Order* than news, I knew the time had come to look a little more closely into what was going on. *Law & Order* was a good story, plausible and realistic, while the news appeared more and more like entertainment or fantasy—or horror, depending on your point of view. I had begun to have the uncomfortable feeling that we, as spectators, were playing a role in someone else's script, or, more accurately, in someone else's commercial.

America's commercialism has been a matter of cliché for some time, its dangerous seductiveness parodied in Kafka's *Amerika,* the hyperrational insanity of it all, its manipulative crassness and good-natured cruelties, its simultaneous cultivation of compassion and indifference. How could a country so boasting of individualism be so conformist? How could people who view themselves as pragmatic be so prone to fantastical thinking? Commercials are bad enough, making you believe they are giving you what you want, but when most everything takes on the feel and texture of a commercial—when the news is there not to give you facts but to seduce and infuriate you—isn't it time to do something? Surely there are other notions of what it means to be American than those offered up by Ann

Coulter and Glenn Beck. When you trust Jon Stewart and Stephen Colbert more than the so-called news offered up by Fox or MSNBC, when you find them fairer and more balanced, when those interviewed on *Face the Nation* and other serious news shows appear more and more like comic parodies, then the time must surely have come, I told Farah with a flourish, to defect in favor of a more appealing America, the one whose founding documents were written by poets and novelists, the one I'd taken to calling the Republic of Imagination.

All this boasting about the American dream—is this dream really as shabby as Dale Carnegie's recipe for success? Remember that episode of *The Simpsons* where Homer is worried because Mr. Burns has threatened him, saying he will destroy his every single dream, and Marge tells him not to worry so much, that when a man's greatest dreams are seconds on dessert, the occasional snuggle and sleeping in on weekends, no one can destroy your dreams? "That is what we've come to," I said triumphantly. "Hence Huck Finn!"

"Hence indeed!" deadpanned Farah. There was a glimmer in her eyes, and I knew she was hooked.

"We have Ferdowsi's 'Book of Kings,'" I said. "America has *Huckleberry Finn*. Only, while Ferdowsi resurrects Iran's history and mythology going back three thousand years, from the dawn of history until the Arab conquest in the seventh century, Twain creates a myth of America in the making. His aim is not to recapture the past but in a strange way to retrieve the future." Then I quoted for her one of my favorite lines from Rilke: "The future enters into us in order to transform itself in us, long before it happens."

"Twain captured the spirit of the future," I went on, "and from then on many great American novelists, from Hemingway and Fitzgerald to Carson McCullers and Raymond Chandler, from Ralph Ellison and James Baldwin to Saul Bellow, have followed suit in their own way, speaking the language of their own times. That is what I mean by 'Huck Finn's Progenies.' They are all spokesmen for the other America, not the rule-bound homeland conjured up by the phony patriotism of politicians, but the more open and inclusive land of our dreams."

Farah was still not convinced it would make a good title, but she was beginning to understand what I had in mind.

# 14

Farah stayed in the house with the large garden at the foot of Evin prison for about a month. Remaining in Tehran was becoming too dangerous for her and for Faramarz's family, as well as for the friends who were giving her asylum, so she decided to leave Iran, along with Faramarz's sister and her six-month-old baby, his brother and sister-in-law, and her own two-and-a-half-year-old daughter, Neda. It was an example of her amazing willpower and levelheadedness that she put her feelings of anxiety and love for Faramarz, as well as her fears of being captured, on hold and tried to focus on how to save her child and herself rather than imagining what was happening to Faramarz.

I have heard this story so many times, in fragments, mainly from Farah and from those who traveled with her, but each time the presence of that other person telling their own story somehow lightened the intensity of the experiences. But now, rereading Mahnaz's account in the solitude of my office, without any hope of calling Farah and hearing her say, "What's up, kiddo," or "Hi, Azi-joon," followed by the inevitable "What's up?" suddenly I feel the intense grief and horror she must have gone through, and the loneliness.

They were to be smuggled to Turkey and were told that they would be traveling by jeep. But that didn't happen. They started with a jeep but soon were told to get out and run across a "plowed field" to meet the guides who would take them across, and that the journey was to be on horseback, riding two to a horse. "I sat behind the rider," Farah explained. "I was forced to stretch my legs across the top of the gunny sacks, which left my belly touching the rump of the horse. Every step the horse took brought pressure on my belly; I soon lost all feeling in my legs, which were sticking out over the gunny sacks." They rode through the night, moving over precarious and narrow paths while crossing the mountains of Kurdistan, one of the westernmost provinces of Iran, bordering Iraq and Turkey. "I kept asking [the smugglers] to stop to let me stretch my legs," Farah said, "but they wouldn't. At dawn I told them that if they didn't stop I would throw myself down. Finally they stopped. I couldn't move my legs to get off. Two smugglers had to lift me off the horse and set me down. Fatemeh [Faramarz's sister's pseudonym] and Simin [her sister-in-law's pseudonym] rubbed my legs until I could move them again." The smugglers threatened them repeatedly, demanding more money, which they wisely refused to hand over.

Soon they reached a village. They spent the day there,

because they could travel only at night. They were put in a stable, the only light a hole in the ceiling. The next morning, Farah insisted on having a horse of her own and was given one. That night, as they snaked their way up a narrow path that plunged into a precipice, she considered the nearness of death: "A slip and I could easily roll down into the valley. I put my faith in the horse. It was a strange feeling to have no control over one's life. The smugglers could do anything they wanted with us. We moved in that twilight area at the edge of the law. No country wanted us. No country was responsible for us."

Later Neda, Farah's daughter, told me how frightened she was to be separated from her mother, sitting behind a smuggler on her own horse. She remembered clinging to her security blanket, and then dropping it and not being allowed to pick it up until she made such a fuss that they had to listen to her. Faramarz's sister's baby had to somehow be kept quiet as they passed through the checkpoints, and her desperate mother gave her a Valium to silence her. "She was holding the baby in one arm and holding on to the smuggler in front of her with the other," Farah recalled. "At one point she felt her arm getting numb and she was afraid she would let the baby slip out of it. I used my scarf to tie the baby to her arm for the rest of the journey." When they were told at last that they were entering Turkey, Farah turned back with a pang in her heart. They were halfway there. "It was painful to look back at the Iranian landscape, knowing I might never return to it, knowing also that I was leaving my husband behind."

On the border with Turkey, they were handed over to a new group of smugglers. Their new guides stole their belongings and abandoned them by the side of the road, in a "flat, desert terrain that seemed to stretch forever." Without food, drink or shade, the baby and Neda soon faced dehydration. To avoid checkpoints, they had to walk in the dark on overgrown paths. They took turns carrying Neda and the baby. Once, when Farah was carrying the baby, "Simin fell flat on her face from exhaustion, asleep before she hit the ground." Farah kept slapping her face to keep her awake. At one point she slipped on a rocky hillside and skidded on her belly all the way down, but at six the next morning, they finally reached the outskirts of Van. "Our clothes were torn and dirty; we could barely walk, and out of habit formed of our recent trek through the mountains, we walked single file, one behind the other, like the remnants of a ragtag army."

They went to a shabby hotel, and Farah fell asleep as soon as she put her head on the pillow. She woke up with a start some hours later, feeling as if she had stopped breathing. She tried to open the door and found it locked from the outside. Simin had locked the door to protect her. She became hysterical. She banged on the door, shouting for someone to let her out. "That moment was the closest I came to breaking down," Farah later recalled. "It marked the beginning of my life in exile."

That image of Farah banging on the door has remained firmly etched in my memory. The price one pays when choosing exile is the loss of so much that defines you as an individual. The only thing that makes this immense loss tolerable is the discovery of a self you did not know existed—of a true independence. That is the real gift of America, not its fabled wealth and prosperity. Farah's independence, I believe, began on that day in Turkey when she started beating against the door.

# 15

On December 1, 2008, I became an American citizen. It was an extremely cold, dry and windy morning, and after I had been asked a few simple questions, mainly on U.S. history, the friendly immigration officer told me I could take the oath if I cared to wait until two o'clock that afternoon.

I spent most of my time before returning to take the oath at a diner next to the immigration office, looking out into a large expanse of land and reflecting on my old and new homes. It had not been an easy choice. Choice implies trust, a leap of faith, and it is difficult for a person who has lost her original home to make that leap regarding a new one. When I went back to Tehran in 1979, I would walk down the streets, feeling the pavement beneath my feet, and tell myself, *I am here, this is my home, I am here, here.* Soon those sentiments turned sour, poisoned by new memories of protests, tear gas, blood and public executions. Walking the streets meant averting my eyes, trying not to see, and hoping that I would not be seen or noticed. I started asking myself, *Is this my home? The home I dreamed of returning to? Where am I, and who are these people now ruling the streets?*

Later, I told Farah and Mahnaz that sitting there alone in that diner, I revisited a question I had been asking myself for the past few years: What does it mean to be an American? I had concluded that to choose a new citizenship is like choosing a partner: it is a choice that binds you, for better and for worse, in sickness and in health. And it seemed to me that no time was as good as this to contemplate both America's sickness and its health. The financial crisis crystallized much that was both good and bad about the country. For me, it never was just a financial crisis, but a crisis of vision and of imagination. You can (at least for a while) bail out the financial giants, but no one seems much concerned with propping up the Republic of Imagination. When I returned shortly before two and joined the long queue waiting to get naturalization packages, I was in a mildly elated mood, although mindful that joy is transient and should not be taken too seriously. I felt that I had the power to do a little "sivilizing" of my own, and this was for me the most exciting aspect of becoming American. We were handed our naturalization packages, which included a booklet containing the Declaration of Independence and the Constitution and a small American flag on a gold-colored plastic flagpole. We then filed into a rather shabby room and sat down. The national anthem played in the background, and a large screen projected images of the flag and of American landscapes.

Soon we were at our seats; my seat number was 30, on my left was number 29, and to my right, number 31, a man with a salmon tie and a pink shirt. It was obvious that, unlike me and the guy to my left, he had taken some trouble with his appearance. He fidgeted and looked in my direction, the movements of a man who is dying to talk. I smiled at him encouragingly and he smiled back, pointing to the small flag in my hand. He waved his, saying, "For the past ten years I have kept an American flag in my apartment. I take it out, dust it and put it back again." He paused and then said, "And now this!"

Obviously he did not mean the small flag, but the occasion, the fact that the next time he took his flag out to dust, he would do so as an American citizen. He went on to describe what awaited us: first there would be the president's message of welcome, some speeches about citizenship, then each of us would be called. "Remember to keep your flag in your hand," he told me, "and smile, because someone will take our pictures." But no one ever did.

Somehow we never properly introduced ourselves, perhaps because the occasion had made such formalities irrelevant. I knew he was Arab, because I had overheard him speaking on his cell phone, but I don't know how I discovered that the man to my left, who was not very receptive to joining in the conversation, was from Latin America.

I listened to my new co-conspirator but did not say much. What did I have to say? Should I have told him that I was becoming an American citizen because of *Huck Finn*? Should I have mentioned Melville, Ralph Ellison, Sherwood Anderson, Kate Chopin and Elizabeth Cady Stanton? Should I have talked about the elections and added that I had some hope, but also many doubts? Should I have asked him if he watched Jon Stewart, *The Simpsons, Law & Order* or *Seinfeld*? Did he like Howard Hawks and the Marx Brothers? What about Dashiell Hammett and Raymond Chandler? Did he listen to the Doors, the Mothers of Invention, Joni Mitchell, Jimi Hendrix, John Coltrane or Miles Davis? Did he really like Edward Hopper? Nothing I could have said, I told Farah later, would have matched his pure, un-adulterated joy, his complete immersion in the moment, transforming the gaudy room, the familiar images and the anthem and the staff, all dressed up, into a magical initiation ceremony worthy of Harry Potter. He was like an ecstatic bridegroom just before his wedding, telling a perfect stranger about his good fortune, about the years he had stolen glances at a picture of his beloved, taking it out every once in a while, and now this!

I left the building and immediately called my husband to let him know that I was now the first American in the family. As I walked down the street, a car stopped and my Arab friend rolled the window down to ask me if I wanted a ride. I thanked him and declined, already a bit nostalgic as I watched the car move on and disappear. I had been too overwhelmed by his feeling of anticipation, his pride at becoming an American, to pay attention to his nationality when he was called up. We had not spoken about the homes we'd left behind. Our brief relationship, if one could call it that, was based not on our shared past but on the present, on becoming American. He had offered me his excitement, his trust, his hope, and what did I have to offer in return except a pair of attentive ears and an approving smile? Could I tell him about my doubts, my arguments with myself, my joy, my guilt? Could I tell him that it seemed to me that in this new place, the past was still very much alive, demanding a space all its own?

And yet there was another aspect to becoming American: I could be an American without casting off Iran. In fact, to be an American you do not cast off the past, but assimilate it into the present. At the time, it seemed that the person of Barack Hussein Obama confirmed my belief that you could cultivate new roots in this land with seeds from another country, that it was possible to not be paralyzed by your past. This was in part Huck's message, or rather what Farah found so appealing about Huck. He left his family, his home—to the extent he had one—and became a stronger person once he was free of the destructive weight of conventions and expectations.

# 16

Farah arrived in the United States on August 30, 1982. "This country offered me a home," she told Mahnaz. "I cannot remain indifferent." The way she confronted the hurdles in this country and overcame what Saul Bellow called the "sufferings of freedom" was to my mind every bit as heroic as her struggle in the face of those other ordeals and hurdles in her country of birth. Writing about Farah, I am reminded of the fact that the United States is a country founded as much on broken dreams as it is on hope and promise; we cannot dismiss one in favor of the other. People come here bringing unbearable pain and anguish with them, and for every story of new beginnings there is one of crushed dreams.

Farah spent the first three months living with her mother in Monterey, California. She told me that those first few days and months in the United States had at times seemed like an extension of her nightmarish escape from Iran. She had tried to busy herself with the simple effort to survive but also to divert herself from the reality of Faramarz's fate, thousands of miles away. She would write letters and place phone calls to Iran, desperate to discover his fate. At the same time, she would later tell Mahnaz, she secured all the necessary forms of identification for her new life—a Social Security card, a driver's license, a library card. She found a child care center and began attending word-processing classes at the local high school. "I tried not to disrupt my mother's life too much," she said. Nema, her son, was born on September 25, less than one month later.

When the government finally announced the arrest of the Amol group, families were allowed to meet with prisoners. Faramarz's family had told him about Farah's escape with Neda and about Nema's birth. The fact that they had seen him gave her hope. Perhaps it was a sign that the trial would be delayed. Perhaps he would be spared. Having heard that the jailers could be bribed, she started raising money for that purpose. Farah knew this was wishful thinking and that she was being unreasonable, but "reason," she told Mahnaz, "had nothing to do with the state of my mind."

I thought of Farah when I first heard on the radio that a number of her former comrades had been arrested. For days I collected the newspaper clippings with their photographs, hiding them by using them as shoe trees in my closet. I watched their show trials with Bijan in silent, inarticulate dread. Faramarz was among them. We, like so many others, had learned not to speculate about their fate. A time comes when even hope is dangerous.

Farah recalled the trials with almost clinical detachment: "Officials had packed a large hall with relatives of the guards who had fought or been killed in Amol. The walls of the hall were draped with slogans against the defendants, who were seated on a stage facing the rowdy crowd that shouted insults at them and demanded their execution. They were not allowed a lawyer." The judge was known as the "hanging judge," because of the number of men and women he had sent to the gallows. All of the defendants were accused of corruption of the earth, fighting against God and (of course), to crown it all, cooperating with the Great Satan. All of the defendants confessed to being communist and to mounting a plot against the regime. They said their actions were wrong. After three weeks, they were all condemned to death.

Mahnaz went to visit Farah in Monterey and finally brought her back home with her. On January 24, the anniversary of the Amol uprising, Farah and Mahnaz went to Clyde's, in Georgetown, for lunch. Farah thought that the execution would happen then. "People were eating and watching the Super Bowl on TV," she said. "The whole place was feverish with excitement. I felt so alien. The world with which my life was interwoven and the world in which I found myself were far apart."

The morning of the twenty-fifth came and went with no news. The next day, Mahnaz got the call from Iran. She hurried home to tell Farah and by the time she reached the house she was crying. Mahnaz later told me that what shocked her more than anything was Farah's reaction. She asked if something had happened to their mother, their friends—she thought of everyone, Mahnaz said, but Faramarz.

At last, she realized that her sister's tears were for her. "The baby was taken away. I was given a tranquilizer. I had depended so much on [Faramarz's] presence. The days became real only when I had recounted every detail of my experiences to him each evening. But part of the experience of losing him involved carrying alone the burden of raising and supporting the children, a burden that would not allow me my time of mourning."

In her quiet and determined way, Farah refused to let Faramarz's death destroy her. She would not give the regime that satisfaction. She moved to Berkeley a few months later and got a job working at a friend's printing press. Then she moved to D.C. in the fall of 1984, found a nursery and a child care center and went to work. Within a year she had found a job as an editor.

"I have learned and grown and found a new identity for myself," she told Mahnaz. "The experience has hardened me. But it has also made me self-reliant. I have grown as a person. I have searched within myself for every ounce of initiative, every resource, every strength in order to empower myself not only to survive but to become whole for my children. I am proud of what I have been able to accomplish. My children are attending good schools and are cheerful, friendly, and optimistic people. I have a successful career. I am not bitter about the past. I think of my years of political struggle not from the vantage point of the tragedy that ended them but from that of the idealism and camaraderie which marked our goals and relationships."

Within two years of arriving in the States, Farah owned a home, had a profession and was raising two healthy, happy children as a single mother, without social stigma. The experience persuaded her that the American myth had a certain reality. "I have come to appreciate the United States in ways I never knew before," she said. "But I have yet to feel completely at home here. . . . I have retained my ethnic identity and nowhere do I realize it more than in my children's clear identification of themselves as Iranian Americans." She claimed she no longer felt implicated by Iran's troubles, and she could not care in the same way about political life in her new home.

"You feel at home when you start grumbling," I muttered when Farah tried that one on me. And, truth be told, she did begin to participate in the political life of this country. After almost twenty years, she finally made peace with her lost love, fell in love again and married another man, who was finally able to give her the home that had eluded her for so long.

# 17

Sometimes I felt as if my conversations with Farah had a life-and-death quality to them—they had become so necessary both to Farah and to me. They led every time to surprise endings and new questions, and old questions in new contexts. We were re-enacting our childhood, the secret exchanges that would fix us for hours to a corner of the living room or under the shade of a generous tree. Our conversations did have a conspiratorial aspect to them, although what we talked about was no secret. We weren't even gossiping when, on that day that we met at Kramerbooks, we both felt kind of dizzy, I with my apple martini and she on her second cup of tea.

I told her I had this strange feeling, difficult to put into words, that although teaching *Huckleberry Finn* in Iran was both rewarding and revealing, and although my students as a whole loved it, they focused mainly on the repressive aspects of the book, wanting to find fault with a society with which they were at war. In my classes in Iran, I had spent a fair amount of time discussing the confinements of life in a "civilized" society and made a point of drawing parallels with Iran, with its rigid structures and conformity, where everything was done *by the book*—and it was always somebody else's book. In America, my focus had shifted to morality, a topic my students returned to both in class discussions and in their journals.

Some of my Islamist students were uncomfortable with Huck's view of Sunday school, but, as one of them put it to me one day after class, "Huck is against not religion but established religion, kind of like what we over here call 'American Islam,' the kind that was prevalent during the shah's time." He handily overlooked the complicating fact that his own kind of religion had now become established. I felt there was little difference between the mentality of slave owners who were in the habit of reminding skeptics that the Bible approved of slavery and of Islamists who claimed that Islam approved of the repression of women and minorities and that the Prophet, after all, was of the view that a woman's testimony should be worth half that of a man. But he seemed so happy with his find that I didn't have the heart to disillusion him, at least not then.

If society's moral edicts are a sham, if they go against the purer lessons of the heart, what should we do? The lessons Huck learns and unlearns go far beyond the immorality of slavery. His trip with Jim is an education, countering the lessons of Sunday school. At every step, Huck is tested.

In one scene in which Jim, having lost Huck, is frantic with anxiety, Huck pretends to have been there all the time. Upon discovering the prank, Jim tells Huck how he felt when he thought he'd lost his friend—"my heart wuz mos' broke bekase you wuz los," he says—and how relieved he was to find him again. Jim goes on to reproach Huck. He says that, while he was thankful to see his friend safe, all Huck was thinking about was "how you could make a fool uv ole Jim wid a lie. Dat truck dah is *trash;* en trash is what people is dat puts dirt on de head er dey fren's en makes 'em ashamed." Huck reports, "Then he got up slow and walked to the wigwam, and went in there without saying anything but that. But that was enough. It made me feel so mean I could almost kissed *his* foot to get him to take it back." It takes Huck fifteen minutes to "humble" himself to a "nigger," but he tells us he did it and "I warn't ever sorry for it afterwards, neither. I didn't do him no more mean tricks, and I wouldn't done that one if I'd a knowed it would make him feel that way."

The real test arrives when Huck contemplates the consequences of helping Jim find freedom. He sees this not as an act of liberation but as a sin, something for which he will be blamed. "I couldn't get that out of my conscience, no how nor no way," he says. As Jim believes he is nearing Cairo and freedom— wrongly, it turns out—Huck tells us, "My conscience got to stirring me up hotter than ever. . . ." He decides to give Jim up, and has a chance to do so when he runs across two men looking for five runaway slaves, but as hard as he tries, he cannot betray Jim. He reports:

"I tried for a second or two to brace up and out with it, but

I warn't man enough—hadn't the spunk of a rabbit. I see I was weakening; so I just give up trying, and up and says:

"'He's white.'"

Although he feels bad for doing the "wrong" thing, he figures he would have felt just as bad turning Jim in, and since he cannot understand why it is that the "wages" of doing the right things and the wrong thing are the same, he decides not to think about it and to just do "whichever comes handiest at the time."

This unresolved dilemma returns to haunt him, as he always seems to impulsively take the side of the "wrong." When he learns that the duke and the dauphin have betrayed Jim for a paltry $45, Huck begins his longest fight with his conscience. He has another "long think," sorting out different possibilities, and he tells us, "The more I studied about this the more my conscience went to grinding me, and the more wicked and low-down and ornery I got to feeling." He knows he could have gone to Sunday school and that there they would have "learnt" him that "people that acts as I'd been acting about that nigger goes to everlasting fire." He tries to pray, but the words will not come, because his "heart warn't right." So finally, deciding to do the "right thing," he writes a note to Miss Watson, giving Jim up.

Once he writes the note, he feels "good and all washed clean of sin for the first time I had ever felt so in my life, and I knowed I could pray now." But his wayward heart would not let him off so easily. For immediately he starts thinking, and as he continues to think he tells us,

I see Jim before me, all the time: in the day and in the night-time, sometimes moonlight, sometimes storms, and we a-floating along, talking and singing and laughing. But somehow I couldn't seem to strike no places to harden me against him, but only the other kind. I'd see him standing my watch on top of his'n, 'stead of calling me, so I could go on sleeping; and see him how glad he was when I come back out of the fog; and when I come to him again in the swamp, up there where the feud was; and such-like times; and would always call me honey, and pet me and do everything he could think of for me, and how good he always was; and at last I struck the time I saved him by telling the men we had small-pox aboard, and he was so grateful, and said I was the best friend old Jim ever had in the world, and the *only* one he's got now; and then I happened to look around and see that paper.

It was a close place. I took it up, and held it in my hand. I was a-trembling, because I'd got to decide, forever, betwixt two things, and I knowed it. I studied a minute, sort of holding my breath, and then says to myself:

"All right, then, I'll *go* to hell"—and tore it up.

That is when Huck decides that he is "wicked" and will remain true to his wickedness, and for a start he will try to save Jim. In doing so, he will turn the civilized world on its head and, hopefully, also make his readers do some deep thinking of their own about words such as "right" and "wrong," "wicked" and "virtuous," "respectable" and "civilized."

While Huck Finn is the quintessential individualist, his individualism does not condone greed. With his rejection of the "Sunday-school" mentality, he also rejects the utilitarian view of religion as a system of reward and punishment. His moral choices are deliberate. He takes conscious risks and accepts responsibility. Huck will find a new home and a new source of moral power, where the authority of the outside world is replaced with an inner authority, one that will help him decide what to do with Jim.

This is the kind of individualism that shapes my idea of America, the one I tried to share with my students in Tehran, explaining to them that moral choice comes from a sound heart and from a constant questioning of the world and of oneself, and that it is just as difficult, if not more so, in a society that appears to give you every freedom. In his study of life in concentration camps, Tzvetan Todorov argues that even under the most adverse conditions, when human beings are at death's door, they still have a choice. Their ultimate choice lies in their attitude toward life and death. It is in this manner that Huck's choice of hell and Jim's decision to risk his freedom in order to remain loyal are essentially choices to be true to that inner self, the rebellious heart that beats to its own rhythm.

If there is a climax to Huck's adventures, it is this. No other scene so poignantly and so perfectly captures Huck and his mate Jim. But the story doesn't end here; we have the Phelps farm to deal with. Once Huck discovers that the duke and the dauphin have betrayed Jim for a paltry $45 and that Jim is now locked up at the Phelps farm (which happens to be home to Tom's aunt Sally and her brood), he decides to go there to free Jim.

# 18

"If I were teaching Huck Finn . . ." I began.

"You *are* teaching Huck Finn," Farah said. "And you have been teaching him ever since your first class in Tehran."

"I am not happy with that anymore," I said.

We were in her living room. She had been feeling unwell and was lying on the couch, with one hand covering her brow. She asked me to move closer so she could see me better. The French windows framed her beloved garden. Before we talked about Huck, she had me pick a tiny lemon from a small tree and put it into a huge bowl. She wanted me to smell its fragrance. She told me that among the things she regretted most was not spending more time on the garden.

That was when she first told me about her desire to get a small dog. She said she felt the dog would motivate her to bear the pain better. Her husband was opposed to this and her siblings worried that looking after a dog might be too much of a burden to her. With a faded smile, reminiscent of the smile forewarning you of some form of subtle guile, she told me her plan to convince Habib to let her have the dog, engaging her two children to conspire with her so that Habib would be confronted with the inevitable presence of the dog. She had spent months trying to choose one and thinking of a name for it.

I told Farah that I didn't want to teach for a while. I felt I needed to take time off, to think things through.

"This is not a marriage you are talking about," she said. "And you are not twenty years old, with time on your hands. Even if you were, you never know how much longer you will live."

"I feel we're all too accustomed to the usual way of teaching these books," I said. "I want something more. I want to create a new course called Creative Reading. What my students need is not another lecture on *Huck Finn*. I don't want simply to bring up the questions we all know we have to ask, about slavery, humor, even Americanism. Those questions should not be posed—they should emerge organically from our engagement with the text." I reminded Farah of Twain's statement that education "consists mainly in what we have unlearned" and told her that I wanted to do a little more unlearning. After all, Huck himself flees the stifling world of cultured indoctrination. He escapes the Widow Douglas's civilizing mission and sets off to shape his own education.

"Maybe I should ask my students, before they write on *Huck,* to write about their most sensual encounter with nature, to express how it feels to touch, to listen, to see, to taste and, of course, to feel. To become conscious of the world around them, because that is what I keep missing: the sensuality that at all periods of my life, no matter where I have lived, I could evoke through a poem, a painting, music or a story."

"Let it be, Azar," Farah said gently. "You and I enjoyed this beauty without seeing the reality that gave birth to it. That was how we were young, and this is how they are young. Just let them be."

"When I give speeches," I said, "the people who come to listen are more frank with me than my students, partly because there is a relationship of trust between readers and writers, some shared intimacy. And of course they are not talking to their teacher but to someone who, despite the curious and immediate feeling of closeness, will leave, after which they will in all likelihood never see them again. The combination of these two elements, of intimacy and distance, conspires to create moments of immense frankness. I feel as open with the audience as they are with me. Teaching is a funny business; you want to share these glimpses of something real and profound, but half the time students want only to know their next assignment and what they will need to study for the test. I wish I could persuade them to be a little less dutiful."

"You might feel this way for a while," Farah said, "but you won't be able to stop teaching for long. It's in your blood." And that was that; she wanted to talk about her garden again.

Before we said goodbye, I said, "By the way, I am thinking of a new subtitle. With all this talk of 'sivilizing' and all that, how about 'Unlearning *Huckleberry Finn* in America?'"

"That's even worse," Farah said. "Take your own advice: being concrete is good. Stop worrying about the subtitle and write the damn book." She was becoming more and more like my real editor.

# 19

In June 2009, I was officially called on to perform my role as citizen of the United States of America: I was summoned to jury duty. Every morning for more than two weeks, I would take the Metro to Judiciary Square and enter the Supreme Court of the District of Columbia, where the main part of my day would be spent with eleven other jurors in a courtroom for the trial of a young African American man named Vincent—known as V—for the murder of another African American man who was just thirty but still older than the accused by ten years. I would avidly write down my questions, my doubts, my "verdict," which kept changing, in the notebook provided by the court, even though, to my chagrin, we had these taken away from us each time we adjourned. That notebook was all I had to write my impressions in, and I was not used to being unable to perform that task.

As I avidly told Farah later that week, a different Washington from the one we lived in was taking shape in my mind, one that I knew existed, that my husband—who worked in northeast Anacostia—had talked about, but I had never felt its existence the way I did during those two weeks. The experience would forever change my view of the city and make me, in a sense, more committed to it, more its citizen than before. The case was about what had happened on the corner of H and 19th streets, among a group of young, mainly male African Americans drinking Grey Goose vodka and at times breaking into fights. But then it was about so many other things, too. It was about gun ownership and inequality, and it was about jobs and dreams and what happens when you have neither.

A little after I started jury duty, Iran broke into an uprising against the rigged presidential election won by Mahmoud Ahmadinejad, and for the first time since I had returned to America, attention was being paid to the Iranian people, as well as to the regime. Farah was very excited and got involved, although she was also very sick. For the first time in a long while, our conversations turned to politics and conditions in Iran. Almost every day, she would call her cousin in Tehran to get the news, and we would spend most of our time together listening to the news, reading the news, talking about the news on Iran. I felt that I was participating in two kinds of justice: one in the court of my new country, and the other played out by the people in the streets of my country of birth. In both, the results could not be foreseen, but there was no doubt about the necessity to participate as engaged citizens.

We felt a great deal of frustration over Obama's hesitation to support the uprising. It had been only a few months since his election, which so many thought of as a turning point, not just for America but for the world. I remember, at the time of the inauguration, a friend sent me a photograph of Barack Obama published in a Persian paper, with a caption reading, "Why can't we have someone like this?" The paper was promptly shut down, and now, less than a year later, Iranians protesting their own presidential elections were chanting, "Obama, Obama, are

you with them or are you with us?" It was a question Obama
could never fully answer, no matter what he might have felt in
his heart of hearts.

Farah had participated energetically in the American election campaigns. She was especially excited about Obama and
had convinced me, despite the fact I could not vote, that I
should participate in fund-raising events in his honor. She asked
me to tell her in minute detail about one of these, a meeting or-
ganized by Jonathan Safran Foer, with Toni Morrison, Samantha Power, Tony Kushner and Jhumpa Lahiri. And so I dutifully
related Samantha Power's story of how Obama had called to
praise her book on genocide and then offered her a job in his
office. "This is going to be a new era," Farah whispered in excitement. As always, I was far more skeptical of politics and
politicians, and therefore less surprised when neither Obama
nor the uprising turned out in our favor, although in Iran, at
least, I knew that the regime would not have the last word
forever.

I believe that Farah never recovered from the defeat of
that uprising, though despite her disappointment in America's
lukewarm support, she still harbored a great deal of hope for
Obama. Her cancer spread like wildfire soon after that, as if she
had lost her will to fight. I have not, as yet, wiped out her phone
numbers and e-mail address from my computer, and every once
in a while I visit her Twitter account and hover over her last
message: "Iranians in Wash. DC support our brave country men
and women inside fighting for all of our rights. Our hearts and
minds are w/ you."

## 20

"Whatever the literary establishment might think, a good story always has a good ending." So says Jessica Fletcher, that knowing and wise fictional murder mystery writer and amateur sleuth of the television series *Murder, She Wrote* who has never failed at solving a crime. And she is right about this particular good story. Only the good ending is not quite what we would expect it to be. Unlike many readers, including Hemingway, who have found the last ten chapters of *Huckleberry Finn* unnecessary, I believe the trip to the Phelps farm is central to the main theme of the book: the triumph, as Twain would put it, of the "sound heart" over a "deformed conscience."

From the moment Huck steps onto the Phelps farm, all of the movement, the variety, the dangerous magic of the river disappear, and we find ourselves once again in the oppressive atmosphere of the opening pages. Phelps farm is a reentry into the real world, where attempts will be made to make Huck complicit in recapturing Jim.

Huck's description of the farm exudes melancholy and boredom. When he gets there, the air is "still and Sunday-like." His mood and the tone of his voice, even his words—"lonesome," "dead," and "spirits"—echo his description of the widow's house. This feeling is reinforced when, a paragraph later, he informs us that he "heard the dim hum of a spinning-wheel wailing along up and sinking along down again; and then I knowed for certain I wished I was dead—for that *is* the lonesomest sound in the whole world."

The Phelps farm is a place where reality and illusion are tested. This becomes clearer when Tom arrives and, since Huck has been mistaken by Aunt Sally for Tom, disguises himself as his younger brother, Sid. When Tom finds out that Jim has been sold to the owner of the farm, he devises an elaborate scheme to free him, ignoring Huck's repeated protests, deriving inspiration from various adventure novels he has read. He ends up treating Jim in a most cruel manner and terrifying the people at the farm by playing pranks on them. When Tom's plans go awry and he is wounded, Jim decides, at great personal cost, to stay on and help. Only then does the reader realize the consequences of Tom's frivolous and self-indulgent desire to impose his fantasies on other people, when the violent words he uses are not games anymore.

Then we learn that Tom *knew* Miss Watson had already freed Jim. It is conceivable that a highly religious person such as Miss Watson, when preparing to meet her maker, would set Jim free, perhaps in a moment of sudden charity, perhaps to earn more points in heaven. But her pardon does not count for much. It is, as the saying goes, too little too late. It does nothing to erase the deeper prejudice bolstering the whole institution of slavery. Twain knew only too well that slavery could be abolished and blacks would still be deprived of their rights. For as long as the attitude that condoned and justified slavery remained, there would be lynching and segregation and the Ku Klux Klan, and, as our own more recent experiences show, that same attitude can reappear clothed in different guises: as fascism, communism or Islamism—or patriotism, for that matter, when it is wielded like a cudgel.

Tom is the only white character in the book who has any hold on Huck. He reads books, he uses big words, he knows all the formulas. He is not a religious fanatic and does not seem to be really bothered one way or the other about slavery. He is, in a sense, more dangerous than an outright racist. He is the ultimate sinner, a dangerous fantasizer who acknowledges no consequences. The difference between Huck and Tom becomes clear in these last chapters: what distinguishes Huck is not just his regard for Jim, but his innate repulsion to cruelty. Yet this does not mean that he is not influenced—or perhaps a better word is intimidated—by authority, especially Tom's authority. Huck feels himself inferior to Tom in terms of knowledge and learning. His courage is rooted in his heart, and he responds to an inner authority he does not know how to define.

Tom is the only one who knows that Jim is a freeman, that Miss Watson freed him on her deathbed, and yet he is prepared to add to Jim's suffering by playing games in order to entertain himself. Huck is the exact opposite. He cannot bear for others to suffer, even if they are murderers or charlatans. All violence is based on blindness, on a lack of reflection and empathy. Miss Watson, Pap and Tom offer up variations on this theme, which I would go so far as to. say is a not just a central theme of *Huck Finn* but a structural element of the novel since its very inception.

Huck wondered all along why Tom, with his respectable upbringing, would commit such a "wicked" act as freeing a slave. He discovers that Tom did in fact act according to his "upbringing," as he knew that Jim was a freeman. And yet in the end it appears as if Tom, who has inflicted so much pain, is also the happiest character. He has learned nothing from his own or others' experiences. Left to his own devices, he tells Huck, he would do the same thing over again, only more elaborately. Before we say goodbye to him, Huck informs us that "Tom's most well now, and got his bullet around his neck on a watch-guard for a watch, and is always seeing what time it is."

Parallel to Tom's unpardonable cruelty, there is Jim and his unforgettable generosity. Although we see Jim mainly as a captive of his white masters and Tom's whims and fantasies, he takes over the story by refusing to act as they do, by refusing to be blind toward others or to be motivated by self-interest. When Tom is wounded and Huck leaves the two of them to fetch a doctor, Jim has a chance to run for freedom. Instead he remains with Tom and, at great risk to his own life, helps the doctor save him. This is where hope lies: not in a rosy future for Jim, whose next step, like everything else in the novel, is left unresolved, but in his refusal to act vindictively, thereby gaining true freedom from his oppressor. Freedom, like happiness, has to be pursued. There is no end to this struggle, so there can be no end to this story. In fiction, as in life, what matters most is not the beginning or the end but the path that leads from one to the other.

In the end, Huck is not yet completely cleansed of his racist conscience, nor is his future necessarily brighter than it was at the start of his adventures. But whatever might happen, no one can erase the bond between Huck and Jim.

# 21

In the morning, I stepped out onto the balcony for a few minutes. The air was crisp and fresh, the sun hovered over the water, the boats silently made their way up the river and a jogger ran by, her body in a determined pose, as if slashing through some invisible obstacle, like a swimmer pushing through water. I heard the sounds of cars, motorcycles, a plane. . . . Life was out there, and I wanted to join in. I wanted to become a part of it all. Soon I would dress and go to Borders to meet Farah, who of late had been feeling pretty good. She'd said we should take advantage of it until the next round came. The next round!

I was impatiently making my way through *The Washington Post* when I heard her familiar voice behind me saying, "What's up?" She was late, as usual, and smiling. She looked good, with her very short hair, her bright lipstick. She used to turn around for us to show off her figure and say, "Look how thin I have become, model thin!"

As soon as she sat down, she said, "Tell me, Azi!" Almost every time I saw her she would say, "Tell me, Azi, tell me!" She wanted to know about my classes, my talks, my travels. More than once she told me she had no public ambition of her own, that she lived vicariously through Mahnaz and me. In fact, she was much more social than either one of us. Farah was one of the most active people I knew. She had what you might call an amazing appetite for life. Cancer had spurred her to take trips with the people she loved—to Northern California with Neda, to Paris and Spain with Habib, to St. Michaels with Mahnaz, Hamid and the family. All of us in her close circle would confide our stories to her, and she participated in our personal dramas so energetically that at times we forgot that she was the one who was facing real obstacles and fighting real demons.

I told her about my morning experience and the fact that, in order to feel at home in a city, I need to have some connection to nature as a point of contact, some mental image to take away with me. In Tehran, it had been the Elburz Mountains, and now, today, I felt I had finally entered a new stage with D.C.: the Potomac River! Every morning when I wake up now, I walk out onto the balcony and pay homage to the river.

"Huck's influence," she said with a twinkle.

"No," I said, "his river is so different, and he lives not by the river but *on* the river. I am a far more domesticated creature."

"Oh, I don't know about that. Now tell me," she said again, "tell me all about it."

That's how it was in that last year. Every time I gave a talk, went to an event or traveled, I had to give her a full account. It was the same with Mahnaz: she was curious about the minutest details of her sister's activities and would interject as if she herself had been present. "Your lives are public, and they are exciting. I cannot live that kind of life, so this is how I experience it," she said. It didn't matter that she could have, at any point, lived that kind of life had she chosen to.

I so miss the girlish enthusiasm and giggles that accompanied our serious discussions on human rights, civic duty and literature, always literature. Farah attended all of Mahnaz's conferences and participated in her workshops, for which she was at times herself a presenter. "Can you imagine," she used to say, "my sister's organization has a branch in Kyrgystan, for heaven's sake!" After the conferences we would spend hours dissecting the meetings and discussing our favorite participants: the legendary civil rights leader Marianne Wright Edelman, Mary Robinson, Rose Styron, Grace Paley. "This abundance of riches!" Farah would say with a sign of satisfaction.

At first reluctantly, and later eagerly, I told her about my own "adventures," as she called them. I would recount the minute details of my travels, meeting writers in different parts of the world. This time she wanted to hear about my first trip to the Mantova book festival, where my old heroine Muriel Spark had adopted me. She had invited me to her hotel, and all the time her mantra was "Poor Doris." Doris was Doris Lessing, who'd somehow had her flight canceled in Zurich or Lausanne and was sent to Italy on a bus with no toilet, all her luggage lost. And Muriel kept saying, with relish, "Oh, I feel so sorry for Doris. If only I could lend her my slacks, but we are not the same size." Coming down the stairs of the hotel, we saw her, like a patient and stoic bag lady, with a brown cardigan and a brown paper bag that must have contained all of her possessions, holding a toothbrush and toothpaste and a few other essentials, looking so dignified, so utterly patient, without any anger or bitterness. . . . Well, Muriel loved it; she appeared to enjoy every moment of it, still at that age.

Another time I told Farah how Salman Rushdie, who had been a popular writer in Iran until the notorious fatwa, had come to my table at a PEN Gala to graciously compliment me on my book, and I, in my zeal to tell him how much I admired his courage, fumbled and said something so convoluted that he thought I had said, "You deserved to die." (What I had meant to say was that in Iran, those targeted by the regime were particularly revered, and so with its fatwa the regime had in effect conferred on him Iran's highest honor.) At the Hay Festival, the writer Lisa Appignanesi laughingly asked me if it was true that I had told Salman he deserved to die, and the question was repeated by others until I saw Rushdie again and swore I'd never said any such thing, and he kindly and mischievously put his arm around my shoulder and said, "Yes you did, yes you did, but it's okay . . ."

Farah always laughed. "Are you having fun?" she would ask, almost anxiously, in the same tone as she would tell me that she worried I was not taking care of my health. I wasn't really having fun—I didn't know why I should be having fun. "For heaven's sakes, woman!" she would say. "Have some fun! It's okay, you might even deserve it." It was not until much later, when she was gone, that I realized how telling her these stories had become a way of remembering, a way even of enjoying events that I had been too preoccupied, too self-conscious, to give in to and simply enjoy, as Farah kept advising me to do.

The night before she died, Bijan and I were invited to Christopher Hitchens's house with Ian McEwan and his wife for dinner. I decided not to call Farah until the next morning; I thought she would want to hear every detail of the dinner and instruct me in what I should have said and not said. McEwan was one of the writers we loved to discuss, his clear and precise lyricism a reflection of his ability to condense so much into an image or scene, while his impartial empathy prevented his stories from becoming merely sentimental. But of course, that night at dinner we talked mainly about the issues of the day and not about McEwan's new novel or Hitch's memoirs. I have never found a good way to discuss writing with my favorite authors; I think you have to be on very intimate terms to talk about such things truthfully. *I will call her in the morning,* I thought, *to give her a full report.* Only there was no call in the morning. Farah died shortly after dawn.

# 22

If I were to find a connection between Farah and Huck, it would be not only what Farah's daughter, Neda, suggested: the vagrant life, part of which was not of her own choosing. There was something deeper. She possessed the kind of courage that shies away from being publicly acknowledged, that does not lend itself to headlines. Unlike some other exiles, Farah did not bank on her misfortunes or boast about her resilience. In fact, she seldom if ever spoke about her experience. Her attributes were of the kind you find represented in the best novels, those that celebrate "ordinary" people, heroic in the struggle to preserve their individual integrity, their right to a life of their choosing, with no other claims. In this sense she could join Dorothy and Huck and all those other "small and meek" protagonists of America's fiction.

We talked so many times about *Huck Finn,* and yet it wasn't until after she was gone that I really understood the source of her fascination. I had been focused on the most obvious aspect, the homelessness. But I had chosen to leave home, she hadn't. All through our discussions, she was fascinated by the idea of Huck's journey, but what was her main focus in her own life? What was it that she most talked about? Her lack of public ambition, her satisfaction with having led an otherwise ordinary life.

Farah wanted time for her garden, she wanted a dog, she wanted to travel, to be with the people she loved most. She wanted Obama to win, and she wanted the Iranian people to have a chance to properly choose their own leader. There was no discrepancy between her wanting a good life for herself and a good life for her people. Being "civic-minded," it used to be called, an attribute that Farah cherished and that so many in America seem to have forgotten. This is what Tocqueville warned us against: a time when Americans would be prosperous and comfortable enough to withdraw from the public domain and satisfy themselves within their own private interests. This was not Huck Finn's idea of America, nor Farah's.

In my experience, in Iran and over here, some of the best people are those who go unnoticed, those who are heroic without knowing that they are, without winning public rewards and recognition. Farah did not want to be a migrant, or without a home, but she would not give in or compromise about certain principles in order to have a home. It was an existential act. Mahnaz was right: she never accepted her role as a tragic heroine, although she had far more reasons to do so than many others. In fact, she was often dismissed by so-called activists and academics, who thought of her only as Mahnaz's little sister.

Contrary to what its ideologically inclined critics claim, the significance of *Huck Finn* is not only a matter of its position on slavery—although Twain made his feelings on that subject abundantly clear—but of how it shifts responsibility for slavery onto us, ordinary people, who can so unwittingly participate in the implementation of unspeakable crimes. Good people, ordinary people, will often fail to protest what society condones. As the Spanish novelist Antonio Muñoz Molina once said, "If a member of the Gestapo can have a normal face, then any normal face can belong to the Gestapo." For Twain, the antidote to this propensity for evil is to be found not in extraordinary heroes—supermen and -women who risk all in search of justice—but in ordinary people, often ignored in real life but celebrated in American fiction. In the end, Tom gets the glory and Huck moves on. The ordinary people, the small and meek, get their rewards in literature, where their moral courage, quietly celebrated, is enduring.

"Why do you insist on springing these weird subtitles on me?" Farah asked me once, impatiently. "'Perfectly Equipped Idiots' . . ."

"Failures," I said. "'Perfectly Equipped Failures,' not idiots."

"Anyway," she said, "it doesn't work. It may have worked for Henry James, in that heavy, convoluted style of his, and I know you love the expression, but it doesn't work as a subtitle. And what does it have to do with Huck Finn?"

I said it seemed to me significant that James and Twain, two very different authors who did not like each other, became the founders of two different schools of American realism and that they both found a common ground in this idea of the successful failure. That is the main point about Huck and his progenies, I insisted. The mongrel is always marginal, never successful in reality or fiction, and then comes Twain, who transforms failure into success, giving us two protagonists (Huck and Jim) who belong to the lowest ranks of society and showing us that their failure to cope with that society, to follow its rules and become successful in a conventional fashion, is their biggest achievement. At the end of the novel, conventional success belongs to the villain of the story, the one who imposes his fantasy on others: Tom Sawyer. But the moral victory is Huck's, and this idea of moral victory is what will become so central to later American fiction, right up to the present, in the writings of Marilynne Robinson, Dave Eggers or Mona Simpson.

Our ordinary heroes have to choose between their heart and their conscience, between what they are told they should do and what they feel to be right. This, to me, is what American individualism, at its best, is all about—not phony adventurism of the kind advertised by *Sarah Palin's Alaska* but a quiet and un-obtrusive moral strength. Huck introduced a new conception of individualism, far more complicated than that of the lone cowboy coming into town, killing off the black hats and moving on while sitting a little askew on his horse. Huck and his progeny fight conformism, as well as the Ayn Randian concept of the superman who rises up against the inconsequential and vulgar mob and is free to implement his own self-serving conception of justice. It was Huck Finn who shaped our moral principles, Huck Finn—solitary but not alone—who desired to be independent but knew that in order to be truly independent he would have to be in constant contact with others, and that he would be shaped through this interaction, both with those he opposed and those he loved. *Huck Finn* is a scathing critique of the kind of society we live in today, not just because racism still exists or because we tolerate it passively, but because of the degree to which we have turned reality into entertainment and embraced the numbing, sanctimonious high-mindedness of Miss Watson's facile indignation.

You can see Huck's progenies in Hemingway, in Faulkner, in Fitzgerald and Ellison and also very much in popular culture, in movies like *Mr. Smith Goes to Washington,* where our hero takes up the fight with all of Congress and is told by the girl that only crazy characters like him are the real heroes. And you can see it in Dashiell Hammett's and Raymond Chandler's or Sara Paretsky's protagonists and their descendants, like *The Wire*'s Omar Little.

Farah could not believe that I would place Chandler alongside the greatest geniuses of American fiction. That was one writer I could never persuade her to read. She had, like so many of my intellectual friends, such a fear of detective tales. I remember I once seriously doubted my friendship with someone who hated *The Long Goodbye,* because, as he put it, "it was not realistic enough." Not realistic? Chandler wrote the best manifesto in defense of realism, an indictment of traditional mystery tales. He followed in Twain's footsteps and did for the mystery— with "The Simple Art of Murder"—what Twain had done for the novel in his denunciation of the sappy, maudlin stories of James Fenimore Cooper.

Chandler's detective, Marlowe, is a loner. He lives in shabby rented homes and dusty offices, his sole ambition to indulge his solitary passion: a search for justice. His attitude toward both victims and criminals is complex, and he has genuine contempt, as does Huck, for "respectable" society. He is seen by them as a "gumshoe," he is condescended to, but it is he in the end who solves the crime, although his success is often bittersweet. In *The Long Goodbye* he takes up the job because of his empathy with the victim, the underdog, but sometimes his empathy deceives him and the victim turns out to be complicit in the crime. Where Chandler falls short is in making Marlowe too perfect. He is *too* moral, and has almost no hesitation. In Marlowe's world, you don't get the girl; you give her up—because she is much wealthier than you are or because you discover in the end that she is a traitor and, although you love her, you will still call the police. Time and again, love stories in American fiction don't end happily. The American novel is a very moral affair, in which love and happiness must be given up for duty, for morality, for honor.

Twain spoofs the immortal Sherlock Holmes in a terribly written and completely biased story called "A Double Barrelled Detective Story," making fun of "that pompous sentimental 'extraordinary man' with his cheap and ineffectual ingenuities." Chandler's view was far more generous, although he believed that in fiction, as in life, there should be no neat solution. His characters are murkier, more conflicted about society and its conventions.

Crime is not just about evil, as Hercule Poirot and Miss Marple are so fond of reminding us. It is about character and motive, about cupidity and stupidity. The American detective tale does not have the luxury of its English counterpart, with its ornate and beautiful backdrops, its stately homes and all the layers that centuries of manners and rituals create. It is more stark, it is angry and it is complicated.

America is a country founded on the noble dream that everyone should be free to pursue happiness, whatever that may be. But happiness and freedom do not always go together, because the idea of the novel, despite everything you hear about "happily ever after," rests on the concept of the integrity of the individual, and that entails choice. If you are a Jamesian or a Whartonian protagonist, your fate is sealed—by your own hands, principally. We, the readers, will watch you make a series of wrong decisions, based on false premises or a weak understanding of what is fundamental. Even if we are free, we sometimes confine ourselves by our choices to a life of hell. This, too, is American realism. In Hammett and Chandler, the detective protagonist is not a happy man—his success at solving the crime does not make him proud or self-satisfied, nor is he a success in the eyes even of those who hire him. In fact, his vain and misled customers make sure to humiliate him for his shabby office, his worn-out suits, but of course, in the end the joke is on them: he is the one who, without bragging, reveals *their* moral and spiritual shabbiness. However ornate and imposing their homes, they lack an inner anchor, an ethical core.

Marlowe himself is a "perfectly equipped failure," that American trope coined by Henry James to describe characters who renounce worldly fame, wealth and power in order to follow the dictates of their own "sound heart," which is, in fact, the most worthy of all achievements. In Marlowe, Huck has returned as a skeptical social critic who might, every once in a while, fall for a classy dame, but who has little respect for society's elites.

I've read detective tales all my life; my father was also a fan, as the saying goes, and the two of us exchanged mystery books, but it was only after the revolution that I realized their significance, when, like so many things I had taken for granted, they suddenly became forbidden fruit. In Iran, mystery tales were popular but despised by the elite, both intellectual and political, the way *One Thousand and One Nights* might have been a few centuries ago. (Farzaneh Taheri, a respected translator of Nabokov and Richard Wright, once wrote an article justifying why she translated detective novels.) I had a theory about why our new leaders were so uncomfortable with scrappy gumshoes like Marlowe. How could such a character be permitted in a dictatorship—someone who stands witness to police stupidity and (in the case of the American detective story) corruption in high places? It was as impossible to imagine as a drama like *Law & Order* in a country where both were sources of most criminal activities.

Twain was wary of conventional morality, and this skepticism extended to his understanding of what it meant to be American. In his memoirs, an assembly of musings transcribed over many years whose genesis was described in a wonderful essay by Lewis

Lapham in *Harper's* in 2011, he distances himself from politics and politicians and maps out his own conception of patriotism:

> I said that no party held the privilege of dictating to me how I should vote. That if party loyalty was a form of patriotism, I was no patriot, and that I didn't think I was much of a patriot anyway, for oftener than otherwise what the general body of Americans regarded as the patriotic course was not in accordance with my views; that if there was any valuable difference between being American and a monarchist it lay in the theory that the American could decide for himself what is patriotic and what isn't; whereas the king could dictate the monarchist's patriotism for him—a decision which was final and must be accepted by the victim; that in my belief I was the only person in the sixty millions—with Congress and the Administration back of the sixty million—who was privileged to construct my patriotism for me.
>
> They said, "Suppose the country is entering upon a war—where do you stand then? Do you arrogate to yourself the privilege of going your own way in the matter, in the face of the nation?
>
> "Yes," I said, "that is my position. If I thought it an unrighteous war I would say so. If I were invited to shoulder a musket in that cause and march under that flag, I would decline. I would not voluntarily march under this country's flag, nor any other, when

it was my private judgment that the country was in the wrong. If the country obliged me to shoulder the musket I could not help myself, but I would never volunteer. To volunteer would be the act of a traitor to myself, and consequently traitor to my country. If I refused to volunteer, I should be called a traitor, I am well aware of that—but that would not make me a traitor. I should still be a patriot, and, in my opinion, the only one in the whole country."

Like all other classics of world literature, *Huck Finn* is a provocation. Those who hate it are disturbed by its heresies, and those who love it are not immune, either; they are provoked by the timeless image in the mirror that the book relentlessly, if compassionately, reflects. Hemingway and all those other American writers who found their own ancestors in a book called *Huck Finn* were right—they were not exaggerating. One by one, the characters in *Huck Finn* would populate the landscape of American fiction, redefining home and homelessness. In the ensuing decades, Jim would light out for his own territory and start telling his own story: he would reclaim his identity, his faith and confidence, and discover his rage and pain. The Widow Douglas, the inhabitants of the smothery towns, even Tom Sawyer—all would appear and reappear in different guises. The small towns Huck and Jim passed by on their raft would acquire new identities, Huck would return and the theme of the solitary individual, his sound heart resisting a monitoring conscience, would be articulated in different times and different manners.

One character remains: the reader. When Mark Twain wrote *The Adventures of Huckleberry Finn,* there were still physical territories to light out to, but in twenty-first-century America, such uncharted terrain is part of fiction as well as fantasy. The only way to light out, to see the "sivilized" world through fresh eyes, is through our imaginations, our hearts and our minds, and that is the real question for us: Will we risk striking out for new territories and welcome the dangers of thoughts unknown?

## PART II

# BABBITT

"next to of course god america i
love you land of the pilgrims' and so forth oh
say can you see by the dawn's early my
country 'tis of centuries come and go
and are no more what of it we should worry
in every language even deafanddumb
thy sons acclaim your glorious name by gorry
by jingo by gee by gosh by gum
why talk of beauty what could be more beautiful than these heroic happy dead
who rushed like lions to the roaring slaughter
they did not stop to think they died instead
then shall the voice of liberty be mute?"

He spoke. And drank rapidly a glass of water

—E. E. Cummings

# 1

Legend has it that Mark Twain said he didn't write a sequel to *Huck Finn* because he was pretty sure a grown-up Huck would have turned out like all the other grown-ups around him, who were mostly crooks and thieves. No one seems to know what happened to Tom Blankenship, the real-life model for Huck, but Twain (perhaps apocryphally) claimed that Tom Sawyer grew up to be "respectable"—in fact, a justice of the peace, which wasn't any better than a crook or a thief, at least in Huck's view.

I have in mind another real-life model for the adult Huck: a writer born in 1885, the year *Huckleberry Finn* was first published, in Sauk Centre, Minnesota. I am thinking of Sinclair Lewis, or Harry Sinclair Lewis, who was called Hal by his first wife and some of his friends and was also known as Red, for the color of his hair and not his political views, though these were famously left of center. His father was not a drunken hobo but an upright doctor, and he himself was anything but a vagrant. Born a generation after Huck, Hal grew up at a time when the untamed wilderness Huck hoped to light out for was scarcer, the "smothery" villages had expanded into a new kind of smothery city, slavery was officially abolished and had been replaced by segregation, and new forms of hope and horror were coming into being.

"Everyone ought to have a home to get away from," Sinclair Lewis once wrote, and homelessness seems to have been ingrained in his very being: he felt it as much when he was with his family as he would at Oberlin and Yale. Among the various groups he attached himself to, he always remained a "furriner," as he used to put it. He was constantly on the move, afraid of settling down, living in many houses, none of which would be turned into a home, and despite the love of two intelligent and attractive women, fame and fortune, blockbuster bestsellers and the privilege of being the first American writer to win the Nobel Prize for literature, he died an alcoholic, alone and on foreign soil.

I somehow find myself returning to unsatisfying words like "poignant" when trying to describe Sinclair Lewis. I find it immensely poignant that upon his death, he left almost no personal possessions behind. "He had no real love of possessions," his first wife, Gracie, said. "The houses he bought one after another were mostly furnished houses; he walked in and he walked out." Gracie reported that when the contents of the Thorvale Farm, in Williamstown, Massachusetts, his last American home, were sold at auction in May 1952, among the six hundred items listed on the auction manifest, the only personal ones were "a leather traveling bag marked with an 'L' and covered with hotel labels, a large typewriter in a heavy leather case, an L-shaped desk and two tennis rackets." A little old woman bid on the tennis rackets—she told Gracie she'd wanted them for her two nephews, who needed to practice more—but someone else got them, for $18. At an exhibition in his honor at the American Academy of Arts and Letters in 1952, the memorabilia were: "bible, soft hat, walking stick, cigarette case, eyeshade, chess set, fountain pen." There were no other keep-sakes, no sentimental treasures, no things.

As a child, Sinclair Lewis was what we would call a "geek." Despite his enthusiasm, he could not participate in the sporting life practiced by his father and older brothers. His one blessing (and curse) was an inability to appear "normal." Both his life and his fiction are reminders of how much who we become is influenced by how we are perceived and defined by others. By all accounts he was spectacularly ugly. His face was pitted with scars from acne that troubled him all his life, made worse by radiation cures. Gore Vidal described him as having a "gargoyle" kind of ugliness, and he was pitilessly portrayed by Hemingway's fourth wife, Mary, as "a piece of old liver, shot squarely with a #7 shot at twenty yards." His tall and disjointed body gave the young writer John Hersey the impression of "a thin man put together with connections unlike those of most human beings." His character seemed disjointed, too. He was plagued by an innate rest-lessness, the inability to settle down or even to sit still or carry on a proper conversation. Rebecca West found his interminable monologues "wonderful, but after five solid hours of it I ceased to look upon him as a human being. I could think of him only as a great natural force, like the aurora borealis." Even some who admired him regarded him amiably as a "freak."

Given all of this, one might expect that, like many of his con-temporaries, he would write what his first biographer, Mark Schorer, called a "Moon-calf novel," the sad tale of a lonely and misunderstood young American male. But rather than withdraw into himself, Lewis set out to discover America. His novels covered the burning issues of the day and touched on much of what still concerns us at the start of this new century: conformity (*Main Street* and *Babbitt*), religion (*Elmer Gantry*), women's rights (*Ann Vickers*), fascism (*It Can't Happen Here*), race (*Kingsblood Royal*), medical science (*Arrowsmith*). Most were controversial and engendered endless debates. *Kingsblood Royal,* appreciated more by blacks than by whites, was even called seditious.

Though Lewis was the first American novelist to win the Nobel Prize, this did not prevent him from being dismissed in his lifetime as a second-rate hack. In some respect, the prize sealed his fate, as the backlash at home was immediate and unrelenting. The American literary set saw the choice as a deliberate poke in the eye: his satirical portraits of small-town America, with its conformity and small-mindedness, perfectly confirmed Europeans' worst prejudices. F. Scott Fitzgerald and Hemingway, whose literary fortunes have fared considerably better, did not mince their words in their assessment of their rival. Never one to elaborate when a few words would do, Hemingway summed up the prevailing view with his crisp statement "Sinclair Lewis is nothing."

But if he is often cast aside from the pantheon of American letters, this disparagement is usually qualified with a "yet" or a "but." Dismissals are generally accompanied by reluctant explanations of why he cannot be ignored. As recently as 2002, John Updike, whose Rabbit Angstrom owes more than a bit to George Babbitt, began his *New Yorker* review of Richard Lingeman's biography (itself inspired partly by such dismissals) by questioning the need for a new biography, only to end by

asking, "Who in the last century more manfully and systemati-
cally attempted to fill the demand, in recent times voiced by
Tom Wolfe and Jonathan Franzen, that American novelists cast
off solipsism and introverted delicacy and embrace the nation as
it exists, in its striving variety and dynamism?"

For Sinclair Lewis, as for Mark Twain and William Dean
Howells before him, this was not a political but an existential
task. A whole host of older writers, like Upton Sinclair and
Theodore Dreiser, and younger ones, like Richard Wright,
F. Scott Fitzgerald, William Faulkner, Saul Bellow and Flannery
O'Connor, would in their own fashion do the same. It was only
three years after George F. Babbitt came into the world, in 1922,
that we would come to know a young man called Jay Gatsby—
who, coincidentally, would die in pursuit of his version of the
American dream in the fictional year 1922, leaving us forever
with that unresolved mystery of the green light at the end of the
dock.

Although Lewis's novels are called sociological, they were
inspired not by politics or ideology but by a passion that gave
him a sense of mission and a reason to live. "Lewis was not to be
talked of at all," Gore Vidal said, "but his characters—as types—
would soldier on; in fact, more of his inventions have gone into
the language than those of any other writer since Dickens."

His literary mission was inspired by his anxiety for America, a
sentiment that links him to Emerson and Whitman and, perhaps
more than anyone else, to Thoreau, whom he admired greatly.
"Have we no culture, no refinement,—but skill only to live
coarsely and serve the Devil?—to acquire a little worldly wealth,

or fame, or liberty, and make a false show with it, as if we were all husk and shell, with no tender and living kernel to us?" Thoreau wrote in a bitter critique of America that he published in *The Atlantic Monthly* in 1863. "Even if we grant that the American has freed himself from a political tyrant, he is still the slave of an economical and moral tyrant. . . . Do we call this the land of the free? What is it to be born free and not to live free? . . . [W]e are warped and narrowed by an exclusive devotion to trade and commerce and manufactures and agriculture and the like, which are but means, and not the end."

America's commercialism is as well worn a trope as its individualism, and writers have gravitated toward this theme. We find it in the work of H. L. Mencken, who relentlessly caricatured the American "Booboisie," as he called it, and the novels of the great American social realists Theodore Dreiser, Frank Norris, John Steinbeck and Upton Sinclair and of course Mark Twain's *The Gilded Age*. It can be said that among the true guardians of American morality, its writers and thinkers have been the most steadfast, challenging readers to question complacent norms, to acknowledge injustice and recognize the underside of this heaving, thrusting, purposeful nation dedicated to making ever more new things.

And so it was that Hal Lewis, the wanderer who never managed to make any of the several houses he occupied into a home, wrote the most scathing critique of the small and smothery homes that Huck had attempted to escape from. In life, he resented "the ghetto-like confinement" of the small town, calling it the "Village Virus." In his first blockbuster bestseller, *Main Street,* he gave us an idealist, Carol Kennicott, the wife of the village doctor, who tries to rectify the mercantile mentality of Main Street America through a futile attempt to beautify and vitalize her small town of Gopher Prairie. Later, in *Ann Vickers,* he would offer up a more liberated and emancipated version of Carol. But it is Babbitt who is his most perfect creation, Babbitt who leaves the pages of his novel and takes on a life of his own, becoming part of the American vernacular.

How did this elusive outsider, by choice and by force, create such a flawless portrayal of the ultimate insider: a character unlike Huck in every way and yet every bit as iconically American? His wife Gracie pointed out that "even though Lewis's first successful novels can be recognized as written by him, it is significant that he created no school of writing as have Hemingway and Faulkner, Henry James and Flaubert. He influenced public thinking rather than public writing." Perhaps Lewis's main contribution to American literature was bringing fiction into the arena of public discourse. *Babbitt* is the product of a culture ever more standardized and atomized, less in tune with the vagaries of the heart, in thrall to monopolies, with their corporate language of efficiency and productivity. If we agree with Ezra Pound that "literature is news that stays news," then we can safely say that Sinclair Lewis was, despite his poor standing in the literary establishment, the ultimate American novelist. We have to be thankful for the minor miracle that after almost a century, *Babbitt* speaks to us still.

# 2

"Garcong! Come here, you bloody garcong! . . . The lazy Frog. Let me tell you, they'd give us better service in Zenith. Gentlemen, have you ever been in the Zenith Athletic Club? Say, that's a swell joint for you." This could be a quote from *Babbitt,* but is not. It is Lewis at a bar in Paris, mimicking his soon-to-be-famous protagonist.

It has been said time and again that Sinclair Lewis captured Babbitt so well because he himself was in essence a Babbitt, but this is too simple an explanation. He does share with Babbitt a very American contradiction: the desire to settle down and the urge to be constantly on the move. But the two men respond very differently to this urge. It would be more accurate to say that Lewis was fascinated by his opposite, a man whose whole aim in life was to conform, to belong to the right club and own the right things. And since he could never be that individual, he conjured him up and entered his world through the large door of his imagination.

Lewis could portray a "standardized" man so well because he was a perpetual, if at times reluctant, outsider for whom normalcy was so inaccessible as to be almost desirable. As John Updike reminds us, mimicking others became a way of covering up his own inability to forge genuine relationships. One can only imagine how frustrated and resentful his second wife, the indomitable Dorothy Thompson, must have felt when, during an attack of DTs, as she was trying to help him into an ambulance, he preempted her rebuke by saying: "You've ruined your life, you're ruining mine! You've ruined your sons, you miserable creature. You're sick, sick."

Writing, like alcohol, became a lifelong addiction. It allowed him to take refuge not just from the world but from himself. In a letter to Gracie, he wrote, "And the East River flows on like the dream of a minor god, below, and all the little brown houses are drowning, and I sit forever working as poetically as a Ford workman pushing buttons."

# 3

We first catch a glimpse of Mr. George Follansbee Babbitt one fine April morning as he struggles to remain asleep. Unlike his creator, Mr. Babbitt, or "Georgie," as his wife, Myra, affectionately calls him, is a solid, hardworking, God-fearing family man who shares a prosperous real estate business with his father-in-law. He comes from a small town but has moved on to better things, an affluent life in a flourishing city, enabling him to view his place of birth, even his close relatives, with affectionate scorn as "the hicks back home." Babbitt can claim to belong to that blessed community of self-made American men who have worked hard to get where they are and, by golly, the world should know how proud they are of their achievements! Soon we will discover that being a self-made man has little to do with independence or individualism: for men like Babbitt to get where they are requires a gradual surrender of the self to a higher ideal. Luckily, this comes naturally to someone whose God was business. Although a vocal champion of individualism, his survival depends on his melting into the background, acquiring the chummy facelessness that his place in society demands.

Babbitt is identified with his city, Zenith, to such an extent that the story begins not with him but with the city. We are told, and this is significant, that the city's austere towers were "neither citadels, nor churches, but frankly and beautifully office-buildings." The city of Zenith, a midsize urban center, the backbone of American business and productivity, is a character in its own right. Indeed, Zenith is *the* all-American city. "A stranger suddenly dropped into the business-center of Zenith could not have told whether he was in a city of Oregon or Georgia, Ohio or Maine, Oklahoma or Manitoba. But to Babbitt every inch was individual and stirring."

Unlike *Huck Finn,* where the break with the past was a deliberate act of liberation, here attitudes toward the past are more in tune with Henry Ford's dictum that "history is bunk." The new buildings seem to have arisen out of a void. All vestiges of the past, the "fretted structures of earlier generations," the post office with "its shingle-tortured mansard," the "red brick minarets of hulking old houses," the factories that have "stingy and sooted windows" and the "wooden tenements colored like mud," are mere "grotesqueries," in deliberate contrast to the "shining new houses" of fortunate souls like Babbitt who have made it. The nature that Huck both loved and challenged is as much a victim here as are history and tradition. As the narrative progresses, we understand that the uncomfortable coexistence of the old and shabby buildings with the new and polished structures of Zenith, of the natural with the artificial, is implied in the conflicts between the city's inhabitants: on one side are the slovenly wage earners and the radical elements that support them; on the other the clean, upright citizens residing in office towers and cheerful new houses, precursors to our McMansions and antiseptically remodeled homes.

After a detailed description of the city waking up, its shining towers that "aspired" from the mist, the streets gradually filling with factory workers, shop assistants and other productive employees, we finally come to the forty-six-year-old George F. Babbitt, on the sleeping porch of his Dutch Colonial house in the residential district of Floral Heights, complete with a master bedroom "right out of Cheerful Modern Houses for Medium Incomes." The occupants of Huck's smothery houses, the respectable, churchgoing citizens, have become more refined and in a sense more formulaic. "If people had ever lived and loved" in this room or "read thrillers at midnight and lain in beautiful indolence on a Sunday morning, there were no signs of it."

The sounds of the city intrude on his sleep. There is the milk cart, the whistling paper carrier thumping the paper against the door, the neighbor's car, and finally the alarm clock that puts a stop to his dreams. Before he is fully awake, that alarm clock is described in great detail: early in the novel we are invited to recognize that this all-American businessman, a defender of individualism and free trade, is best defined not by any peculiarity of temperament or cherished keepsake but by his ownership of the best of the "nationally advertised and quantitatively produced alarm-clocks, with all modern attachments," making its owner "proud of being awakened by such a rich device." In terms of social status, it is "almost as creditable as buying expensive cord tires."

Once Babbitt begins to stir, we follow him from the sleeping porch through his bedroom to the bathroom. Every object he encounters along the way is described with the pointed detail of an advertising brochure. Like the city itself, everything in this house is "up-to-date" and of the moment, devoid of the messiness of personal taste or the burden of history. The shiny and meticulous quality of the surfaces produces a spooky refracted light of the kind we will later come across in films such as *The Truman Show* and *American Beauty,* where a fabricated reality intrudes on the protagonists' souls. The objects Babbitt transfers from one suit to another—a fountain pen, a silver pencil, a gold penknife, a silver cigar cutter, seven keys all hanging from his watch chain—are of "eternal importance" to him, "like baseball or the Republican Party." Without them, he feels "naked."

Next we meet Myra Babbitt, George's loyal wife. We are told that she "no longer had reticences before her husband, and no longer worried about not having reticences." So she appears in a petticoat, unaware of her "corsets which bulged." Although Myra is a "good woman, a kind woman, a diligent woman," no one but her youngest daughter really cares much about her or is "entirely aware that she was alive." At breakfast we meet the Babbitts' three children: the "dumpy brown-haired" twenty-two-year-old Verona, a graduate of Bryn Mawr College and ardent advocate of social causes; Theodore Roosevelt, known as Ted, who at seventeen is a typically wild teenager; and finally Babbitt's favorite, the ten-year-old Katherine, called Tinka, whom her father greets each morning with "Well, kittiedoolie!"

Babbitt looks out the window and considers his city. Surveying the top of the Second National Tower, a building thirty-five stories high, he is inspired "by the rhythm of the city" and beholds "the tower as a temple-spire of the religion of business, a faith passionate, exalted, surpassing common men; and as he clumped down to breakfast he whistled the ballad 'Oh, by gee, by gosh, by jingo' as though it were a hymn melancholy and noble."

# 4

The first time I read *Babbitt,* during my college days, I associated it with E. E. Cummings's poem "next to of course god, america i." I loved Cummings and felt I had found the poetic equivalent of the "Babbitt experience." At the time, I had little connection to the world outside my university, and I was too embroiled in its politics to care to know much about America beyond its precincts. *Babbitt* was a fun book to read, a critique of America, and that was enough. But something remained in the back of my mind, nagging me, or perhaps "beckoning" is a better word—something that made me return to *Babbitt* once I was more comfortably settled back in Iran. This time I saw things I had missed, the complications and paradoxes of being an American, or of life in a democracy, now that I found myself living in a totalitarian state. But it was not until I had returned to America and begun the process of becoming a citizen that I came to appreciate *Babbitt* fully. By that point I had come to feel as if certain aspects of that fictional universe were shimmering reflections of the reality I was then living. It was as if Lewis had perfectly captured our hollow, thing-filled times, as if the characters he created almost a century ago mimicked us, gloating over the fact that we had turned out to be their true progenies. Like the Red King in his confrontation with Alice, I am tempted to ask, Who dreamt up whom? Did the characters in *Babbitt* dream us up, or are we imagining them? I often find myself wondering: What is George Babbitt (or Myra or Ted) doing here, parading on my television screen, in new clothes, with a new haircut, using the same old words?

"What the country needs—just at this present juncture—is neither a college president nor a lot of monkeying with foreign affairs, but a good—sound economical—business—administration, that will give us a chance to have something like a decent turnover." This is not a speech by Mitt Romney, George Bush, or a conservative talking head on *Hannity;* it is George Babbitt himself, in conversation with his neighbor and friend Howard Littlefield, the great scholar, with a B.A. from Blodgett College and a Ph.D. from Yale in economics. He is an "authority on everything in the world except babies, cooking, and motors." His real job, however, is as the "employment-manager and publicity-counsel of the Zenith Street Traction Company."

There is a strict, if largely unspoken, hierarchy in Zenith. There are those above Babbitt in wealth and power, the ones he aspires one day to join—they belong not to the Athletic Club, as Babbitt and his regular cronies like Littlefield do, but to the Union Club, a notch above it, classier and more posh. These are men like Charles McKelvey, the contractor, and Colonel Rutherford Snow, owner of the *Advocate-Times.* Right above them is old money, represented by William Washington Eathorne, president of the First State Bank of Zenith. "Out of the dozen contradictory Zeniths which together make up the true and complete Zenith, none is so powerful and enduring yet none so unfamiliar to the citizens as the small, still, dry, polite, cruel Zenith of the William Eathornes; and for that tiny hierarchy the other Zeniths unwittingly labor and insignificantly die."

It is not politics that rules Babbitt's world—this is not the Soviet Union or the Islamic Republic of Iran, where the state reshapes its citizens' social, cultural and personal lives. A different, more generous if equally ruthless god controls this universe. It is Mammon, the god of buying and selling. Babbitt has made "nothing in particular, neither butter nor shoes nor poetry," but he is "nimble in the calling of selling houses for more than people could afford to pay." The word "calling" is significant, because business is Babbitt's true calling, and he embraces it with the zeal of a new convert. He speaks about real estate in terms of vision and poetry; he is not a broker but a "realtor," whom he defines as a "seer of the future development of the community . . . a prophetic engineer clearing the pathway for inevitable changes." Translated into more concrete terms, "a real-estate broker could make money by guessing which way the town would grow." Babbitt calls this guessing "Vision." He also helps elect the mayor, slandering and browbeating the antibusiness politicians and activists, talking about "Zip and Bang" and the "Standardized American Citizen," his words for the model Rotarian. In short, his is not a world ruled by politics; if anything, politics is ruled by the business of selling. In Babbitt's world, as in our own, a metaphorical Botox coats all walks of life: if a party loses an election, it will repackage itself and revisit its messaging rather than engage in meaningful reflection.

Long before Mitt Romney's closed-room expression of disdain for the 47 percent of Americans he branded as "takers," George F. Babbitt had it all figured out. In Babbitt's view, "all this uplift and flipflop and settlement-work and recreation is nothing in God's world but the entering wedge for socialism." He opines that "the sooner a man learns he isn't going to be coddled, and he needn't expect a lot of free grub and, uh, all these free classes and flipflop and doodads for his kids unless he earns 'em, why, the sooner he'll get on the job and produce—produce—produce! That's what the country needs."

Babbitt's utilitarian philosophy is consistent with his attitude toward work. We are told that he is "conventionally honest," and not kind. When Stan Graff, a lowly, overworked, underpaid employee, complains about his working conditions and wages, Babbitt, seeking to justify refusing him a raise, wants to know whether Stan is the kind of fellow who "kicks about working overtime, that wants to spend his evenings reading trashy novels or spooning and exchanging a lot of nonsense and foolishness with some girl" or "the kind of upstanding, energetic young man, with a future—and with Vision!" He ends his fatherly admonition by asking, "What's your Ideal, anyway? Do you want to make money and be a responsible member of the community, or do you want to be a loafer, with no inspiration or Pep?" If he were with us today, I have no doubt that George Babbitt would be a regular guest or consultant on Fox News.

In a society like Iran, "Inspiration" and "Pep" come at the barrel of a gun, a very straightforward method of persuasion.

There is nothing complicated about the brute force of an ideological state. Babbitt's god wants to sell, not to kill; its main weapon is seduction. It is full of guile and promise and yet remains efficient and impersonal, like the up-to-date alarm clock gracing the Babbitts' sleeping porch. Babbitt is persuaded that without that clock and his other gadgets, his life would be lacking, incomplete. "Just as he was an Elk, a Booster, and a member of the Chamber of Commerce, just as the priests of the Presbyterian Church determined his every religious belief and the senators who controlled the Republican Party decided in little smoky rooms in Washington what he should think about disarmament, tariff, and Germany, so did the large national advertisers fix the surface of his life, fix what he believed to be his individuality. These standard advertised wares—toothpastes, socks, tires, cameras, instantaneous hot-water heaters—were his symbols and proofs of excellence; at first the signs, then the substitutes, for joy and passion and wisdom."

Sinclair Lewis's genius was in capturing the spirit of modern advertising when it had not yet come to dominate the American landscape and define the soul of the nation. Advertising was in essence a twentieth-century phenomenon, and, like so many things belonging to that century, it was made in America. Its genius lies in its ability to hijack our "joy and passion and wisdom," repackaging them and returning them to us as fantasies, transforming everyday instruments, from cars to vacuum cleaners, into exotic objects of desire. Novelists, who are in the business of joy, passion and wisdom, were the first to grasp the power of advertising and technology in their best and worst forms. From Jules Verne's fantastic journeys to the macabre worlds of *1984* and *Brave New World,* they would become prophets (often Cassandras) of the modern world.

Most of us citizens of the twenty-first century cannot simply mock and deplore Babbitt. Can we deny the fact that we feel a certain empathy for him, an uncomfortable sense of identification? After all, our iPhones, iPads and Kindles are sophisticated descendants of that up-to-date alarm clock. These and thousands of the other products we have come to depend on evoke passion, guilt, anxiety. We are told that Olay Regenerist will restore our youth, a Citi card will prevent us from being boring and Alcatel and Verizon will allow us to fulfill our dreams. Meanwhile, insurance companies think day and night about nothing but our well-being.

I can imagine standing in one of those interminable lines with a Babbitt-like figure waiting for the latest iPhone and sharing his "enormous and poetic admiration, though very little understanding, of all mechanical devices." How many owners of a Mac who look nothing like Babbitt and might strongly disapprove of his lifestyle would feel, with him, that these devices are "symbols of truth and beauty?" Anyone who has gazed with longing at a clean, well-lighted Apple Store on her way to work may understand why Babbitt yearns "for a dictaphone, for a typewriter which would add and multiply, as a poet yearns for quartos or a physician for radium."

In fact, our relationships with our cell phones and iPads are far more intimate than Babbitt's to his gadgets. These objects have almost become extensions of our physical selves, threatening to take the place of actual contact with others and with the world around us. They are our intimate companions: in the streets, in our cars, in supermarkets and at restaurants, even during family meals and in bed, we communicate with them and through them, we ask them for advice and direction, feeling lost, almost bereft, without them.

Possessions have always been symbols of class and status, or mementos of love and friendship. But America has come up with a new role for them: they are now our pals, and although we may find ourselves addicted to them, they are ultimately dispensable. You love your iPhone, yet in the blink of an eye you can exchange it for something newer, better, more desirable. Excitement, free of commitment, is the basis for our most intimate relationships these days. This constant need—greed—for the new is both our strength and our vital flaw; it is what makes America a country of manufacturing dreams, or, more correctly, all kinds of dreams, and one that can also be shallow, unthinking, even fragile. What is surprising is not how much things have changed since the beginning of the last century, but how much they are alike. The gadgets in question have changed, but the mentality that packages them and buys them is basically the same. Are we all becoming Babbitts now?

# 5

It seems quite simple, this condemnation of consumer society, until one realizes that we are, of course, part of the problem. What are my exact grievances against my laptop, cell phone and now my iPad? How far am I implicated in the creation and preservation of the very world I find so easy to dismiss and despise?

*Babbitt* is full of surprises, small complications, forewarning of future dilemmas. It is deceptively simple. We don't like to think that innovation and vitality go hand in hand with complacent commercialism, and yet here we are, and it is this unexpected revelation that has made *Babbitt* gnaw at me for so many years. Much has been said about the corrosive nature of consumer society, its hazards and the inevitable conformity it generates. *Babbitt* does not merely condemn this consumerism; it lays open the paradox at the heart of American society: the urge (perhaps "addiction" is a better word) for novelty, for movement, for constant change that creates "Pep" and motivates "invention" while at the same time being an impediment to imagination and reflection.

In her review for the *New Statesman,* Rebecca West wrote that *Babbitt* has "that something extra, over and above, which makes the work of art, and it is signed in every line with the unique personality of the writer." She goes on to quote one of Babbitt's public speeches, adding, "It is a bonehead Walt Whitman speaking. Stuffed like a Christmas goose as Babbitt is, with silly films, silly newspapers, silly talk, silly oratory, there has yet struck him the majestic creativeness of his own country, its miraculous power to bear and nourish without end countless multitudes of men and women. . . . [T]here is in these people a vitality so intense that it must eventually bolt with them and land them willy-nilly into the sphere of intelligence; and this immense commercial machine will become the instrument of their aspiration."

Interestingly enough, it is Seneca Doane, the radical lawyer, friend of the workingman and astute critic of Zenith and its corrupt leaders, who most understands and appreciates this intense vitality. Responding to a foreign friend who condescendingly criticizes American conformity, Doane reminds him that there is standardization in every country: in England ("every house that can afford it having the same muffins at the same tea-hour"), in France (with its "sidewalk cafes") and Italy (where the "love-making" is standardized). For him, "Standardization is excellent, *per se.* When I buy an Ingersoll watch or a Ford, I get a better tool for less money, and I know precisely what I'm getting, and that leaves me more time and energy to be individual in." Doane goes on to explain how when he saw, in London, the picture of an American suburb in a toothpaste ad on the back of a *Saturday Evening Post,* "an elm-lined snowy street of these new houses, Georgian some of 'em, or with low raking roofs and—the kind of street you'd find here in Zenith, say in Floral Heights," he felt homesick. He thought to himself, "There's no other country in the world that has such pleasant houses. And I don't care if they *ARE* standardized. It's a corking standard!"

"What I fight in Zenith," Doane proclaims, "is standardization of thought, and, of course, the traditions of competition. The real villains . . . are the clean, kind, industrious Family Men who use every known brand of trickery and cruelty to insure the prosperity of their cubs. The worst thing about these fellows is that they're so good and, in their work at least, so intelligent. You can't hate them properly, and yet their standardized minds are the enemy." This was Sinclair Lewis's dilemma. The only way to prevent the harmful aspects of "standardization" is by cultivating its opposite, that which is unique and wayward, independent and individual: ideas and imagination. Unless we have independence of mind, how can we confront the illusions of advertising or see through the false promises of conformity?

We may laugh at Babbitt as he irritates us and invites our sympathy, but what is at stake is not just a matter of socks, shoes, cell phones and alarm clocks; the real danger lies in the commodification of our souls. Now, mind you, Babbitt himself would in no way agree with this. He, like his latter-day descendants, has his own definition of the problem. "Trouble with a lot of folks," he informs his son, Ted, is that "they're so blame material; they don't see the spiritual and mental side of American supremacy; they think that inventions like the telephone and the aeroplane and wireless—no, that was a Wop invention, but anyway: they think these mechanical improvements are all that we stand for; whereas to a real thinker, he sees that spiritual and, uh, dominating movements like Efficiency, and Rotarianism, and Prohibition, and Democracy are what compose our deepest and truest wealth. And maybe this new principle in education-at-home may be another—may be another factor. I tell you, Ted, we've got to have Vision."

There is something irresistible about Babbitt's innocent hijacking of words and ideas. He transforms familiar concepts beyond recognition through his odd pairings—"real thinker," "spiritual . . . Efficiency." And yet you have only to pay a little attention to what goes by the name of "spiritual" these days to see that his philosophy has had many converts. Whatever the field or arena, the language we use to describe (or, in today's parlance, "market") our policies, our ideas and feelings, is the same, re-duced to a single, deceptively sincere and utilitarian slogan.

Take "The Sermon on the Amount," which tells us, "The next time you get paid, you write the first check to God. . . . And then you watch God take care of you," and exhorts us to "Get involved with God financially," because if you do, "God will provide for you." You may think these words belong to *Babbitt*'s fictional preacher Mike Monday, the "Prophet with a Punch" and the "world's greatest salesman of salvation," who has "converted over two hundred thousand lost and priceless souls at an average cost of less than ten dollars a head." But the Sermon on the Amount is a real sermon, delivered by the very real Dr. David Jeremiah, radio show host, televangelist and pas-tor of Shadow Mountain Community Church, in San Diego. On his Sunday television show, Dr. Jeremiah will educate you about "God's economic plan," and offer to take you on a cruise along with his wife, and sell you *30 Days to Understanding the Christian Life in Just 15 Minutes a Day.* He has also helpfully writ-ten a book called *The Worst Financial Mistakes in the Bible and How You Can Avoid Them,* advertised as a "'What Not to Do' guide for your finances from a biblical perspective!" Once your money problems are solved, you can then turn to ChristianMingle.com to help you find your true love: "God's match for you!"

We have come a long way from Babbitt's desirable dicta-phone to Christian Internet speed dating, but the mind-set that came up with the concept of "investing" in God is still very much with us. Slowly, imperceptibly, it has reshaped our thoughts and feelings. "I don't see why they give us this old-fashioned junk by Milton and Shakespeare and Wordsworth and all these has-beens," Theodore Roosevelt Babbitt complains to his parents. Young Ted, who has to study "plain geometry, Cicero, and the agonizing metaphors of Comus," concedes, "I guess I could stand it to see a show by Shakespeare, if they had swell scenery and put on a lot of dog, but to sit down in cold blood and READ 'em—These teachers—how do they get that way?" His mother sympathizes and consoles him with the recollection that "when I was young the girls used to show me passages that weren't, really, they weren't at all nice."

The ever utilitarian Babbitt tells his son he should soldier on and slog through the courses because they are required for college entrance. But he does not see why "Shakespeare and those" are required for college or "why they stuck 'em into an up-to-date high-school system like we have in this state." He believes it would be better if "you took Business English, and learned how to write an ad, or letters that would pull." This argument is now all too familiar: learning "Shakespeare and those" won't help you pull in a paycheck down the road.

Despite Ted's dislike of college and his desire to take up "mechanics," Babbitt wants him to go to college and study law—no doubt because when he was young, his own ambition, derailed by his unexpected marriage, was to become a lawyer. "Trouble with you, Ted," he tells his son, "is you always want to do something different! If you're going to law-school—and you are!—I never had a chance to, but I'll see that you do— why, you'll want to lay in all the English and Latin you can get."

Babbitt is a fan of home-study courses, "which the energy and foresight of American commerce have contributed to the

science of education." These courses entice the discerning mind
with advertisements that begin like this:

$$$$$$$$$$

## POWER AND PROSPERITY IN PUBLIC SPEAKING

One in particular is taught by Professor W. F. Peet, "author
of the Shortcut Course in Public-Speaking" and "easily the fore-
most figure in practical literature, psychology & oratory." Babbitt
figures that this "correspondence-school business had become a
mighty profitable game." We now have many versions of home-
schooling, where the student does not have to actually attend
school but can pay an online provider to get a degree. Had he
been alive today, Babbitt would have been a sucker for for-profit
education and a great mentor to those who are shaping and for-
mulating our system of education. His terms "Business English"
and "practical literature" would fit beautifully into the educa-
tional plans our policy makers have been dreaming up. Babbitt
believed "somebody'd come along with the brains to not leave
education to a lot of bookworms and impractical theorists but
make a big thing out of it." And how right he was!

# 6

Almost a century after Babbitt was conjured into being, what he
could only dream of is on the point of being actualized. In college
we are encouraged to learn "Corporate Communications," and

Democrats and Republicans have come together to relieve young kids like Ted of that "old junk." The American public school system is being Babbittized, with learning increasingly seen as a means to an end, a vehicle for job creation. We all need jobs, and there is nothing wrong with wanting to help people who are struggling to find them, but why should earning wages be at odds with nurturing genuine knowledge and independent thought? It is no longer literature, philosophy or history that will preserve the nation in these complex times; it is practical-minded college graduates, comfortable in their new language of acronyms and shortcut, brandishing their diplomas and awash in debt.

A heated controversy has broken out in education circles in the past few years over the "Common Core State Standards," new guidelines released in 2010 and now endorsed by forty-five states and the District of Columbia. Although the Common Core was formulated and implemented by a Democratic administration, it was both supported and opposed by members of both parties. To understand its philosophical underpinnings, it is helpful to take a step back to the Obama administration's "Race to the Top" initiative, and one more step back to the Bush administration's "No Child Left Behind." Both of these programs were predicated on the belief that public schools in America were broken (one big worry was that we were falling behind China) and that the solution lay in instituting new systems of evaluation that would enable school administrators to punish the teachers of poor-performing students and reward those whose students passed the new tests. The idea was that this would motivate them to teach better, though by all appearances it has instead persuaded them to teach their students to fill out multiple-choice tests, which cannot be the best approach for preparing young people to live rich and meaningful lives. According to Diane Ravitch, an impassioned critic of these reforms, teachers have been encouraged to "teach to the tests," resulting in a narrowing of the curriculum in most schools and a focus on reading and mathematics at the expense of art, history, civics, literature, geography, science and physical education.

Where Bush opted for sticks, Obama chose to lure with carrots, and so Congress allocated an additional $5 billion to the Department of Education, and "Race to the Top" was born. States were made to compete for the jackpot and had to agree to certain rules as a condition for participation: they would have to evaluate teachers' performances based on the results of students' test scores and agree to adopt "College- and Career-Ready Standards." This nebulous directive was the seed of the future Common Core. Suddenly, the goal of school was no longer to prepare children for the world and to turn out fully formed and informed citizens, but to create employable, college-worthy test takers capable of passing multiple-choice math and English tests.

The Common Core was formulated by a nonprofit organization called Student Achievement Partners, headed by Dr. David Coleman, now president of the College Board. Its most significant supporter was the Bill and Melinda Gates Foundation, which has spent around $200 million to help develop and promote the Common Core. Many people have complained that the new standards were developed with the active participation of the testing-and-textbook industry and little input from actual teachers, but the problem is not so much one of corporate influence as of a creeping Babbitt-like mentality, which has no time for imaginative knowledge in its eagerness to create an efficient and productive "standardized man." Coleman has worked at McKinsey and started several companies involved in educational policy, and he is by all accounts intelligent, affable and well-intentioned. But he has never stood in front of a classroom and does not seem to be much interested in what most good teachers hope to achieve: to kindle curiosity, passion, a desire to learn and know and live a full and meaningful life. Students are more than future employees.

The most controversial aspect of the Common Core is its mandatory division of reading into nonfiction (redefined as "informational text") and fiction. For high schools, the required ratio was set at 70/30 in favor of informational texts, which range from Plato's Allegory of the Cave to Ronald Reagan's 1988 speech at Moscow State University to material from the San Francisco Federal Reserve Bank. Now, don't get me wrong: I would have welcomed a more interdisciplinary approach, one in which Martin Luther King Jr.'s "Letter from Birmingham Jail" might be taught alongside James Baldwin's *Go Tell It on the Mountain* and poems by Langston Hughes, but this was not the intention. The goal was not so much to illuminate the intersection between history and fiction or to demonstrate the rhetorical underpinnings and literary influences of historical speeches and documents as to replace anything that might invite subjective interpretation—the realm of imaginative knowledge—with tangible facts. Yet imaginative knowledge is one of the most potent ways of understanding and communicating with the world. This is something that was powerfully understood by those who wrote two of these informational texts: the Declaration of Independence and the Gettysburg Address.

There is something distasteful about the current fashionable buzzwords in educational circles. The goal is to promote "higher-order thinking skills." Students are "workers in the global economy" and need to be "career- and college-ready." In our tech-friendly times, we are told that students must be fed "data-driven instruction," and they need to be "evidence-based learners" familiar with "key academic concepts." While they do need to think clearly—which may be what is meant by "evidence-based critical thinking"—even more than that, they need their teachers, as one university professor so eloquently put it, to "mess them up," by which she meant that students should be made to feel uncomfortable. They should be given a desire to think and to know, and asked to articulate their own questions rather than simply scratch a pencil across a page and regurgitate the "right" answers.

When I recently stumbled upon a piece by Coleen Bondy, an English teacher who participated in a training session for the implementation of the Common Core—an "exemplar for instruction," to use the McKinsey-inflected terminology—I began to understand more clearly why fiction had been marginalized and found wanting: it is too subjective and insufficiently "evidence-based." The "exemplar" for teaching the Gettysburg Address to ninth and tenth graders comes with a number of "text-dependent questions." Teachers are forbidden from telling students about the context of its delivery; a trainer told Bondy that it was better "to give a cold, hard, assessment" of the text, saying, "we need to 'remove the scaffolding sometime.'" Teachers are instructed to refrain from asking students whether they have ever been to a funeral, despite the fact that this was, of course, the occasion for the Gettysburg Address. Such questions, touching on "individual experience and opinion," should not be asked. After a series of steps in which the students, to quote David Coleman, are made to "stay within the four corners of the text," they will then be asked to write an essay about the "structure" of the address. This same dry methodology is to be applied to all "informational" texts; the suggestion is that the "facts" they contain will speak for themselves if teachers are sufficiently rigorous in their demands for their extraction and students sufficiently diligent in their efforts to retrieve and collect them. This "cold reading" as one high school teacher, Jeremiah Chaffee, writes, "mimics the conditions of a standardized test on which students are asked to read material they have never seen and answer multiple choice questions about the passage." He adds that such "pedagogy makes school wildly boring. Students are not asked to connect what they read yesterday to what they are reading today, or what they read in English to what they read in science." As one critic complained, this is "New Criticism on steroids."

There is to be no interaction between the reader and the text, or the text and its context; students are simply asked to glean objective "evidence," and all subjective interpretations are frowned upon. Is it any wonder that fiction—rife with exactly the kind of unanswerable questions that face us in life—is the unloved stepchild? Let us consider the teaching methods recommended in this "exemplar." In an ideal classroom, would all students come to the same conclusion after reading the Gettysburg Address? Would the "evidence" point them all in the same direction?

We are not, as some critics have suggested, dealing with a conspiracy involving policy makers, billionaires and the chamber of commerce, but something far more insidious and difficult to

liberal arts, "I want to spend our dollars giving people science, technology, engineering, math degrees . . . so when they get out of school, they can get a job." How could this also become the mantra of the Obama administration, which rarely condescends to mention its own liberal arts formation? How did such a utilitarian attitude come to replace the creative American pragmatism embodied by the educational philosophy of John Dewey? Our public schools, especially in poverty-ridden neighborhoods, have been under pressure to give up music, arts, literature and all the subjects related to the humanities. But the administration's admirable goal has been to raise the standards in these schools and provide equal opportunities for all. How can this goal be realized if these subjects are not taught alongside science and mathematics? I begrudgingly took note that the humanities were pointedly absent from the president's last State of the Union speech, while mathematics, science and engineering at least got an honorable mention.

Then we have Bill Gates, the philanthropist whose money has been one of the biggest factors reshaping the educational system. In a speech to the National Governors Association emphasizing the importance of using data-based metrics to increase educational standards and bring down the costs in K-12 education, Gates noted: "The amount of subsidization is not that well correlated to the areas that actually create jobs in the state—that create income for the state. . . . Now, in the past it felt fine to just say, Okay, we're overall going to be generous with this sector," but now, he said, we should ask, "What are the categories that help fill jobs and drive that state's economy in the future?" His response to this rhetorical question was perhaps self-evident, but should we really be surprised to hear this soul-crushing evaluation from a man who has argued that donating money to a new museum wing, rather than spending it on preventing an illness such as blindness, is morally equivalent to saying, "We're going to take 1 percent of the people who visit this [museum] and blind them"?

Of course, not all of our tech entrepreneurs think like Bill Gates. This, for me, was one of the consoling aspects of delving into the controversy surrounding the Common Core: discovering how many tech people disagree with this view and see the liberal arts as central both to who they are and to their working lives. "It's in Apple's DNA that technology alone is not enough," said Steve Jobs. "It's technology married with liberal arts, married with the humanities, that yields us the result that makes our heart sing, and nowhere is that more true than in these post-PC devices." In a famous, much-circulated graduation speech to the Stanford graduating class in 2005, Jobs urged students to follow their passion. He told them how he had dropped out of the expensive college he was enrolled in because his parents couldn't afford it anymore. From then on, he followed his "curiosity and intuition," despite the fact that he was very poor, sleeping on the floor in his friends' rooms, walking seven miles across town every Sunday night to get "one good meal a week at the Hare Krishna temple." None of the things he did was in conscious pursuit of money or success. He was not preparing himself to be "college- and career-ready." Instead, after dropping out, he attended seemingly useless classes that interested him, like calligraphy, on the side. He found it fascinating—"beautiful, historical, artistically subtle in a way that science can't capture." Later, this interest resurfaced when he was designing the Mac, the first computer with a range of elegant fonts. He told Stanford students, "You've got to find what you love," and ended his speech with a quote from the final issue of the *Whole Earth Catalog:* "Stay Hungry. Stay Foolish."

Bill Gates took a risk, and so did Steve Jobs. Neither one of them could ever have imagined that he would make so much money and have so much influence, but the lesson one should take from this is not simply "Drop out of college" or "Take a few more computer science classes," but to be innovative, follow your passions—"Think different," as Apple would have it. That spirit is sorely absent from the Common Core.

"Do people know the two most popular forms of writing in the American high school today?" a group of educators was asked rhetorically in a question-and-answer session shortly after the release of the Common Core. "It is either the exposition of a personal opinion or the presentation of a personal matter. The only problem—forgive me for saying this so bluntly—the only problem with these two forms of writing is as you grow up in this world you realize people don't really give a shit about what you feel or what you think. What they instead care about is can you make an argument with evidence? Is there something verifiable behind what you're saying or what you think or feel that you can demonstrate to me?"

This statement comes to us courtesy of David Coleman, the main engineer of the Common Core. With the arrogance that comes partly from self-importance, Coleman—who boasts of a Rhodes Scholarship and degrees from Yale, Oxford and Cambridge in philosophy and English literature, proving perhaps that there is some flaw in the teaching of those subjects—has determined that literature is insufficiently useful to the formation of future wage earners, which is perhaps one reason why, instead of reading a whole play by Shakespeare, students will now be limited to one or two speeches, making them the envy of Ted Babbitt.

The absurdity (because this goes beyond irony) of the Common Core is that its main architects were not teachers and educators. In introducing David Coleman in 2011 at the Institute for Learning, Lauren Resnick said, "Okay, so this is the kind of person we are going to be privileged to hear tonight. He has been involved in virtually every step of setting the national standards, and he doesn't have a single credential for it. He's never taught in an elementary school—I think. You know, I actually don't know. He's never edited a scholarly journal, but I think he has written scholarly papers."

Really? You must be kidding! But then, as he took the stage, Coleman merrily concurred that he and other lead composers of our nation's new scholastic guidelines are

> unqualified people who were involved in developing the common standards. And our only qualification was our attention to and command of the evidence behind them. That is, it was our insistence in the standards process that it was not enough to say you wanted to or thought that kids should know these things, that you had to have evidence to support it, frankly because it was our conviction that the only way to get an eraser into the standards writing room was with evidence behind it, 'cause otherwise the way standards are written you get all the adults into the room about what kids should know, and the only way to end the meeting is to include everything. That's how we've gotten to the typical state standards we have today.

In his speeches, Mr. Coleman uses the word "evidence" a great deal, reminding me of the way in which the magnificent Gradgrind, the headmaster of an experimental school in Dickens's *Hard Times,* uses the word "facts." Gradgrind wants his children and students to learn only facts—mathematics and physical science. "Wondering" and "fancy" are forbidden in his school. "Now, what I want is, Facts," he announces. "Teach these boys and girls nothing but Facts. Facts alone are wanted in life. Plant nothing else, and root out everything else."

Now, I have nothing against a few good facts, or making an argument based on evidence—our twenty-first-century version of facts—both are essential to any good assessment of literature or just about anything else. And I would agree with Dr. Coleman that there is a problem as this skill is not in evidence in the papers of a good number of American college students. But must he be so dismissive and reductive? Must he decide that students no longer need to learn about metaphors and that the concept of a synonym is "esoteric"? Must we really believe, with him, that no one should care about what others think and feel?

"It is rare in a working environment," he memorably opined, "that someone says, 'Johnson, I need a market analysis by Friday, but before that, I need a compelling account of your childhood.'"

## 7

Now, we all know that there is more to a liberal arts education than telling childhood stories, and I doubt that is the problem facing either Coleman's imaginary Johnson or his boss. It might help both of them if Johnson had chosen a job he loved, something that engaged him and that he had a passion for, which would guarantee his devotion to his job far more than the offer of all the money in the world. But regardless, however proficient Johnson may be at making money, would he be satisfied with the notion that he should be prepared to give up his life for his country only because it gave him a job, a car, a house? Or would he, in the back of his mind, think that the material aspects of life might be secondary to more abstract concepts such as meaning and fulfillment? When the physicist Robert Wilson, the founding director of the Fermi National Accelerator Laboratory, the site of the world's most powerful particle accelerator, appeared before Congress to ask for the allocation of a considerable sum of money, he was asked to justify his demand by explaining its contribution to national defense. "It has nothing to do directly with defending our country," he said, "except to make it worth defending." If Johnson were ever to study what the nation's founders had to say about education, he might find this answer just as applicable.

In his parting words to his fellow countrymen as he stepped down as America's first president, George Washington told them they should be thankful that their nation had been created at such an auspicious time, when it was possible to realize the legacy of the Enlightenment. The era had arrived when a majority of people could benefit from privileges that until then had belonged to only the few. Among these were the right to education, by which he meant an education both in science and the liberal arts, for, as Washington said succinctly, "there is nothing which can better deserve our patronage than the promotion of science and literature. Knowledge is in every country the surest basis of public happiness."

Most of the founders were proficient in Greek and Latin, and Benjamin Rush, the patron of America's first public schools, recommended the study of the "dead languages" as central to the practitioners of "law, physic or divinity." It now occurs to me that Johnson, should he wish to know more about the foundations of his country, might want to spend more time reading Locke and Cicero than "informational texts" like "Recommended Levels of Insulation," issued by the Environmental Protection Agency, and the "Invasive Plant Inventory," courtesy of the California Invasive Plant Council. I say this not to belittle environmental issues, which are at the heart of so many contemporary problems, but rather to point out that if you want children to care for the environment, you need to educate them by providing them with knowledge and not simply information.

The "critical thinking" that the Common Core claims to wish to instill in our youth will not come from simply teaching them to decipher informational texts. Anyone, especially nowadays, can find information about almost anything in the world with a few keystrokes on Google, but not everyone can understand the nuances of that information, and even fewer will have the patience to place it in a relevant context or to be objective enough, responsible enough and passionate enough about the truth not to mind what its discovery might mean for their beliefs or short-term benefits. If our children have not been learning how to think critically, you cannot blame this on their being stuffed with too much poetry or history. Far from it. You can blame it on a culture that makes access to free thinking costly and irrelevant. You can blame it on overloaded and underpaid teachers, on a lack of public funding for education, a lack of discipline or respect either for learning or for teachers; you can blame it on a culture too focused on money, on success, on entertainment, on making life more easy than meaningful.

In a letter to his grandson, Francis Wayles Eppes, Thomas Jefferson advised him to "undertake a regular course of History and Poetry" in both Greek and Latin. This does not mean that Jefferson was not concerned with science or the material aspects of public life. Far from it. In fact, in a letter to Joel Barlow in 1807, he wote, "People generally have more feeling for canals and roads than education. However, I hope we can advance them with equal pace." He knew there could be no innovation and progress, no canals and roads, in the long term without a well-rounded education.

I am not suggesting that we should all be reading Latin and Greek, or that we should revive the educational curriculum of the founding fathers, but it is a long way between mastering Tacitus, Virgil, Horace and Herodotus and reading about recommended levels of insulation. The trouble with the Common Core is that it treats all these texts as simple texts. It asks for passages from Ovid, the Gettysburg Address, *Romeo and Juliet* and EPA reports all to be taught in the same manner, a dry and brittle exercise that takes no account of the need, as even Babbitt understood, for a little "vision" and fantasy.

# 8

Imagine that Mr. Coleman's hardworking Johnson had been persuaded to stop fidgeting in the history class in which he was assigned the Gettysburg Address (assuming it was in fact a history class, as history is a low priority these days). He might have been interested to learn that Lincoln's language—which is as inspiring and heartbreaking now as it must have been then—was colored by his readings of Milton, Shakespeare and the Bible. But alas, this is something his successors will never know if their teachers meticulously follow the instructions mapped out by the progenitors of the Common Core. And if he had stuck with that history lesson, he might also have learned that every movement for equality and justice—the civil rights movement, the women's rights movement, the environmental movement and, more recently, the gay rights movement—was affected (or perhaps "infected" is a more suitable word) by this same spirit. Words, ideas—they can be quite powerful, at least as powerful as math and science. They move people to dream and do exceptional things.

If we want our children to learn, they'll need more than rigid guidelines and "evidence-based" standards; they'll need good teachers. And if we want good teachers, we will have to treat them with respect and appreciation and give them a say in how the school curriculum is shaped and implemented. While I have not studied educational pedagogy, I have taught students for more than thirty years, and I cannot help but think that cutting art, music and fiction from the classroom is not the best way to foster creativity or innovation, or to inspire future voting citizens. "The vocation of teacher is among the highest known to [man]," said Frederick Douglass, in a statement that now sounds so very naive. He called it a "permanent vocation," claiming that "neither politics nor religion present to us a calling higher than this primary business of unfolding and strengthening the powers of the human soul."

Benjamin Franklin, Abraham Lincoln, Frederick Douglass, Elizabeth Cady Stanton, Susan B. Anthony, Albert Einstein and Steve Jobs were not mere spinners of words, someone you might begrudgingly read to get a good grade on your final exam before moving on to bigger and better things, as Babbitt advises his son, Ted, to do. They were inspiration for great deeds, reasons to seek and achieve, reminders of what it means to be human.

Now, the founders were on the whole a group of aristocratic gentlemen, and it is true that they did not think of democracy in the way we do. But they saw democracy as inextricably linked to education. Washington wanted to create a national university in the nation's capital, and his successor, John Adams, was if anything even more emphatic on the subject. In a letter to Mathew Robinson Jr. in 1786, he addresses Robinson's ideas on "American affairs" and begins by expressing hope that a time will come when the "Sciences and the art of Government" will be rid of superstition and imposture and "Authority" will come from the people and not from the "the skies in Miracles and mistery." Adams continues, explaining that before such time arrives and before any great things are accomplished, a memorable change must be made in the system of education and knowledge must become so general as to raise the lower ranks of society nearer to the higher. . . . The education of a nation instead of being confined to a few schools and universities for the instruction of the few, must become the national care and expense for the formation of the many." In another letter he said, "The whole people must take upon themselves the education of the whole people and be willing to bear the expenses of it. There should not be a district of one mile square, without a school in it, not founded by a charitable individual, but maintained at the public expense of the people themselves."

So much for Rand Paul's contention that schools are fine and great but should not be funded by the federal government. Speaking of Senator Paul's state, Kentucky, he might be interested to know that in 1822 James Madison commended the State of Kentucky for appropriating funds for a general system of education. In a letter to William Taylor Berry in August of that year, he stated that "a popular Government, without popular information, or the means of acquiring it, is but a Prologue to a Farce or a Tragedy; or, perhaps both. Knowledge will forever govern ignorance: And a people who mean to be their own Governors, must arm themselves with the power which knowledge gives."

By now it should be clear to Johnson that prosperity and enlightenment were the two pillars of both the idea of America and the American dream, and the most important achievement of American pragmatism was to recognize that one could not survive without the other. "If a nation expects to be ignorant and free, in a state of civilization," Jefferson remarked, "it expects what never was and never will be."

"Liberty" and "knowledge": one finds these two words repeated time and again in the early years of the republic. Johnson might be as surprised as I was to discover how farsighted some of the founders were. They knew the value of engineers, of people who build roads, canals and bridges, but they also knew that dictatorships could build roads, canals and bridges, and they believed that what a free society needed was an enlightened and civic-minded public that could prevent tyranny from taking root. "In despotic governments, the people should have little or no education, except what tends to inspire them with a servile fear," said Daniel Webster. "Information is fatal to despotism. . . . In our American republics, where [government] is in the hands of the people, knowledge should be universally diffused by means of public schools." He believed that "the more generally knowledge is diffused among the substantial yeomanry, the more perfect will be the laws of a republican state." And here is Madison: "Learned Institutions . . . throw that light over the public mind which is the best security against crafty & dangerous encroachments on the public liberty."

Why was Giordano Bruno burned at the stake, and why did Galileo face the Inquisition? Why is it that today countries with rigid educational systems, such as China, Saudi Arabia and even Japan, have realized that without more liberal education they will not progress beyond a certain point? Why does the supreme leader in Iran attack universities, threatening to close them down and accusing them of fomenting unrest?

To a writer, a philosopher, a teacher, a musician or an artist, freedom of expression is like bread and water—it is that without which they cannot survive. This is why in every tyrannical society, they become the first targets and are the first to raise their voices. Rather than worry that Chinese students are surpassing us in mathematics, we should perhaps celebrate the fact that the Chinese and the Saudis and so many others come to the United States looking for a blueprint from which to build new liberal arts colleges. Oil-rich countries can buy technology and import engineers from all over the world, but they cannot buy original thought. What these societies lack—what citizens in Iran and China go to jail and are tortured for, what tyrants are afraid of when they talk about Western democracies—is not technology or scientific prowess but a culture of democracy, a culture that understands and respects freedom of expression, of ideas, of imagination.

The only engineers and computer scientists in jail in totali-tarian societies are the ones who speak their minds. There are more writers, artists, musicians and poets than mathematicians and businessmen, and that is part of the reason why the hu-manities are so much more valued in these societies than in our own. But do we need the stark contrast with a totalitarian so-ciety to be reminded of the value of free thinking? Why do tyrants understand the dangers of a democratic imagination more than our policy makers appreciate its necessity?

Many things change with time, but certain basic human traits remain eternal: curiosity and empathy, the urge to know and the urge to connect. These twin attributes are our means of existence and tools for survival. They are the keys to knowledge, whether scientific or literary. Those who think the humanities are old-fashioned and out of date in the era of technology should perhaps take a look at their own history—and fairly recent his-tory at that, let us say twentieth-century history—and consider the results of divorcing technology from its human implications.

Now, perhaps, we can better understand George Babbitt's in-tuitive aversion to ideas and works of fiction. In the novel, when Myra Babbitt takes their youngest daughter, Tinka, and goes east,

Babbitt finds himself alone in the house for the first time in a long while. He wanders into his daughter's room, trying to amuse himself, and finds her books: Conrad's *The Rescue,* a book of "quite irregular poetry" by Vachel Lindsay, and "highly improper essays" by H. L. Mencken that poke fun at "the church and all the decencies." He dislikes these books, finding in them "a spirit of rebellion against niceness and solid-citizenship."

One can see why Babbitt would be both attracted to the joys of freedom and frightened by its perils, for freedom does have many perils, and the best way to confront them is not to avoid being free but to cultivate independence of thought, the kind of freedom that, incidentally, has been the great engine of American creativity and vitality in all fields, from engineering to literature. It is not enough to study chemistry. For that breakthrough to come, you need to have that precious and ineffable thing, so difficult to capture, that cannot be trained: you need to have imagination.

What every reader has in common with Babbitt is that, like him, we are faced with choices, from trivial matters like choosing toothpaste to decisions about what to do, whom to see or be, where to live or work. Freedom of choice lies at the heart of every democratic society. Against the onslaught of consumerism, against all the overwhelming siren voices that beckon, our only weapon is to exercise our right to choose. And to make the right choices, we need to be able to think, to reflect, to pause, to imagine, because what is being sold to you is not just toothpaste or deodorant or a bathroom fixture, but your next president or representative, your children's future, your way and view of life.

Now that David Coleman has let Johnson loose upon the world, my hope is that he will go places his creator never dared, freeing himself from the straitjacket of those tedious informational texts. If he is to be a good and upstanding citizen, Johnson will need to understand what it means for his country to go to war and what kind of peace is a just peace. He will need to reflect on what is moral and what is not, and to understand that he cannot simply blame the president or Congress for an aberration like Guantánamo, because he has a choice to vote for one and not the other; he has a choice to voice his opinions. He can boycott, he can protest, he can tweet. But what he cannot do is shirk his responsibility—that is what Johnson would learn if he were to undertake to travel with Huck Finn and his progenies through the imaginary landscape of American fiction. Who knows, if his boss were to ask him to do something that he considered immoral, he might even, without fear, tell him where to go.

And should he be free, despite the new curriculum, to follow his curiosity, he might learn—to quote the immortal words of William Stoner, the eponymous hero of John Williams's *Stoner,* an anti-Babbitt if ever there was one—that "as his mind engaged itself with its subject, as it grappled with the power of the literature he studied and tried to understand its nature, he was aware of a constant change within himself; and as he was aware of that, he moved outward from himself into the world which contained him, so that he knew that the poem of Milton's that he read or the essay of Bacon's or the drama of Ben Jonson's changed the world which was its subject, and changed it because of its dependence upon it."

# 9

*Paralisi Cardiaca:* these are the words inscribed in the records of the Clinica Electra, on the outskirts of Rome, explaining the cause of death for America's fugitive Nobel laureate. It means "paralysis of the heart," an apt description for the author of *Babbitt,* which, flipping *Huckleberry Finn* on its head, tells the story of a conflict in which a "sound heart" loses to a "deformed conscience." When I first read *Babbitt,* in college, I was too caught up with the obvious satire on conformity to pay much attention to the murmuring of its protagonist's heart. It is easy to catch the satire, less so the pathos. Perhaps I felt more secure laughing at Babbitt and despising him than feeling pity.

At the time, like so many of my age, I was immersed in avant-garde works of fiction, which seemed far more complex and rewarding. It was Beckett, with his scrappy and disjointed characters, and Ionesco, whose condemnation of bourgeois conformity kept me up at night and ignited my imagination. But the heart is there, from Babbitt's first appearance; we hear its faint pulse running throughout the entire story, challenging the incessant medley of distracting noises, belying the inhabitants of Zenith's seemingly confident complacency. The regular interplay between the underground life of Babbitt's heart and his surface existence, between his secret silences and his loud proclamations, is what rescues *Babbitt* from being an oversimplified exposé.

Unlike the surface world, which is full of hurried words,

the language of the heart is silent and inarticulate. At first we hear it as Babbitt struggles to sleep despite the racket outside. He is dreaming again "of the fairy child, a dream more romantic than scarlet pagodas by a silver sea." This fairy child, "so slim, so white, so eager," awaits him in "the darkness beyond mysterious groves," until he can get away from his "crowded house" and his "clamoring friends." She believes in him, soothes him, cries that he is "gay and valiant, that she would wait for him, that they would sail—" but here his romantic thoughts are interrupted as life intrudes into his dream: "Rumble and bang of the milk-truck."

Babbitt asks himself one question: Why? Why, despite his success, his loyal family, his status among his community, his prosperity and the promises of the future, does he feel so dissatisfied? This *Why?* runs throughout the story, following Babbitt from his sleeping porch into the office, returning home with him after a successful if shady transaction and persisting in the midst of jolly banter with his friends, at home, during parties, at the moment of his most satisfying deals. He can find only one response: "I don't know." Perhaps the answer is simply the fact that "he who had been a boy very credulous of life was no longer greatly interested in the possible and improbable adventures of each new day." This is where the heart comes in, to help Babbitt find an answer, or perhaps to disturb him and deprive him of his sense of complacency, to warn him that he does have a choice—there are alternatives to his way of life.

Panic comes to him in unexpected places, like a series of short strokes followed by minor epiphanies, as when, in the midst of a party with his gang of Good Fellows and their wives, they decide to hold a séance and summon the "Wop poet" Dante, "the fellow that took the Cook's Tour to Hell." Suddenly and in the "impersonal darkness," the "curst discontent" revisits him, and his friends' hackneyed jokes at the expense of the poet's "spirit" are no longer funny to Babbitt. As their shallowness and ignorance are revealed to him, he is "dismayed by a sudden contempt for his surest friends." He has a glimmer of Dante's immortality and wishes he had read the dead poet. One more lost chance, because he knows he never will.

After that party, having succeeded in finally persuading his wife to allow him, for the first time in their marriage, to go on a fishing trip with his best friend, Paul, to Lake Sunasquam, in Maine, Babbitt does not feel triumphant. Instead, "for many hours, for a bleak eternity," he stays awake, "shivering, reduced to primitive terror, comprehending that he had won freedom, and wondering what he could do with anything so unknown and so embarrassing as freedom."

When his wife and daughter Tinka leave him to visit relatives, he is "free to do—he was not quite sure what." He wanders around the silent house, asking himself what he wants. "It was coming to him that perhaps all life as he knew it and vigorously practised it was futile; that heaven as portrayed by the Reverend Dr. John Jennison Drew was neither probable nor very interesting; that he hadn't much pleasure out of making money." And so Babbitt tramps in "forlorn and unwanted freedom," childishly desiring the company of the fairy child.

Sinclair Lewis introduced a different kind of fear into American fiction: not the cosmic challenges of Melville or the puritan qualms of Hawthorne or the very real physical dangers of Twain or the insecurities and fears induced by poverty and injustice in Dreiser. With *Babbitt*, he gave us the first novel of anxiety. Alfred Kazin describes this other kind of fear, the one that is part of our everyday life, rooted in our terror of freedom at the very moment we most desire it: "There is indeed more significant terror of a kind in Lewis's novels than in a writer like Faulkner or the hard-boiled novelists, for it is the terror immanent in the commonplace, the terror that arises out of the repressions, the meanness, the hard jokes of the world Lewis had soaked into his pores."

Lewis had something in common with his protagonist. He appears to have felt, for very different reasons, the same fear when confronted with his solitary existence. As Updike put it, "His frenetic activity—all those books, all those addresses, all those binges—seems in the retelling one long escape, an anesthetic administered to a peculiarly American pain, just before the last screw of his talent could be turned."

Babbitt is a different kind of mimic from Lewis. His public self, the incessant conversations that are in actuality long monologues, his jauntiness, the jollity and physical vitality that so impressed many impressive readers like Edith Wharton—all are attempts to cover a gaping void, to forget that Floral Heights and Zenith are mere decorations and props for a life that in essence is a paltry show. Like Jim Carrey's Truman, he has a feeling that his real inner self, the one he catches only in glimpses, the one that appears in the guise of the fairy child, constantly eludes him—or perhaps it is the reverse, and he is the one eluding it?

While reading *Babbitt*, interrupted by the clamor of a world that at times appears ever more like David Coleman's dream universe, where "people don't really give a shit about what you feel or what you think," I was reminded of my conversation with Ramin in Seattle. And then I would think of Babbitt's hidden heart, and of that fairy child, and I came to believe that those books that we hungered for and risked our lives for in Iran matter just as much right here in America, even if not everyone sees it that way.

# 10

While Sinclair Lewis is not much read in English classes or by book groups today, Babbitt has had a long afterlife. He has, like Huck, engendered all manner of progeny—lonely, dissatisfied, career-minded family men yearning to escape from the seemingly desirable entrapments of their mundane lives. We find him in various guises in the characters of John Cheever, John Updike, Richard Ford and Jonathan Franzen.

David Foster Wallace gave a commencement speech at Kenyon College, which I can only hope will become one of the informational texts our students are asked to read. In it, he reminds us that neither Babbitt himself nor what he represents will go away in the foreseeable future, and that his life and dissatisfaction have lessons for every one of us as we face that vital moment of choice:

> The so-called real world will not discourage you
> from operating on your default settings, because the
> so-called real world of men and money and power

hums merrily along on the fuel of fear and anger and frustration and craving and the worship of self. Our own present culture has harnessed these forces in ways that have yielded extraordinary wealth and comfort and personal freedom. The freedom all to be lords of our tiny, skull-sized kingdoms, alone at the center of all creation. This kind of freedom has much to recommend it.

But of course, there are all different kinds of freedom, and the kind that is most precious, you will not hear much talked about in the great outside world of wanting and achieving and displaying. The really important kind of freedom involves attention and awareness and discipline, and being able truly to care about other people and to sacrifice for them, over and over, in myriad petty, unsexy little ways, every day. *That* is real freedom. *That* is being educated, and understanding how to think. The alternative is un-consciousness, the default setting, the rat race, the constant gnawing sense of having had, and lost, some infinite thing.

I know that this stuff probably doesn't sound fun and breezy or grandly inspirational the way a commencement speech is supposed to sound. What it is, as far as I can see, is the capital-T Truth, with a whole lot of rhetorical niceties stripped away. You are, of course, free to think of it whatever you wish. But please don't just dismiss it as some finger-wagging Dr. Laura sermon. None of this stuff is really about morality or religion or dogma or big, fancy questions of life after death. The capital-T Truth is about life *before* death. It is about the real value of a real education, which has almost nothing to do with knowledge, and everything to do with simple awareness—awareness of what is so real and essential, so hidden in plain sight all around us, all the time, that we have to keep reminding ourselves over and over . . .

"It is the conflicting fate of an American artist to long for profundity while suspecting that, most profoundly, none exists," Updike writes; "all is surface, and rather flimsy surface at that." In this story of surfaces and mirrors, certain characters stand in for alternative paths that Babbitt might have chosen. He has chosen the path of the Good Fellows, but there are temptations. Take Paul Riesling and Seneca Doane, two former schoolmates, one of whom he loves and the other he begrudgingly respects.

Babbitt's best friend, the sensitive and fragile Paul, wanted to be a musician—a fiddler, to be precise—but marriage to a boisterous girl who later turned into a nagging and disparaging shrew forced him to take up his father's business: tar-roofing. With Paul, Babbitt becomes a different person: tender, protective and genuinely concerned, like a loving older brother. Paul is the only person who shares Babbitt's past and his dreams, for Babbitt once wanted to be a lawyer, a governor maybe, a champion of the poor and the oppressed, before he married the good-hearted and placid Myra and became a salaryman.

When he sees Paul, Babbitt is "neither the sulky child of the sleeping-porch, the domestic tyrant of the breakfast table, the crafty money-changer of the Lyte-Purdy conference, nor the blaring Good Fellow, the Josher and Regular Guy, of the Athletic Club." They shake hands solemnly and smile "as shyly as though they had been parted three years not three days," greeting each other:

"How's the old horse-thief?"

"All right, I guess. How're you, you poor shrimp?"

"I'm first-rate, you second-hand chunk o' cheese."

Paul is swiftly moving toward destruction, despite a wonderful fishing trip with Babbitt and his friend's love and support. He dreams of leaving his shrewish wife and has an affair with a faded woman in Chicago that at first sounds scandalous to Babbitt. When Paul is discovered by his wife he tries to kill her, wounds her instead, goes to jail and dies.

As the story moves inexorably forward, the urge in Babbitt to try to escape not simply in his dreams but in real life becomes ever more overpowering. He turns to Seneca Doane after a chance meeting on a train. At first he attempts to avoid the radical lawyer, but gradually he realizes that Doane is a human being like any other, who enjoys dancing and pretty women, only he also likes to see "the meetings of the Garment Workers held at the Ritz, with a dance afterward. Isn't that reasonable?" he asks.

Doane reminds Babbitt of who he was, telling him how, at some point during their student years, Babbitt and his enthusiasm were an inspiration for Doane. In those days, Doane tells Babbitt, he was "an unusually liberal, sensitive chap." He adds that at the time, Babbitt used to tell him that he intended to be "a lawyer, and take the cases of the poor for nothing, and fight the rich," and that Doane would be "one of the rich," buying paintings and living in Newport.

Babbitt painfully follows in the footsteps of both Riesling and Doane. He finds a woman and tries to love her and be part of her world—a group of Bohemians called "the Bunch"—only to discover that she is conventional in her own way. Next he takes a more dangerous step by speaking rebelliously at the Athletic Club, defending and quoting the radical lawyer. His friends start to look at him with suspicion, and during a workers' strike he even dares to defy the church and denounce the preacher's sermon about "How the Saviour Would End Strikes." He becomes so insolent that the most powerful men in Zenith threaten him with bankruptcy and ruin if he does not straighten up and join the new Good Citizens' League, formed to fight the unions and workers. Despite his fears, he resists. But now he is isolated, his business is suddenly not as prosperous as it used to be, and people are whispering and avoiding him.

The pathos of Babbitt's return to the fold is that it is motivated not only by fear of being ostracized by the Good Fellows but by his heart. His complicated feelings for his complacent wife, Myra, form a central motif in both driving him away and bringing him back. Even at the very beginning of the novel, although negligent and irritated by her, he does feel moments of tenderness, admitting that poor Myra has not had it easy, either. But it is when she becomes sick and has to be taken to the hospital and operated on that Babbitt finally gives in. "Instantly all the indignations which had been dominating him and the spiritual dramas through which he struggled became pallid and absurd before the ancient and overwhelming realities, the standard and traditional realities, of sickness and menacing death, the long night, and the thousand steadfast implications of married life." And so "he crept back to her."

As he kneels down before his wife, before she is taken to the hospital, he knows clearly and swiftly that he will have "no more wild evenings." He is honest enough to admit that he will miss them. Myra survives, the Good Fellows return, the prodigal son is forgiven and becomes the most rabid critic of Doane and the godless workers. The strike is put down, and Babbitt joins the league, whose members, the most influential and powerful citizens of Zenith, believe that "American Democracy did not imply any equality of wealth, but did demand a wholesome sameness of thought, dress, painting, morals, and vocabulary."

The novel, in its simple and direct manner, at times veers into science fiction. It has about it something of *Invasion of the Body Snatchers,* whose protagonist finally succumbs to an alien who sucks out his soul, transforming him into a programmable drone. Babbitt gives up the fight with a whimper: "They've licked me; licked me to a finish!" he says. At the end we see him encouraging his son, Ted, to stray and follow his dreams, while admitting, "I've never done a single thing I've wanted to in my whole life!"

It is a rather feeble and disappointing ending. We are given the satisfaction neither of complacently judging Babbitt as a villain nor of his redemption and transformation. Ted will never be reconciled to reading Shakespeare, but he does choose what his heart desires. Yet his choice, like his father's, is limiting.

So few American novels have happy endings. Perhaps this is not surprising in a nation whose declaration of independence provides its citizens not with the right to happiness but the right to its pursuit. And yet there is a glimmer of hope, just as there is in *Gatsby,* with its green light at the end of the dock, because Babbitt, despite everything and despite himself, does stray, proving that the faint murmur of the heart cannot be silenced.

At the party where Babbitt and his friends try to summon the spirit of "the WOP poet," Dante, for a minute Babbitt has, "without explanation, the impression of a slaggy cliff and on it, in silhouette against menacing clouds, a lone and austere figure." And that is where the hope lies: no matter how many utilitarian business-minded educators may try to erase the image of the poet, to make it irrelevant, it will endure. It will disturb us in our waking hours and haunt our dreams, because poetry, like love and lunacy, is as much a part of the human condition as fear and the courage to be free.

# PART III

# CARSON

"No live organism can continue for long to exist sanely under conditions of absolute reality; even larks and katydids are supposed, by some, to dream."

—Shirley Jackson, *The Haunting of Hill House*

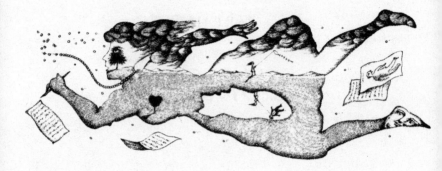

# 1

Every novel has a setting, but the American novel is unique in its conception of the landscape as an integral part of its moral universe. This is something I first came to understand when I started teaching *Huckleberry Finn* to my students in Iran. To teach a novel is not the same as to read it for pleasure. You notice things that would otherwise slip your attention and you probe it more vigorously. When one thinks of the landscape of *Huckleberry Finn,* the first thing that comes to mind is of course the river, the abundant Mississippi carrying our two heroes and offering up a spectacle of beauty and horror. But there is another landscape, equally if not more enduring: that of the smothery town with its deadening stillness from which Huck is so desperate to escape. Was this listlessness a particular southern condition or could that fictional town of St. Petersburg, Missouri, stand in for any small town across America? This is a question that occupied my imagination in my own college days when, at some point between sophomore and junior years, I started hanging out with a tall, lanky girl with mousy hair and wonderful long legs with whom I carried on intense and at times heated discussions about art, literature and a boy named Ben Holder.

Joanna was an art major, a painter to be precise. I first met her in an art history class when our young teacher, unabashedly biased in favor of modern art, introduced us to Mark Rothko and Claes Oldenberg, but we spent most of our time talking about fiction—southern fiction, if you will, though at the time I was almost allergic to the term. Some of my favorite American writers, even my favorite among favorites, William Faulkner, belonged to that group, but they were great writers, not great *southern* writers. This visceral reaction, which took me some time to shake, was provoked not by a professor or a class but by Joanna, who would sit in the front row near the door, a study in provocation. I never did figure out how she managed to look so comfortable slumping over that unyielding wooden chair. I wouldn't put it past her to have hoped that one day she might be rewarded when a careless classmate would trip over her long legs, making a fool of himself.

"My name is *Joanna*," she would tell me time and time again—not Joan-*anna*, as I sometimes jokingly called her, in honor of another artist friend, Joan Frederick, or Joe-Anna, as she claimed I pronounced it, a habit that seemed to both irritate and amuse her. I fell back on my privilege as a foreigner, though, truth be told, I had given up correcting myself when I mispronounced names, reasoning that since few people bothered to pronounce my name correctly, I was simply returning the compliment. For a while, the two of us felt a competitive kinship as foreigners, or more precisely as people who came from somewhere else.

At first I was bewildered that Joanna, who was born in America, should feel that she too had traveled from another country thousands of miles away, with a different past and a different story. She grew up in Tennessee, although she had only a faint southern accent—in itself an act of rebellion, as her mother had insisted she should remain loyal to her southern heritage. I can't really say what either one of us was doing at the University of Oklahoma. (Contrary to common belief, she would remind me, Oklahoma is *not* in the South.) For her it was a short pause before going east—that was her destination, though she never really specified where in the East she was heading.

My friend Mike Wright, a fellow activist who was not much interested in literature, firmly believed that any focus on regional differences would hurt the unity of the "movement," as we called it back then. People are people, he would say. We should differentiate among them according to the causes they support and not their geographic origins. "This land is my land *and* yours, Azar," he would tell me, quoting his beloved Woody Guthrie—though this didn't stop him from promptly contradicting himself by announcing that Woody was an Oklahoma boy, and neither East nor West could claim him as theirs. Mike had grown up in Norman. No one knew exactly what year he had graduated, and for some reason he had never moved on. He had been president of Students for a Democratic Society and was active in the Committee to End the War in Vietnam, and he made sure we all knew that in the sixties he had participated in the civil rights movement. He was respected and liked by various student groups, who were constantly fighting among themselves, but seemed to be a loner—at least that is how I remember him.

Mike lived in a small place near the post office. I would sometimes bump into him at Campus Corner, whose shops were the center of university life, most often at the intersection of Boyd and Asp. I was usually coming from a coffee shop or going to the post office, and I have no idea what Mike was doing, walking alone.

He never told me where he was coming from or where he was headed; he would just turn around and start walking with me.

Those short walks, which generally ended at Ernie's Town Tavern and once or twice at the Library Bar, were the only occasions when Mike and I discussed matters other than those pertaining to the Vietnam War or the civil rights movement. (He was the one who interested me in the case of the Scottsboro Boys and the history of protest around them.) I used to think he liked to talk more than listen, because he seldom looked you in the eye when he spoke. His gaze was fixed straight ahead, as if he were searching for something in the distance visible only to himself. And because he so liked to talk—in a droning, monotonous voice, a bit like slow-motion typing, if you can imagine that—much later I was surprised by how much he had been listening, and how carelessly I, in turn, had been listening to him.

Joanna would from time to time sit in on my English class, and when she did she talked a great deal, usually managing to bring the topic back to what she called the "southern climate"— a term she used in both its literal and metaphorical senses. I thought she was overly focused on where a writer happened to have been born, through no fault of his or her own. I was the only foreigner in the English department and took it as a personal affront that she thought I could not understand Twain or Faulkner as well as she did. She was too narrow, I felt, too possessive of the South and its writers. Of what value is a novel if you had to have been born in a certain latitude in order to enjoy it?

Joanna tolerated my objections in silence, waiting for me to finish my sentence so that she could return to her point. There is a southern sensibility, she would say, that's key to southern fiction. I would rattle off a list of authors—Mark Twain chief among them—whose landscape, while ostensibly southern, was undeniably universal. For a while we hovered in an uneasy truce, but we finally parted company over *The Heart Is a Lonely Hunter,* which we read together for that class in the spring of my sophomore year. At some point Joanna became obsessed with Carson McCullers, who had not been my favorite author but whose *Heart Is a Lonely Hunter* had interested me enough to want to follow up with *The Member of the Wedding* and *The Ballad of the Sad Café*. Chance and choice, my friend Ladan was fond of saying. How much of what we think we are choosing is already chosen for us by chance? A medley of unrelated encounters reminded me of Joanna and of our conversations: Oprah Winfrey's selection of *The Heart Is a Lonely Hunter* for her book club, after a number of my favorite novels cropped up on her list (*One Hundred Years of Solitude, Anna Karenina,* three books by Faulkner . . .); a throwaway remark by a student—("Oh, her—we read that book in high school; what's the point of her?"); someone's use of the word "freaks"; but perhaps most of all, the unexpected news and circumstances of Mike's death. I had not thought of McCullers for twenty-five years, and here I was suddenly checking out her books from the local library, then buying them, then rereading and underlining them once again.

As I resurrect Joanna, sorting through hazy memories that appear deceptively lucid, I am less irritated by her brashness and her obsessions and more impressed by how much those oh-so-serious discussions over hamburgers at Across the Street; or eggs over easy, hash browns and coffee at Ernie's Town Tavern; or those walks around campus, ending on the South Oval, have remained as exciting and important to me as they were then. Maybe in choosing to write about Carson McCullers today, I am trying in part to retrieve the freedom and enchantment of those youthful conversations, when it was possible to seriously fight and fall out over a novel, only to make up, mainly in order to pick up the fight where we had left off. Joanna was the one who led me to coin the term "Southern Syndrome," which I later amended to the more specific "Joanna's Carson McCullers Syndrome." At some point it became our Carson McCullers Syndrome, and now it is all mine.

# 2

Despite our vocal disagreements, in a vague and confused way I empathized with Joanna. She felt like an exile in her own country. And even then I felt like an exile myself, so far from home and from people who could understand the texture of my life in Tehran. Joanna and I were not exiles in the true meaning of the word, at least not then—we were both free to return to our places of birth—but we recognized a kinship in each other and knew or suspected we would never simply settle down back home.

Anyone who has experienced exile knows that in the aching desire to retrieve the lost land, the first thing that comes to mind is not what forced you to leave, but what kept you from leaving. This desire manifests itself as a sensual urge, a desperate longing for certain tangible things whose absence makes them so hauntingly present. Even then, whenever I thought of Iran, I yearned for that special quality of the light, the way it gave a cool, sun-drenched taste to the peaches and apricots and brought out the crisp scent of jasmine at night. Did it smell so strong and so sweet, our jasmine, because of that sun?

The sun acts in different ways in different places. For me it was a cool light, for Joanna a persistent heat, heavy and suffocating, like the weight of sameness and boredom we find in Faulkner's *Light in August* or the murderous and relentless heat in the Algerian desert that incites the protagonist of Camus's *The Stranger* to kill a man. Light plays a dominant role in the works of Faulkner, Welty and McCullers, and yet its texture, which ultimately decides its function, is radically different in each one. This is something that Joanna, with her artistic temperament, particularly appreciated. Characters respond to what she called "the climate" not just physically but psychologically.

Recently I returned to *Light in August* to find the passage in which the Reverend Hightower, sitting by the window, reflects on his past. It is at the start of chapter twenty, near the very end of the novel, and is narrated in the present tense: "Now the final copper light of afternoon fades; now the street beyond the low maples and the low signboard is prepared and empty, framed by the study window like a stage." Hightower is reminded of his youth and of "how that fading copper light would seem almost audible, like a dying yellow fall of trumpets dying into an interval of silence and waiting."

"In August in Mississippi there's a few days somewhere

about the middle of the month when suddenly there's a foretaste of fall," Faulkner said in an interview when asked to explain the title of his novel. "It's cool," he said, "there's a lambence, a luminous quality to the light, as though it came not from just today but from back in the old classic times. It might have fauns and satyrs and the gods and—from Greece, from Olympus in it somewhere. It lasts just for a day or two, then it's gone, but every year in August that occurs in my country. . . ."

In almost every one of Faulkner's novels—I am thinking most especially of *The Sound and the Fury* (Shakespeare), *As I Lay Dying* (Book XI of Homer's *Odyssey*) and *Light in August*—the present time is simultaneously transient and ancient. It is linked to the more immediate past but also to the literary past of our human civilization. "The past is never dead," says a character in *Requiem for a Nun*. "It's not even past." This notion of the perpetual presence of the past is perhaps best expressed by the narrator's incantatory statement in *Light in August:* "Memory believes before knowing remembers. Believes longer than recollects, longer than knowing even wonders." All of Faulkner's major novels, be they about a crumbling aristocratic family or a rootless vagrant, are illuminated by that light. There is something in the quality of his prose that captures this twilight effect, at once beautiful and sad, in ruins and yet eternal, like the voice of Addie Bundren in *As I Lay Dying* coming to us after her death.

In Eudora Welty's fiction, the light is not quite so thick; it does not have so many layers. In the first chapter of *Delta Wedding* we are told that the land, which is "perfectly flat and level," shimmers "like the wing of a lighted dragonfly." Again the senses intermingle to create a feeling, an impression, so this shimmering land seems to be "strummed, as though it were an instrument and something had touched it." Welty's descriptions of nature and the play of light are so loving, so tender, as if drawn with the lightest touch of a watercolor brush. Her writing is impressionistic, like the writing of that altogether non-southern writer she loved so much, Virginia Woolf.

McCullers's light comes from a different place. It lacks the weight of Faulkner's past and the shimmer of Welty's dragonflies. It is a new sun, blazing, ruthless in its glare, and angry. The heat in *The Heart Is a Lonely Hunter* is not tropical and lush; it is urban, the reflection of a scorching sun on the asphalt. This sun acts more like a fury than a guardian. It is not the same sun as the one we find lighting the way for Huck and Jim or beating down on the poverty-ridden sharecroppers in Erskine Caldwell's *Tobacco Road,* documenting the cruel transition to industrial farming, a transformation responsible for another kind of poverty, another kind of loneliness.

*The Heart Is a Lonely Hunter* is an urban story, unmistakably set in the South, but this is a South where the sense of community and familial affinities are broken, where even exploitation has taken on a new tone and texture. McCullers's characters are solitary misfits who cannot create a bond. They might speak in a more "civilized" manner than Huck and Jim, but they do not know how to interact, how to connect, how to communicate—they are spiritually inarticulate, having discovered a new kind of urban loneliness that will cast a long shadow over American fiction.

"The South has always been a section apart from the rest of the United States," McCullers wrote in an essay published in 1941, "having interests and a personality distinctly its own. . . . Economically and in other ways it has been used as a sort of colony to the rest of the nation." In the year that America entered the Second World War, McCullers proclaimed that modern southern writing was "the progeny of the Russian realists," an affinity she attributed to the strikingly similar circumstances under which the two societies functioned: "In both old Russia and the South up to the present time a dominant characteristic was the cheapness of human life," she wrote. "Life is plentiful; children are born and they die, or if they do not die they live and struggle. And in the fight to maintain existence the whole life and suffering of a human being can be bound up in ten acres of washed out land, in a mule, in a bale of cotton."

I found the essay almost by accident and was only a few paragraphs in when I felt myself transported back to those muggy spring days in Oklahoma when Joanna and I argued about the southernness of Faulkner and Flannery O'Connor. Joanna was not terribly interested in this central theme of Carson McCullers's most famous novel, the special kind of loneliness that she described as peculiarly American. What she wanted was to retrieve its texture. At times, frustrated by my abstractions, she would almost shout out, "Yes, but how would you *paint* that?"

# 3

In her outline for "The Mute," the working title for *The Heart Is a Lonely Hunter,* McCullers writes that the town that forms the backdrop to her story could exist anywhere in America, at any time, but "there are many aspects of the content which are peculiar to the America of this decade—and more specifically to the southern part of the United States." This town, never mentioned by name, "is located in the very western part of Georgia, bordering the Chattahoochee River and just across the boundary line from Alabama"—much like Carson's own hometown of Columbus. Its population is around forty thousand, about one-third of whom are "Negroes." It is a "typical factory community and nearly all of the business set-up centers around the textile mills and small retail stores. Industrial organization has made no headway at all among the workers in the town," who are "conditioned to a very apathetic, listless state." Rather than blame himself for his own misfortune, the worker turns on the "only social group beneath him—the Negro."

From this skeletal description grew that haunting town somewhere in "the middle of the deep South," whose stagnant air carries something of the dangerous and dusty heat of the Phelps farm in *Huckleberry Finn.* The same motionless air chases all the characters, penetrating their pores and setting them in frantic motion, as if in flight from some invisible burden: "The summers were long and the months of winter cold were very few. Nearly always the sky was a glassy, brilliant azure and the sun burned down riotously bright. Then the light, chill rains of November would come, and perhaps later there would be frost and some short months of cold. The winters were changeable, but the summers always were burning hot. The town was a fairly large one. On the main street there were several blocks of two- and three-story shops and business offices. But the largest buildings in the town were the factories, which employed a large percentage of the population. These cotton mills were big and flourishing and most of the workers in the town were poor. Often in the faces along the streets there was the desperate look of hunger and of loneliness."

This same aura of desperation will resurface in McCullers's later fiction. In *The Ballad of the Sad Café* she writes, "Yes, the town is dreary. On August afternoons the road is empty, white with dust, and the sky above is bright as glass. Nothing moves—there are no children's voices, only the hum of the mill. . . . There is absolutely nothing to do in the town. Walk around the millpond, stand kicking at a rotten stump, figure out what you can do with the old wagon wheel by the side of the road near the church. The soul rots with boredom." We have come a long way from Dorothy's Kansas and the celebrated myth of the hard-working pioneer.

I once tried to convince Joanna that the small towns in American fiction all have something in common, thinking of Sherwood Anderson's *Winesburg, Ohio,* Sinclair Lewis's *Main Street,* and the unnamed towns in Georgia of *Lonely Hunter* and *Ballad of the Sad Café.* This was a pet theory of mine, one I still find myself returning to. She shot back that I didn't understand a thing about America. They are not the same, she cried,

Winesburg and that town in Georgia! Her tone implied that such a thing should be very obvious, like the color of snow. "Can't you see?" she would ask earnestly, leaning slightly toward me, her hands outstretched as if in supplication.

For a long time, I did not see. I could not bring myself to share her view that all southern characters are lonely outcasts—this was certainly not true of the characters populating Eudora Welty's novels, or Robert Penn Warren's *All the King's Men.* And yet I was forced to concede that Faulkner's major characters are outcasts in the sense that they have been cast away from a past that is not just irretrievably lost but also somehow poisoned by a lie. "There was something definitely rootless about him," the narrator says of Joe Christmas in *Light in August,* "as though no town nor city was his, no street, no walls, no square of earth his home."

At the time I staked out my position, but over the years I have come to appreciate that there are certain elements that make southern fiction distinct. Faulkner, O'Connor, Richard Wright, Erskine Caldwell—they were born in the only part of America that had lost a war and been occupied, a loss that remained central to their self-definition. Their unique history was a burden but also a source of inspiration. Many other southern writers, like Peter Taylor and Walker Percy, tackle this admittedly southern theme of a lost past to different degrees, but the past is not a major concern for McCullers. Her characters suffer from loneliness and isolation, but their conditions are rooted firmly in their present states of mind.

# 4

Joanna wasn't a friend in the usual sense of the word. Most of my close friends, like Joan and Steve, were sympathetic to "the cause," if not part of a specific political group or ideology. Joanna would have none of it. Whenever I would mention a protest meeting or the war in Vietnam she would shake her head and lean forward, as if ready to physically cut me off, and then she would change the subject to what she really wanted to talk about.

Mike was on the other side of the spectrum. He was a committed activist. At the time there were so many different organizations and groups mobilized to change the world. Although I officially belonged only to the Confederation of Iranian Students, I participated in some of the other radical activities around campus. Mike, of course, sympathized with each and every cause. He would tease me about my literary "tendencies," which he saw as a distraction from what really mattered. For a while I was on the English department's speakers committee, and he'd appraise the speakers we brought to campus, dragging out his curt evaluation in slow motion: "Allen Ginsberg, good. Norman Mailer, not so good. Amiri Baraka, good. Fredric Jameson, gives Marxism a bad name. Adrienne Rich, good, I guess. And who is this John Barth you are so crazy about?" I would try to cajole him into appreciating literature by quoting from his favorite thinkers: Hegel on form and content, Marx in praise of Greek tragedy, Brecht on the fact that Paul Claudel was a reactionary but nonetheless a great poet.

"Facts, Mike," I would tease him. "Your facts are mere skeletons, without the flesh and blood of imagination."

"Fancy talk," Mike would say, "fancy talk."

He would tell me that stories do not put bread on the table, and I would say they're not meant to do that, and your "facts" are in the eye of the beholder. And besides, man does not live by bread alone.

Mike was, as others later described him, a Norman "fixture." I have the same mental image of him throughout my years at the University of Oklahoma: slim and straight, with a long face, frizzy hair, a beard that covered most of his face, and granny glasses. He and Joanna represented two poles of my existence in Norman, one having to do with art and literature, Fellini, Bergman and playing the guitar, and the other with protests, taking over the administration building, long meetings and singing old labor songs.

# 5

In her outline for "The Mute," McCullers describes the main theme of the novel as that of "man's revolt against his own inner isolation and his urge to express himself as fully as is possible." The characters could belong to any place at any time, as their isolation and inability to communicate takes on a larger, more universal meaning. Or could they? This was what Joanna and I never could agree on. She held the view that what gave these characters blood, flesh and bones and shaped their souls—in short, what made them "real"—was rooted in a particularly American psychosis and, more specifically, in the character of the American South.

"Inner isolation," "man's revolt," "the urge to express"—these are charged words, both intense and abstract, almost intimidating, but what endures is a compelling human drama and not an existential thesis concocted by a precocious twenty-year-old who, aside from a short trip to New York, had only ever been to Charlotte, North Carolina. Yet she did touch on all of those abstractions, with the ruthless eye of a writer, accomplishing what one of her characters, Biff Brannon, strives for, which is "to store up a whole lot of details and then come upon something real."

There is something about each one of her four principal characters that is slightly off, slightly self-tortured, as they struggle to understand the meaning of life and to give their own lives meaning. Rereading the book, I found many aspects at once comical and tragic and began to feel that the whole novel was, in many ways, encapsulated by what the narrator says at one point about Jack Blount: "There was something very funny about the man, yet at the same time another feeling would not let you laugh."

This is McCullers's secret strength: creating something "very funny" that cannot be laughed at. McCullers invented her own style, what the German writer Klaus Mann called "a strange mixture of refinement and wildness, 'morbidezza' and 'naïveté.'" She would later describe southern realism as a "bold and outwardly callous juxtaposition of the tragic with the humorous, the immense with the trivial, the sacred with the bawdy, the whole soul of a man with a materialistic detail." While farce and tragedy have always been foils for each other, it is rare, she maintains, other than in works of Russian and southern literature, that "they are superimposed one upon the other so that their effects are experienced simultaneously."

McCullers describes her book as "the story of five isolated, lonely people in their search for expression and spiritual integration with something greater than themselves. One of these five persons is a deaf-mute, John Singer—and it is around him that the whole book pivots." The other four are a restaurant proprietor, Biff Brannon; a self-proclaimed activist and labor agitator, Jake Blount; an African American doctor, Benedict Mady Copeland; and a twelve-year-old girl, Mick Kelly, whose large family barely makes ends meet by turning part of their home into a boardinghouse. "Because of their loneliness," McCullers writes in her outline, these four "see in the mute a certain mystic superiority and he becomes in a sense their ideal." Singer himself has a parallel relationship with another deaf-mute, Antonapoulos, who is his roommate and only friend until he begins to behave strangely and is taken to a mental hospital in another city.

I did not at first imagine, when I went searching for Huck's progenies, that I would find myself revisiting Carson McCullers. But when I did, I was struck by their affinity, with one crucial difference. Huck's solitary journey was enriched by Jim's presence. Here there is no Jim, no soul mate and moral compass. What each character is left with is a secret passion and the need to communicate it. This makes them feel both alone and hopeful. It also accounts for their jittery restlessness. McCullers's characters do not ponder the past; they spend their time dreaming of the future, or rather of a future other than the one they have been dealt.

# 6

When Oprah picked *The Heart Is a Lonely Hunter* for her book club, she devoted a segment to interviewing two "deaf divas," the actress Marlee Matlin and former Miss America Heather Whitestone McCallum. Both expressed their excitement about the novel, and the former Miss America said she admired McCullers for offering "the hearing world a glimpse of what it may have been like to be deaf in the 1930s." Both said how impressed they were with McCullers's ability to "capture deafness," not in today's terms, but "accurately for her time and place." Whitestone McCallum mentioned the isolation she had suffered while growing up and said, "Today, people have a better attitude towards deaf people. Technology is much better, and that's what makes such a difference." I would have liked to hear more about her feelings of isolation as a child, that experience being so central to the book.

Singer is deaf, and he can read lips, but is that really the point of the book? Is it a book about deafness? Maybe, but not as literally as that would suggest. McCullers did not model Singer on research about deafness. When, a few months after their marriage, her husband suggested that he could take her to a convention on deafness in Macon, Georgia, so she could authenticate her conception of John Singer, she refused to go. She said she wanted to keep "her own imagined image."

This conversation with the deaf divas caught my attention because it seemed to be a straightforward representation of a common point of view in our culture today—one quite inimical both to the fictional world and the real one. It has in fact become so dominant not just in academia but everywhere that we don't even notice it anymore. Implicit in this approach is a certain guideline for how to read a novel, whereby you are expected to identify with the characters, to see them as representative of certain types or social conditions. Of course, readers, like writers, are unpredictable. They are unruly, and no matter how many guidelines you give them, they will find their own way of connecting with a book. The problem with this utilitarian mind-set is that it distorts both fact and fiction in order to arrive at a certain predetermined conclusion, one that most often ends with uplift and a happy ending.

I have been teaching American fiction to sometimes reluctant and often eager students ever since I moved to Washington from Tehran in 1997. Some of my students over the years have asked me, "What's the point of reading these books?" or "How will they help me solve my problems?" The question is not generally posed in such stark terms, but that is the gist of it. Often, in response, I will turn the question back to them: What is it that we are looking for when we read a novel? Must it be useful? Must it teach us something concrete? I am tempted to quote Nabokov: "Fancy is fertile only when it is futile."

If our main expectation from a work of fiction is that it be factually correct or that it correlate to real life, that it cure us of our anxieties, improve our relationships with our mothers—in short, be aspirin for the soul—then we risk treating the novel as nothing more than a manual, in this case a manual for understanding deaf people—with not very successful results, because, unlike the former Miss America, Singer does not feel his life to be full of "blessings" and does not say, "I am happy even though I'm deaf."

Singer is real. He has feelings and can touch people, which is why readers empathize with him. And on a metaphorical level, he reminds us of a larger, more universal truth that is as relevant in this century as it was in the last—this despite the technology that not only has improved hearing aids and facilitated our lives but has provided us with so many new ways of communicating. As human beings, we have a profound need for empathy. We need to be listened to and understood. And so the book is less about the challenges of a deaf person than it is about our difficulty communicating meaningfully with one another, a difficulty that no technology can heal. No hearing aid would help us understand the kind of isolation human beings feel when they cannot communicate and articulate their inner feelings, their desires and aspirations. Because the terrible truth is that you can learn to lip-read the world, but the world around you still might not hear you.

## 7

In her own life, Carson McCullers elicited from people either tenderness and a desire to protect or outrage and bitter resentment— "viper" and "bitch" were among the terms used to describe her. Joanna would have said that these twinned and contrary emotions were, on a larger scale, what the rest of the country tended to feel about her native South, tempting me to disagree. I was of course well aware of Flannery O'Connor's statement that "anything that comes out of the South is going to be called grotesque by the Northern reader, unless it is grotesque, in which case it is going to be called realistic."

According to McCullers's first biographer, Virginia Spencer Carr, her mother claimed that she, while pregnant, had been "alerted by the oracles that her firstborn would be unique." She was convinced the child would be a boy and decided to name him Enrico Caruso, in honor of the famous singer. The birth was difficult, which some believe accounted for her slightly misshapen head. In any event, the baby was not a boy, but a boyish girl, so she was named Lula Carson—Lula (which she later dropped) in honor of her beloved grandmother, and Carson after Caruso. And she did become a genius of a kind. Oprah's Book Club called her a "southern belle," a term that would have amused more than irritated her.

If her life was charmed, it was not so much in the way of most southern belles, but more like that of a heroine in a Tim Burton movie. To the conservative society into which she was born, Lula Carson was an odd specimen of a girl. To begin with, there was her appearance. She was tall and lanky, and as she grew into adolescence she would deliberately emphasize her boyish appearance by wearing white socks and sports shoes, which she even wore to her own wedding, along with a tailored suit and a sailor cap. Beginning at a young age, she was fond of carrying around a flask of sherry and hot tea.

From the start, she was different from the "normal" kids

around her, enjoying the kind of status as an outsider that she would later pass along to her favorite protagonists, Mick in *The Heart Is a Lonely Hunter* and Frankie in *The Member of the Wedding*. She was the type of odd girl whom boys were forced by their well-mannered parents to promise they would ask to dance. Most of her high school classmates thought her eccentric. Her skirts and dresses were always a little too long, and she wore dirty tennis shoes or brown Girl Scout oxfords when the popular girls were wearing hose and high heels. When she was young, some of the girls threw rocks at her when she walked by, snickering loudly and calling her "weird," "freakish-looking" and "queer." So perhaps it wasn't so surprising that she would later empathize with "freaks," who to her mind were not just people with physical disabilities but those who refused to act according to the norm. "Nature is not abnormal, only lifelessness is abnormal," she would write in her essay "The Flowering Dream: Notes on Writing," first published in *Esquire*. "Anything that pulses and moves and walks around the room, no matter what thing it is doing, is natural and human to a writer."

Life in Columbus, Georgia, might have seemed limited and narrow, but Carson spent hours in her inner world, infinitely rich and various, keeping company with Mozart and Beethoven, Flaubert, Joyce and the Brontë sisters, D. H. Lawrence, Eugene O'Neill, Chekhov, Gogol and Tolstoy. Like Mick Kelly, she had an outer world and an inner, more private world of her own construction. I have sometimes thought of her as my ideal student. In her unfinished autobiography, *Illumination and Night Glare,* she writes, "When I was about eleven my mother sent me to the grocery store and I carried a book, of course. It was by

Katherine Mansfield. On the way I began reading and was so fascinated that I read under the streetlight and kept on reading as I asked for the supper groceries." Later, she was apparently fired from a job because she was too busy reading Proust.

Like Mick, she spent many hours playing the piano. She was precocious, learning to play without any training. In 1932, when she was only fifteen, she caught rheumatic fever and was bed-ridden for a long time and started to contemplate her options in life. That was when she first considered becoming a writer. Her friend Helen Jackson said that when, in December of that year, she visited her at her home in Columbus, Carson told her, "I've got something important to tell you, Helen. I've given up my dream of being a concert pianist. But it's O.K. I'm going to be a writer instead."

Her childhood fever was misdiagnosed and mistreated, leading to a series of terrible strokes that would leave her almost half paralyzed by the age of thirty. By forty her body would be a wreck. In her last years, she would suffer though a number of intricate operations to relieve the spasms of an atrophying left hand, wrist, elbow and leg; to repair a shattered hip and elbow; to cope with repeated sieges of pneumonia, a severe heart at-tack, breast cancer. . . . And yet, through it all she was as busy as ever, writing and giving interviews. If in her first book, written when she was barely out of her teens, she could capture the life of the senses and portray pain in such a concrete manner, it was in part because pain was an organic part of her life; she resisted it most effectively by making it her own.

# 8

In September 1937, when she was twenty, Lula Carson Smith married the dazzlingly handsome Reeves McCullers. ("It was the shock of pure beauty, when I first saw him," she would later write; "he was the best looking man I had ever seen.") They had been introduced through a common friend, Edwin Peacock. Reeves was an aspiring writer, but he never did write, and to the end of his life he would be bitter about the fact that he spent so much time taking care of his wife and trailing after her. Three years into their marriage, she published *The Heart Is a Lonely Hunter,* and after that she became a literary sensation. They had what is called a tumultuous love-hate relationship, with extramarital affairs, a divorce and a remarriage, all of which ended on a note as morbid as Carson's own stories. They had been living for a while in Bachvillers, near Paris, going through a period of contentment and activity followed by depression. In the summer of 1953, Reeves suddenly started talking about suicide, then one day he attempted to take his life by hanging himself from a pear tree in their orchard. The limb broke under his weight. Carson's response, as she reported it, was, "Please, Reeves, if you *must* commit suicide, do it somewhere else. Just look what you did to my favorite pear tree."

After that unsuccessful attempt, Reeves came up with another idea: a suicide pact. He took Carson to the barn to show her a rope. He picked it up and, pointing to the beam overhead, said, "See that rafter, Sister. It's a good sturdy one. You know what we're going to do? Hang ourselves from it. I tell you, it's the best thing for us both." Carson told Tennessee Williams, who was by then a good friend, that she thought she had dissuaded him from the idea of a double suicide, but a few days later, on their way to the American hospital in Paris, she noticed two lengths of rope in the back of the car. Reeves told her that instead of taking her to the hospital, he was going to the forest so they could hang themselves, but first they would stop to buy a bottle of brandy. "We'll drink it for old times' sake . . . our one last fling."

While Reeves was in the liquor store, Carson jumped out of the car and hitchhiked to a friend's house. She immediately made arrangements to leave Paris for New York. Two months later, on November 18, 1953, Reeves told friends he would be "going west" the next day. He sent a telegram to his wife in Nyack, New York, saying, "Going West—trunks on the way."

During the First World War, when a man felt his death was imminent, he would say he was "going west." Reeves was found dead the next day—he had committed suicide in his hotel room, alone.

After Reeves's tragic death, Carson tried to banish him from her life. It may have been the easiest way to deal with the anguish and the pain. Meanwhile, her physical ailments continued to torment her. She could rarely sit and suffered from circulatory problems. For about a year, she had to elevate her left leg and hold it straight out in front of her. She was told at one point that she would have to have it amputated, though she was kept ignorant of the reason why. Only later did she learn that she had developed bone cancer. Despite this, she never stopped traveling and never stopped writing.

Notwithstanding her growing physical disabilities and the intensity of the pain she constantly suffered, Carson McCullers was very busy, so busy in fact that her workload might have made a healthy person ill with exhaustion. She struggled with writing and finally published a new novel, *Clock Without Hands*. She also wrote a play, *The Square Root of Wonderful,* and a collection of poems, *Sweet as a Pickle and Clean as a Pig;* worked on her unpublished memoirs, *Illumination and Night Glare;* wrote a number of essays and articles and even participated in the translation of her stories into plays and films, composing the libretto for a musical based on *The Ballad of the Sad Café.* In between surgeries and writing, Carson found ample time to tend to her social life and keep up with her friends—good old-fashioned American sturdiness, giving the finger to both life and death, something so little encouraged today, so little appreciated.

A few months before her death, in the spring of 1967, Carson traveled to Ireland to meet the director John Huston, who was making a film of her book *Reflections in a Golden Eye,* starring Elizabeth Taylor and Marlon Brando. The invitation excited her so much that each morning she would wake up thinking about her love of Ireland, rereading Joyce's *Dubliners,* listening to *Tristan und Isolde* because of its Irish setting. After months of strategic planning, finally she left in April 1967. She had to be driven from Shannon Airport to Huston's estate in an ambulance. Yet she was determined to enjoy her time, drinking bourbon and smoking menthol cigarettes. She read Joyce, O'Casey and Yeats while holding court from her bed for a whole host of people who wanted to visit the famous American author. She even dictated "A Love Letter from Ireland." A huge hassock stuffed with foam rubber was made to fit in the plane cabin for her return, creating a sort of chaise longue. She boarded first, and once she was made comfortable, Aer Lingus uncorked champagne for the first-class passengers to toast the famous author.

Despite the pain and anguish she suffered both physically and emotionally, McCullers maintained a certain youthfulness, which came to her rescue at her worst times. In life she was childish, egocentric and needy, depending on others to be with her and to take care of her. Perhaps nowhere does she combine this childlikeness and childishness, this state of protracted adolescence, which she invoked time and again to describe her native South, as effectively as in *The Heart Is a Lonely Hunter.* And nowhere else does she identify so clearly this mix of childish petulance, freshness, resilience and transient growing pains with her beloved country, America.

# 9

In 1949, McCullers published an essay in *The Week* entitled, "Loneliness . . . An American Malady." It was a short piece, but I have come to think of it as her credo, and I've returned to it many times over the years. She writes that Americans "tend to seek out things as individuals, alone. The European, secure in his family ties and rigid class loyalties, knows little of the moral loneliness that is native to us Americans. While the European artists tend to form groups or aesthetic schools, the American artist is the eternal maverick—not only from society in the way of all creative minds but within the orbit of his own art. . . . Whether in the pastoral joys of country life or in the labyrinthine city, we Americans are always seeking. We wander, question. But the answer waits in each separate heart—the answer of our own identity and the way by which we can master loneliness and feel that at last we belong."

I don't think it is an exaggeration to say that this very American form of solitude is essential to our democracy, springing forth as it does from a native self-reliance. I am reminded of Elizabeth Cady Stanton's short and searing pamphlet "The Solitude of the Self," in which she proclaims that the need for equal rights comes innately from the seclusion of every woman in America who is born alone, is solely responsible for her own life and will die alone. Therefore, she needs to be able to sustain herself. Cady Stanton begins her essay by championing "the individuality of each human soul" and goes on to elaborate why every woman must live "in a world of her own, the arbiter of her own destiny, an imaginary Robinson Crusoe with her woman Friday on a solitary island."

In words that are more poetic and anguished than ideological and polemical, she writes, "The isolation of every human soul and the necessity of self-dependence must give each individual the right to choose his own surroundings." Then she relates how she once asked Prince Kropotkin, a Russian political prisoner, "how he endured his long years in prison, deprived of books, pen, ink, and paper." He responded, "In the pursuit of an idea I took no note of time. When tired of solving knotty problems I recited all the beautiful passages in prose or verse I had ever learned." He had a "world of my own, a vast empire, that no Russian jailer or Czar could invade."

McCullers was deeply musical, and in her outline she writes that the novel's form is "contrapuntal throughout." She goes on to explain: "Like a voice in a fugue each one of the main characters is an entirety in himself—but his personality takes on a new richness when contrasted and woven in with the other characters in the book." The main characters all suffer from an inner isolation. Their suffering is unique, but they are all too preoccupied with their own obsessions to listen to one another or to anyone else, so they share this listless isolation.

As Joanna used to say, there are many different forms of loneliness. In some respects, the loneliness of solitude is far less chilling than the loneliness we feel when we are alone together. Joanna and I would pore over paintings by Toulouse-Lautrec, Picasso and Edward Hopper showing people sitting or standing, within touching distance, and yet appearing to be lonelier than if they were by themselves. In all of these paintings, that feeling of loneliness is accentuated by silence—no one makes eye contact or speaks—by the evident inability to communicate and by the simultaneous awareness of the other person's physical proximity.

Lately I have discovered a new kind of loneliness, peculiar to our time, for which I have yet to find proper artistic expression. I have seen it in photographs on the Internet of groups of young people who sit very close together, each one busy texting. What disturbs me most about these photographs is that the youth seem to have no consciousness of where they are or whom they are with. They are not lonely; they are wholly somewhere else. Toulouse-Lautrec, Picasso and Hopper all attempted to convey a consciousness of this terrible isolation, and a certain anguish stays with you long after you have stopped looking at the painting, but we seem in our own time to have become numb to our surroundings.

In *The Heart Is a Lonely Hunter,* the principal characters are equally unaware of their environment; they are too wrapped up in their own obsessions to see or hear one another, but their distractions give them no entertainment or comfort. They are disturbed by their inability to express themselves or communicate with others. It makes them restless. It also keeps them from knowing themselves, because for McCullers, the search for the self is inseparable from the need to connect with others. "For a baby," McCullers writes, "the question of identity shares urgency with the need for milk. The baby reaches for his toes, then explores the bars of his crib; again and again he compares the difference between his own body and the objects around him and in the wavering, infant eyes there comes pristine wonder." This consciousness of the self is indispensable not just philosophically but also pragmatically.

If, in the work of Hopper and Raymond Carver, loneliness is expressed through silence, in McCullers this solitary pain is communicated in words. Jake Blount, the agitator, best demonstrates the manic urge to pour out words, words that seem to have no hinges, no past or present to them—they do not reveal or clarify but confuse and frustrate. Biff stands behind the counter, observing, as Jake eagerly talks to Singer, the words coming "out of his throat like a cataract." Biff notices that "the accent he used was always changing the kinds of words he used." Jake is all over the place; he jumps from subject to subject and seems to belong everywhere and nowhere, and that, of course, is the problem.

# 10

I did not really properly say goodbye to Mike when I left the United States for Iran in 1979. I had told him what I had said to my other friends: "See you next year, or the year after." I promised to come back for summer vacations. But once I was in Tehran, there was no coming back for summer vacations. I did not see him again until I returned to Oklahoma for two days in 1991 to give a talk on Iranian culture and film before heading on to Washington and then back to Tehran. To call that trip an emotional event is an understatement. I was elated and saddened and curious and absolutely dislocated. All I remember is faces: Dr. Gross, Dr. Yoch, Dr. Velie and Dr. Elconin, my beloved English teacher, who was very sick and died before my next visit to Norman, in 2001. There were some unfamiliar faces, too, telling me they had heard about me, had started to wonder what had happened to me. I saw Mike briefly on that visit—he was not there and then he was, standing a little aloof from the crowd after the discussion of an Iranian film I had just screened.

We had coffee together later and, like David Gross, my professor, fellow protester and dissertation chair, Mike told me that for a long time he'd thought I had died or been killed. After the revolution I had changed addresses in Tehran and he didn't know how to find me. We talked a bit about old times, and at one point he said, "Don't you remember, you wanted to seduce me into loving literature?" "Seduce" was a strange word for him to use, because Mike was so un-seducible in so many senses of the word—or so I believed. He was the type of person who was always on the periphery of one's attention, not outstanding for being handsome or intelligent or particularly passionate; he was, if anything, outstanding despite or because of his lack of these qualities. There was an oddness about him; even when he was young he appeared older than his years; his shadow would fall somewhere between your line of vision and those good-looking, boyish young men who attracted your attention. He was there, and one got the impression that he would always be.

I reminded Mike of how he had taught me about Woody Guthrie and told me about his participation in the civil rights movement. I said I had thought of him and our conversation about African American writers and the civil rights movement when my first published work, a translation of two poems by Langston Hughes, came out and later when I wrote an introduction to Richard Wright's *American Hunger,* a book I had taken with me to Iran. He remembered that Melville had been one of my favorite authors and reminded me of how I had once called him "Mr. I Prefer Not To" in reference to the character in *Bartleby, the Scrivener*—I'd told him he was as stubborn as old Bartleby. I had also called him Mr. Gradgrind, after Dickens's character, because he would repeat so many times in our discussions "facts, Azar, it's all about the facts. . . ." He remembered my love of Katherine Anne Porter's "The Jilting of Granny Weatherall" and Faulkner's "A Rose for Emily," and then there was Flannery O'Connor's "A Good Man Is Hard to Find." "And the British," he said. "You loved them, too, and some of the French, like Flaubert and Balzac. For a while you talked like a real proletarian, when you were reading Mike Gold and Henry Roth."

He told me that the times had changed; there were the Reagan years, and now? "What now?" I asked. "We've come a long way from the civil rights movement," he said. "That was an exciting time." He started filling me in on the years since I had left. "It all started with Reagan," he said, casting his eyes about him now, "followed by Bush and the Gulf War."

Mike had always talked a lot, but as time went by, most of those who had listened or pretended to listen dispersed and left, and he was left talking to fewer people and then mainly to himself. His "enemy" did not kill him or put him in jail; it simply ignored him. Indifference, as McCullers reminds us, is among life's worst punishments.

Norman had remained progressive, or at least there were progressive pockets. "You think New York and Chicago are hubs of protest," Mike said, "but we have our own tradition right here. It goes back—yes, it goes back." Then he told me how the other night at a bar, some rednecks had beaten two Pakistanis, thinking they were Iranian. I mentioned this anecdote in my speech that night, asking the audience to please not do that sort of a thing to me. It gave me an opening to remind them of how little they knew about these other countries, that they could not tell the difference between a Pakistani and an Iranian.

When it came to politics, Mike talked for so long, and I was so tired, that everything was becoming more jumbled and confused in my mind. A long time had passed since I had been away from America, from Norman, from Mike and from drinking coffee dressed that way with a man who was not my husband. It had been eleven years since I had left all of that behind. Perhaps since I was coming from Tehran for the first time in so many years and knew that I would return in a few days' time, I felt Mike had little to complain about. He seemed dissatisfied with the U.S. government, but I pointed out that there were no morality squads and public executions. I felt that I had changed a great deal since we had last met but that he had not changed so much. He had remained the same Mike, without roots or attachments, ready to talk to you at the drop of a hat and always looking for that invisible something in the distance that tempted and eluded him.

I felt slightly depressed after seeing Mike, and although I had promised I would keep in touch, I did not give him my contact information, or ask for his. I wanted to forget him, to not be disturbed by something so very sad that I sensed in him but could not touch.

# 11

What connects a restaurant owner, a drunken agitator from out of town, an African American doctor and a young teenage girl living on the edge of poverty? The answer appears to be a deaf man, John Singer, and their insatiable need to be close to him, to talk to him. They believe he is the only person in that town who genuinely understands them.

They don't know that Singer is simply puzzled by them. In a letter to his friend Antonapoulos, Singer writes that the four are "very busy people," so busy that "it will be hard for you to picture them." He adds, "I do not mean that they work at their jobs all day and night but that they have much business in their minds always that does not let them rest." It is words that torment them: "Those words in their heart do not let them rest, so they are always very busy." He cannot understand why they are so eager to talk to him, when most of the time he does not understand them, although he nods in response and is distantly sympathetic.

Of these four people, Biff Brannon, the restaurant owner, is different from the other three. His focus in life is on one word:

Why? "The question flowed through Biff, always, unnoticed, like the blood in his veins. He thought of people and of objects and of ideas and the question was in him." The word is echoed throughout the story, gradually gaining volume as it takes on a more universal meaning. Biff is different from the others. While the others take refuge from their inner turmoil in constant, agitated physical movement, Biff's restiveness has little outward manifestation. Jake is a drifter, moving from one shabby, smelly room to another. Mick finds no free and private space in her home and takes to spending a great deal of her time wandering the streets. And then there is Dr. Copeland, whose cold, lonely home cannot appease his terrible feeling of uprootedness. Even Singer is a roamer. He has a room in the Kelly family's boardinghouse but spends most of his time when he is not working roving the different parts of the town. None of these characters feel at home in their own home. Biff is the only one who pays any attention to where he lives, who takes care of his home and makes it presentable. He is the only one who remains, at the end of the novel, in the same place we first found him.

We meet Biff Brannon at his restaurant, the New York Café, named for the elsewhere that so many inhabitants of small towns all across America dream of, the fantasyland to which the eighteen-year-old Carson fled the first chance she got. The summer night is "black" and "sultry," it is midnight and all the streetlights have been turned off, so "the light from the café made a sharp, yellow rectangle on the sidewalk." The streets are deserted, and inside, the café is busy with the half dozen customers drinking while Biff waits "stolidly, his elbow resting on the counter and his thumb mashing the tip of his long nose." As is his habit, he is watching. Singer differentiates him from the other characters, writing to his friend that those others "all have something they hate. And they all have something they love more than eating or sleeping or wine or friendly company. That is why they are always so busy." But as for Biff, what he does is "watch."

Biff's eyes are "cold and staring, half-concealed by the cynical droop of his eyelids. On the fifth finger of his calloused hand there was a woman's wedding ring." Early in the novel, there is a scene in Biff's bedroom in which he and his wife, Alice, quarrel about one of their customers, Jake Blount, who his wife complains has been eating and drinking and talking wild for a week without paying a cent. She wants him kicked out, for "he's nothing but a bum and a freak." Biff responds that he likes freaks. "I reckon you do!" Alice shouts back, "I just reckon you certainly ought to, Mister Brannon—being as you're one yourself." In response, Biff accuses his wife of not having "any real kindness. . . . Or maybe it's curiosity I mean," he elaborates, adding, "You don't ever see or notice anything important that goes on. You never watch and think and try to figure anything out." His list keeps growing: "The enjoyment of a spectacle is something you have never known. . . . You don't know what it is to store up a whole lot of details and then come upon something real."

Watchfulness, thinking, curiosity, "enjoyment of a spectacle," "real kindness"—might these be qualities similar to those of a writer of fiction? One who does not participate in the spectacle but is almost always watching, asking, curious to know, who has to place himself in the minds and hearts of others, all the time piling up a whole lot of details? Biff has the urges of a writer; what he lacks is the ability to express and articulate them, to "store up a whole lot of details" and, through his imagination, come up with "something real." His artistic ability is limited to decorating his room or the café window.

Through the café doors they come and go under Biff's watchful gaze, in search of something, as if hoping to find a way to fulfill the dreams gnawing at their hearts, evasive and yet so real. There is John Singer and the agitator Jake Blount, and the thirteen-year-old Mick Kelly, and for a brief moment Dr. Benedict Mady Copeland. Soon we, the readers, find ourselves asking: Why? Why are they so restless, so uncomfortable in their own skin? Why?

# 12

Joanna wanted to study painting in order to find her own style. Capturing "southern heat" was her main obsession. We spent hours tracing the way the heat chased the characters around the city. I had discovered the metaphorical use of the word "dazzle"—both Jake Blount and Mick Kelly are dazzled by the glare of the sun, which seems to follow them almost like a fury in Greek mythology, in sync with their inner urges or, in Jake's case, his indecipherable rage.

Joanna and I went over several passages again and again, like the one in which Jake walks down the "quiet and hot, almost deserted" main street on a Sunday morning, when "the awnings over the closed stores were raised and the buildings had a bare look in the bright sun." He doesn't have any socks on, and "the hot pavement burned through the thin soles of his shoes. The sun felt like a hot piece of iron pressing down on his head. The town seemed more lonesome than any place he had ever known. The stillness of the street gave him a strange feeling. When he had been drunk the place had seemed violent and riotous. And now it was as though everything had come to a sudden, static halt."

Jake is an anticapitalist; he is full of facts and figures about the oppression of labor, the need for workers to unite, but the people he wants to liberate do not understand his agitated words, and they pay attention only to tease him. Biff, observing Jake carefully through half-closed eyes, comes to the conclusion that although Jake gives the impression of being a "freak," he is not one. "It was like something was deformed about him—but when you looked at him closely each part of him was normal and as it ought to be. Therefore if this difference was not in the body it was probably in the mind. He was like a man who had served a term in prison or had been to Harvard College or had lived for a long time with foreigners in South America. He was like a person who had been somewhere that other people are not likely to go or had done something that others are not apt to do."

That same night, Jake comes in with a "tall Negro man carrying a black bag." Jake tries to bring him to the counter for a drink, but the black man refuses and leaves. When someone objects to his bringing this man to a place where white men drink, Jake responds, "I'm part nigger myself," and goes on to say, "I'm part nigger and hop and bohunk and chink. All of those." They laugh at him while he continues: "And I'm Dutch and

Turkish and Japanese and American," ending with "I'm one who knows. I'm a stranger in a strange land."

"Why?" Biff asks, and this time he has an answer. "Because in some men it is in them to give up everything personal at some time, before it ferments and poisons—throw it to some human being or some human idea. They have to. In some men it is in them—the text is 'All men seek for Thee.' Maybe that was why—maybe—He was a Chinaman, the fellow had said. And a nigger and a wop and a Jew. And if he believed it hard enough maybe it was so."

Faulkner, who wrote to a friend that he did not "care much for facts," believed there was no room in a writer's profession to "be afraid," no room, as he proclaimed in his Nobel Prize acceptance speech, "for anything but the old verities and truths of the heart, the old universal truths lacking which any story is ephemeral and doomed—love and honor and pity and pride and compassion and sacrifice." Central to *The Heart Is a Lonely Hunter* are those "old verities and truths of the heart"—in fact, we wouldn't be far off the mark if we were to claim that the main themes in the novel are "love and honor and pity and pride and compassion and sacrifice." Is this not the real reason we read Carson McCullers or William Faulkner or Flannery O'Connor—or any novelist, for that matter, whether from the South or from Tahiti?

# 13

I was reminded of Mick Kelly the other night by a young girl on a segment of *60 Minutes* whose parents had lost their jobs and their home as a result of the economic crisis. They had lived with dignity and relative comfort, and suddenly they were homeless, living in their car. They were not complaining—not because they had nothing to complain about, but out of a certain sense of personal integrity. Their protest was implied in their description of how they were forced to live, struggling to keep clean and find a safe place to sleep, how they avoided being discovered by the authorities and worried about the consequences—one problem, you see, is that to go to school you have to have a permanent address, and of course they had none. They were not '"moochers," nor did they feel "entitled"—terms some of our elites have been throwing around indiscriminately about Americans without jobs or homes, when really they would more appropriately describe Kim Kardashian and her fellow reality stars.

That young girl and her family were no Kim Kardashians; they were just plain Americans, more like descendants of Dorothy and her sober relatives in Kansas, or of the Joad family in *The Grapes of Wrath*. What caught my attention was the expressions on the faces of the children, in particular that girl with short blond hair, who seemed to beam forth a desperate resilience and personal integrity that made her say, not because of the camera but in all sincerity, that they would survive, and that for her the American dream was still valid—and I believed her.

That expression has stayed with me and made me think of Mick Kelly. The two girls, one fictional and one real, certainly have something in common. It has something to do with passion and integrity—something that makes you hopeful and breaks your heart.

There is another passage Joanna and I pored over a great deal. Mick has taken her two younger brothers out for a walk. There's no one in the street on this "very hot" late Sunday morning, and her brother Bubber "was barefooted and the sidewalk was so hot it burned his feet. The green oak trees made cool-looking black shadows on the ground, but that was not shade enough. . . . The long summer-time always gave Bubber the colic. He didn't have on a shirt and his ribs were sharp and white. The sun made him pale instead of brown, and his little titties were like blue raisins on his chest."

Joanna would cry out in frustration, "How do you capture heat? How can you paint it like Carson McCullers does in her stories? That sort of loneliness," she would add. "It's not a Hopper kind of loneliness." She said this knowing that Hopper was my favorite painter, at a time when Andy Warhol reigned supreme. So it just may be that I owe to Joanna an idea I later became obsessed with: the different forms of loneliness in American art and fiction and their relation to a certain idea of America.

That morning, Mick had been woken up early by the sun. Too hot to even drink coffee, she had ice water with syrup and cold biscuits before leaving home. She set off with her brothers for a building site. When she got there, she left the boys and started climbing a ladder to the top, where she stood up "very straight. She spread out her arms like wings. This was the place where everybody wanted to stand. The very top. But not many kids could do it. . . . The sky was bright blue and hot as fire. The sun made everything on the ground either dizzy white or black." Mick has an urge to sing, and "all the songs she knew pushed up toward her throat, but there was no sound." This urge, the search for song, is what makes Mick so restless. She belongs to a large family, all of them hard workers who barely make ends meet. Mick is too poor to afford a radio, a gramophone or a musical instrument. She roams the streets listening in on houses with a radio or a gramophone and occasionally indulges herself by listening to their lodger Singer's radio. Like her creator, she can read and play notes without training, and she spends her lunch money learning to read music from another girl, practicing long hours after school on the piano in the gym, amid the noise of her schoolmates playing sports. She even takes a cracked ukulele that's been strung with two violin strings, a guitar string and a banjo string and tries to refashion it as a violin. "But all the time—no matter what she was doing—there was music. Sometimes she hummed to herself as she walked, and other times she listened quietly to the songs inside her. There were all kinds of music in her thoughts. Some she heard over radios, and some was in her mind already without her ever having heard it anywhere."

Like all young girls of her age, Mick has her daydreams. On that day, alone in the unfinished building, Mick dreams about how, when she is seventeen and very famous, she will write her initials, M.K., on everything, how she will drive a red and white Packard with her initials on the doors, how she will have them on her handkerchief and underwear. She daydreams about inventing a radio the size of a green pea that people will carry around and stick in their ears, and flying machines, but her real dream is music, and the thing she wants most in the world is to have a piano.

She has recently discovered one fellow whose music "made her heart shrink up every time she heard it." The fellow is called something like "Motsart." Standing in the empty room, she takes two stubs of chalk out of her pocket, one green and the other red, and writes on the wall, in big block letters, "EDISON, and under that she drew the names of DICK TRACY and MUSSOLINI. Then in each corner with the largest letters of all," she writes her initials. Finally, on the opposite wall, she "wrote a very bad word—PUSSY." She hums one of the tunes she remembers, "and after a while in the hot, empty house by herself she felt the tears come in her eyes. Her throat got tight and rough and she couldn't sing any more. Quickly she wrote the fellow's name at the very top of the list—MOTSART."

In her outline, McCullers states that Mick is "perhaps the most outstanding character in the book. Because of her age and her temperament her relation with the mute is more accentuated than any other person's." Mick "commands more space and interest than anyone else." This is partly because her "essential traits" are "great creative energy and courage. She is defeated by society on all the main issues before she can even begin, but still there is something in her and in those like her that cannot and will not ever be destroyed."

McCullers bestows her with her own most distinct attributes: her appearance, her love of music, her desire to be loved and tended to, her complex relationship to sex, her need for tenderness and capacity for life, her resilience and courage. In her secret inner room, Mick keeps her paintings and drawings, her notes and the notes to the music she is either hearing or composing. Nothing is clear to her yet; she is at a transitional time in her life, something both frightening and exhilarating, on the verge of discovering herself and the world.

Mick's prominent role also comes from the fact that she is a metaphor for the main theme of the story: growing pains. She is the only real teenager in the book, but the other characters in one way or another suffer from stunted growth: they are grown-up adolescents with urges and emotions they are unable to express. Like Mick, they are haunted by an inner voice whose language they have not learned to speak: "The feeling was a whole lot worse than being hungry for any dinner, yet it was like that. I want—I want—I want—was all that she could think about—but just what this real want was she did not know."

# 14

After the publication of *Reflections in a Golden Eye,* one of whose characters was gay, McCullers was visited on her return to Columbus, Georgia, by a Ku Klux Klan member who told her that she should leave town immediately or else he and his friends would come and "get her" before morning: "We know from your first book that you're a nigger-lover," he said, and "we know from this one that you're queer. We don't want queers and nigger-lovers in this town." Her father stayed up all night on their front porch with a loaded shotgun, but the Klansmen never showed up.

Twenty-five years later, McCullers wrote that in her first book she had tackled several moral problems, most notably "the problems of prejudice and poverty in the South." Jake represents the search for social and economic justice, but it is in the figure of Benedict Mady Copeland, the most critically acclaimed character in the novel, that we find a man grappling with the most enduring of all urges: the desire for dignity, both for his race and for himself. McCullers should be praised as much for her minor characters—the Copeland family, Antonapolous, Mick's brother Bubber, and her friend Harry Minowitz—as for the major ones, each in their own way attempting to preserve their dignity, and each being defeated in the end.

In the August 1940 issue of *The New Republic,* Richard Wright compared McCullers to Faulkner, writing, "To me the most impressive aspect of 'The Heart is a Lonely Hunter' is the astonishing humanity that enables a white writer, for the first time in Southern fiction, to handle Negro characters with as much ease and justice as those of her own race. This cannot be accounted for stylistically or politically; it seems to stem from an attitude toward life which enables Miss McCullers to rise above the pressures of her environment and embrace white and black humanity in one sweep of apprehension and tenderness."

Dr. Copeland's house, while more substantial than those of other African American characters in the novel, lacks the warmth and comfort of a real home. It is bare and dark, for although the doctor has electricity, he barely uses it, even at night. Even on very hot nights, he sits close to the fire, in a straight-backed chair, "motionless. . . . Even his eyes, which stared from behind the silver rims of his spectacles, did not change their fixed somber gaze." Then he picks up a book and, because the room is very dark, he has to hold it close to the stove to make out the print. "Tonight he read Spinoza. He did not wholly understand the intricate play of ideas and the complex phrases, but as he read he sensed a strong, true purpose behind the words and he felt that he almost understood."

Dr. Copeland is an educated man, familiar with Spinoza and Karl Marx, an honest and hardworking physician, and yet the sense of injustice is so strong and deep in him that he cannot find the words to express it. His frustration is exacerbated by the silence of his own people, even his children, who refuse to participate in his social protest, who do not understand him and take refuge in the church and in God, trying not to step on the white man's toes. His rage and their silence feed upon each other. His daughter, Portia, who works for Mick's parents, tells Mick that her father is not like the other "colored" men, explaining that "most of the time he were very quiet. But then some nights he would break out in a kind of fit. He could get madder than any man I ever seen." Her diagnosis is that "he full of books and worrying. He done lost God and turned his back to religion. All his troubles come down just to that."

Dr. Copeland has tuberculosis and must take his temperature four times a day and get an X-ray once a month. He begins work very early in the morning, going "from one house to another and the work was unending." "All his life he knew that there was a reason for his working. He always knew that he was meant to teach his people. All day he would go with his bag from house to house and on all things he would talk to them." If he were able to rest, he might be able to heal, but he cannot. "For there was another thing bigger than the tiredness—and this was the strong true purpose. He would think of this purpose until sometimes, after a long day and night of work, he would become blank so that he would forget for a minute what the purpose was. And then it would come to him again and he would be restless and eager to take on a new task. But the words often stuck in his mouth, and his voice now was hoarse and not loud as it had been before. He pushed the words into the sick and patient faces of the Negroes who were his people."

Dr. Copeland's father was a preacher, and his mother a slave who, after securing her freedom, became a washerwoman. They had taught him and made enough money, out of their weekly savings of two or three dollars a week, to provide him with eighty dollars to go up north. He had made money in a black-smith's shop, then as a waiter and a bellboy, then he had gone to school and after ten years become a doctor. He married the woman he loved and had four children whom he also loved, but his mission, his desire to set his people free, would get in the way of his personal feelings. "The hopeless suffering of his people made in him a madness, a wild and evil feeling of destruction. At times he drank strong liquor and beat his head against the floor. In his heart there was a savage violence, and once he grasped the poker from the hearth and struck down his wife." She took the children, went to her father's house and never re-turned, leaving him "an old man in an empty house."

During a family gathering, his relatives all talk of miracles and God. His father-in-law, a crafty tenant farmer and the family patriarch, explains to his children that while working the fields, he likes to dream of Jesus appearing to him and his telling Jesus that "us is all sad colored peoples." Jesus would then place "his holy hand upon our heads and straightway us will be white as cotton." Portia's husband, Highboy, when sick with pneumonia, had seen God's face looking at him through the fireplace, and God had "a large white man's face with a white beard and blue eyes."

Dr. Copeland, listening to them, "felt the old evil anger in him. The words rose inchoately to his throat and he could not speak them. . . . These are my people, he tried to tell himself—but because he was dumb this thought did not help him now. He sat tense and sullen." He stares at them with "angry misery" and knows that if he could find a way to tell his children how "the sight of their faces made a black swollen feeling in him," the act of telling them "would ease the sharp ache in his heart. But they would not listen or understand." So he sits in silence, and leaves the house without saying goodbye, because "if he could not speak the whole long truth no other word would come to him."

Unlike her father, Portia tries to stay clear of racial issues. She lives with her brother Willie and her husband, Highboy, and is proud of the way they work and live together. She finds every opportunity to repeat how Highboy pays the rent, Portia provides the food and Willie pays for their Saturday-night outings. "Us has always been like three-piece twinses," she says. But the churchgoing and the God fearing, the not stepping on the white man's toes—none of this will save them from the

white man's wrath. One night, Willie gets into a fight with another black man, whom he injures. The police arrest him and
send him to prison, and from there to a chain gang near Atlanta,
and then the family hears that he and two of his friends whom a
white guard kept picking on had been punished for fighting
back and that all three had been locked in an "ice-cold room"
with their feet bound by a rope suspended from the ceiling.
Their cries for help went unheeded for three days. When their
jailers finally came for them, their legs were frozen and they had
gangrene, so both of Willie's legs were sawed off. This incident
brings Copeland the kind of peace that comes with the loss of
all hope. "In this he knew a certain strong and holy gladness.
The persecuted laugh, and the black slave sings to his outraged
soul beneath the whip. A song was in him now—although it
was not music but only the feeling of a song. And the sodden
heaviness of peace weighted down his limbs so that it was only
with the strong, true purpose that he moved. Why did he go
onward? Why did he not rest here upon the bottom of utmost
humiliation and for a while take his content?"

# 15

In the Kellys' kitchen, Portia tells Mick what happened to Willie.
Her father is with her, sitting on a stool in the corner. Soon
Singer also comes in. As Mick hears the story, she becomes more
and more angry. Mick is concerned; she asks questions; she wants
those prison guards to be punished. She says, "They ought to be
treated just like they did Willie and them," she says. "Worse. I

wish I could round up some people and kill those men myself."
Portia believes that this is unchristian and takes consolation in
her belief that "us can just rest back and know they going to be
chopped up with pitchforks and fried everlasting by Satan."
Mick is unconvinced. She hands Dr. Copeland a cup of coffee
and says, "I wish I could kill them."

In her outline, McCullers writes that the four main characters, although very different, share a great deal in spirit. They all
have something to give without expecting anything in return.
Portia expresses the same idea more poetically. She says that
Mick "favors" her father more than anyone Portia has known.
Then she goes on to clarify: "I don't mean in the face or in any
kind of looks. I was speaking about the shape and color of your
souls." This is what Richard Wright must have meant when he
wrote that McCullers's portrayal of African Americans was
rooted not in any political belief but in an attitude, one that is
very difficult to preserve in real life, and which, in a sense, is the
essence of the novel. Because a great novel will allow you to
transcend the social, racial and political limitations imposed by
the vicissitudes of life and to find a deep fraternity based on empathy.

Jake responds more politically. He wants to capitalize on the
event and to use it to mobilize people, rushing to Dr. Copeland's house and asking a startled and uncomprehending Willie
to go on a tour with him so he can tell his story and thus agitate
and educate the masses about the injustice of the system. Mick's
reaction, like Huck's response to Jim, is more from the heart. It
is rooted in Willie's wound. A month after she hears the story of
what happened to Willie, she still has nightmares at night.

Throughout the years of Carson McCullers's childhood and adolescence, Dr. Mady Copeland, his daughter, Portia, her brothers and husband and the whole African American community around them were growing inside her. Like Mark Twain, she had her first encounter with racial injustice during childhood, when her maid Lucille, "who was one of the kindest and youngest of our nurses, she was only fourteen and a marvelous cook," worked late one night and called a cab to go home. Carson and her brother watched as Lucille left and the cabdriver refused to drive her, yelling, "I'm not driving no damn nigger." Seeing "Lucille's embarrassment, and the feeling of ugliness of the whole injustice" made her brother run under the house, weeping, but Carson, "torn with fury," screamed to the driver, "You bad, bad man." Then, she recalled, "I went to join my brother, and we held hands in order to comfort ourselves, because there was nothing, nothing else we could do." Decades later, not long before her death, she would write, "We were exposed so much to the sight of humiliation and brutality, not physical brutality, but the brutal humiliation of human dignity which is even worse. Lucille comes back to me over and over; gay, charming Lucille. She would stand at the window and sing a current tune which went 'tip toe to the window.' Blues tunes were not her taste as she was much too gay for them."

Dr. Copeland feels that something more should be done to protest Willie's treatment. For him it is a matter of "the strong, true purpose, the will to justice." He goes to court and asks to see the judge. The deputy sheriff and two other white men make fun of him, and when he insists, he's taken in and booked and beaten with clubs, but "a glorious strength was in him and he heard himself laughing aloud as he fought." He was kept in jail overnight, his fever came back and the next morning he was freed. Portia, Highboy, the pharmacist Marshall Nicholas and Mr. Singer were there when he was released.

"Dignity" is the password that links the young man Ramin to the young girl on *60 Minutes* to the fictional Mick and Mady Copeland. For Ramin and for Dr. Copeland, worse than the physical pain inflicted on them was the humiliation they had to suffer, and the added shame of having to remain silent. Dr. Copeland tells Jake Blount, "In the face of brutality I was prudent. Before injustice I held my peace. I sacrificed the things in hand for the good of the hypothetical whole. I believed in the tongue instead of the fist. As an armor against oppression I taught patience and faith in the human soul. I know now how wrong I was. I have been a traitor to myself and to my people. All that is rot. Now is the time to act and to act quickly. Fight cunning with cunning and might with might."

But Dr. Copeland, despite his rage, is wiser than that. He later tells Jake, "The most fatal thing a man can do is try to stand alone." Despite his fury, his solution is "to lead more than one thousand Negroes in this county on a march. A march to Washington. All of us together in one solid body." He is mocked by Jake, as he would have been by many. Years later, close to her death in 1967, McCullers was reminded that she had anticipated the 1963 March on Washington—another instance, as Nabokov would put it, of life imitating art.

# 16

I tried to find Mike Wright in 2012. He was the only person I could think of who might be able to help me track down "the other Mike"—that was what we called him back then. We were all in the movement against the war in Vietnam together, and "the other Mike" was a Vietnam veteran. He seldom talked in any of our numerous meetings, formal or informal, where almost everyone had something to say and few were too shy to interrupt and make themselves heard. Only Mike would sit in a corner and withdraw into a fetal position, or as close as one can come while sitting in an upright chair. Sometimes it seemed as if his body were curled to prevent an imminent imaginary blow. This made me notice him. I wanted to know what had made him so withdrawn, what it was that he was trying to avoid or hide. He was the gentlest among us, quiet, soft-spoken, kind, and he seemed so very vulnerable.

Perhaps I would have forgotten him were it not for an incident that refused to be forgotten. One day I was told by a friend that Mike had forced his beloved dog into a sack, tied the sack tightly, and begun furiously beating it with a stick. The act seemed all the more violent because it was committed by such a mild and gentle person. I couldn't get it out of my head, and afterwards, all those times we were arguing, planning protests and denouncing the war atrocities, I wondered in the back of my mind, What is Mike thinking? Did he ever talk to anyone, to his veteran buddies, at least, about what had happened?

I had not kept Mike Wright's information, so I went online and the first thing that caught my eye was a blog post on which someone had written, "I heard 2 or 3 days ago that local Norman 'character' Mike (Michael Phillip) Wright was found unconscious on a bench in Norman and that he was not expected to live. And I just heard that he has died and already been cremated." This was followed by a few comments about this "town character," Mike Wright, and the confirmation of his death. With a few more keystrokes I found an obituary, which stated blandly that Michael Phillip Wright had died on "September 16, 2009, consequent to a stroke."

I thought I knew Mike, but I learned from his obituary that he had been a National Merit Scholar at OU, that he had a master's in sociology and that he had "developed a social science and market research firm. His work has been published in the *American Journal of Preventive Medicine,* the *Journal of the American Medical Association, AIDS Education and Prevention,* and the *Proceedings from the Oklahoma Symposium on Artificial Intelligence.*" As I sought, now that it was too late, to retrieve Mike, to learn more about him, I discovered that in his later years he had become obsessed with the president of the University of Oklahoma, former senator David Boren. When I left Norman, he had been an activist and a loner, but in time protesting seems to have become his profession in life. His mild manner made me think of him as a Woody Guthrie type, not a "character" or a nice, if a little crazy, man.

It was only after his death that I discovered Mike's website, *In Michael's Opinion,* and began to read his posts. They were filled with conspiracy theories about the CIA and the FBI, with

David Boren somehow always in the middle of it all. Mike had theories about 9/11 and AIDS research, about air pollution and noise pollution, and he believed that Nick Berg, a University of Oklahoma graduate who became an American contractor and was killed in Iraq, was a CIA infiltrator who provided Zacarias Moussaoui—the would-be "twentieth hijacker" on 9/11—with his airline ticket. Later, the theory went, the CIA had set him up in Iraq so that he would be killed and "the secret would die with him."

The one unifying thread throughout was David Boren. Mike believed that the OU president was gay and that he had both favored and harassed young men in the workplace. He believed that Boren's friend and protégé George Tenet was either gay or bisexual and that they were coconspirators. *In Michael's Opinion* offers up gossip and "facts": Boren and Tenet were "reported by TIME to be having a 'leisurely breakfast' together in a Washington hotel on the morning of the 9/11 attack." In the ceremony in which George W. Bush presents Tenet with the Presidential Medal of Freedom, Bush "talks about the fact that Tenet was always seen around the CIA with an unlit cigar in his mouth." Mike asks us to note "the knowing smile from General Tommy Franks" in the video and the fact that Boren, sitting in the audience, is seen "rubbing his hand over another man's back and resting it on his shoulder." There was no way I could fully understand his treatises on AIDS, the CIA or 9/11. Minute details were meticulously marshaled and assembled into a text packed with equal parts facts and fantasy.

I found a post on another website about this "old" lonely man, who one person claimed had had a heart attack and died on a bench at his favorite haunt, the OU campus library. One recent graduate remembered him "quite fondly." He mentioned that when he had worked at the library for three years, Mike would come in to use the computers, typing his "latest conspiracy theories." To this young student Mike was "by and large benign."

# 17

Carson McCullers loved the snow. It became the symbol of her elsewhere, a place of tranquillity, as opposed to the restless rage of the southern heat. She loved to live in cold places, and despite the fact that the cold was so inimical to her fragile health, she took every opportunity to walk in the snow and often paid for it by becoming sick. She gave this love of snow to the two characters closest to herself, Mick Kelly in *The Heart Is a Lonely Hunter* and Frankie in *The Member of the Wedding*.

"Early in the mornings it was a little cool and their shadows stretched out tall on the sidewalk in front of them," Mick muses. "But in the middle of the day the sky was always blazing hot. The glare was so bright it hurt to keep your eyes open. A lot of times the plans about the things that were going to happen to her were mixed up with ice and snow. Sometimes it was like she was out in Switzerland and all the mountains were covered with snow and she was skating on cold, greenish-colored ice. Mister Singer would be skating with her. And maybe Carole Lombard or Arturo Toscanini who played on the radio. They would be skating together and then Mister Singer would fall through the

It was whispered in one browbeaten textile union that the mute was an organizer for the C.I.O. A lone Turk who had roamed into the town years ago and who languished with his family behind the little store where they sold linens claimed passionately to his wife that the mute was Turkish. . . . One old man from the country said that the mute had come from somewhere near his home and that the mute's father had the finest tobacco crop in all the county. All these things were said about him."

In fact, more than the deaf divas or the fact that she had urged her viewers to read this book, what made me think of Oprah was my association of her with Singer. Both fulfill our need to find someone who understands, who listens, who knows. And that someone cannot be too intimate. They have to be real enough for us to feel that they can understand us, but distant enough, evasive enough, that we can be allowed to make of them what we wish, to believe that they stand for us, that they feel what we do, that they are the incarnation of who we want to be. Oprah creates her audience as much as they create her.

When Oprah speaks to millions, she appears to be addressing each one of us individually, speaking not just to us but also for us. We believe that she has a personal message for each one of us, but in fact she is looking into the camera, not into our souls. Like Singer, she is sympathetic—she does have a real curiosity about people and their lives—but she is only human. She is not really the healer we would like her to be. In truth, we don't really want her to speak back. We want her to reassure us, to comfort us, to console us, to prove that here is one person in this world who understands us. There is much more to Oprah the real person, just as there is more to Singer—much more than the smiling, reassuring image we find every month on the cover of O magazine. It is not that we don't know about that real Oprah; it is that we don't want to know. We are not curious, and if we are, it is in that predatory, voyeuristic manner that pries into her love life and tracks her weight gain in the magazines sold alongside her own. In the end, the icon and her disciples are both alone. As Elizabeth Cady Stanton reminds us, each one of us, king or beggar, comes to the world alone and leaves it alone. We are all responsible for our own lives.

How would Mick and Biff and Dr. Copeland have reacted if they had known that "the mute," like them, was desperate to talk and unable to connect—that he, like them, had his own mute, his friend Antonapoulos, who also did not understand him? Did they know that he roamed the streets at night for hours, wandering the different parts of the town, trying to keep his hands, which were eager to speak, quiet and under control? He partially listened to them, and he helped them when he could, but "the want for Antonapoulos was always with him— just as it had been the first months after his friend had gone— and it was better to be with any person than to be too long alone." Would they have found it ironic that this man whom they had elevated to such heroic stature, this man who seemed to listen and understand, who lightened their burden, was himself so much in need of understanding?

One day, Singer, who on a much anticipated surprise visit to his friend discovers that Antonapoulos is dead, returns to town, leaves his luggage in the middle of the train station, goes straight to the jewelry shop where he works and comes out with something heavy in his pocket; we are told that for a while he "rambled with bent head along the streets." But the narrator adds that "the unrefracted brilliance of the sun, the humid heat, oppressed him. He returned to his room with swollen eyes and an aching head. After resting he drank a glass of iced coffee and smoked a cigarette. Then when he had washed the ashtray and the glass he brought out a pistol from his pocket and put a bullet in his chest."

At some point the snow has to melt. The illusion of comfort and softness is broken. And then, when the snow melts, as Carson's French editor André Bay would ask, where does the whiteness go?

# 18

Having neglected to ask questions of Mike in real life, I now became greedy to know and collect every scrap of information I could find about him. What had happened to turn a committed activist into an obsessed and obsessive old man? Many in the movement had moved on and now led apolitical lives. Some had become Republicans, some were liberal or progressive, but Mike seems to have stopped at some point. When all the rest of us grew up and got on with our adult lives, he "preferred not to." The movement he had fought for had long since vanished, but not his cause—that had stayed with him, only at some point the "enemy" he so hated had come to take over his life, and he became a prisoner of his own worst imaginings.

On the Internet, where our residues have a way of remaining, Mike's website still exists, forlorn and orphaned. You can still find *In Michael's Opinion,* and on YouTube a video of a song he sang parodying Merle Haggard's "Okie from Muskogee." You remember that song? Mike's answer to it was:

> *I'm proud to be a hippie here in Norman,*
> *A place where long-haired fellers have a ball,*
> *I still wear old jeans and ragged T-shirts,*
> *'Cause I like living free and standing tall.*

Was this enough? No matter how I looked at it, I couldn't get around the fact that the world Mike had so much wanted to pay attention had ignored him. Even his nemesis, David Boren, had remained indifferent; he had not sued him for defamation or even bothered to respond. This resounding indifference would have destroyed Mike had it not been for his obsessions, for his belief.

I found a few videos on YouTube called "GhostofMikeWright" where cartoon characters discuss some of the issues Mike wrote and talked about. Apparently the videos, one of which portrays a debate between Boren and Mike, were inspired after his death. In another video, "Light Pollution at OU Campus," which Mike posted before he died, he shows us how the football stadium became a "festival of light" and how historic houses around the stadium were destroyed.

Maybe Mike wasn't, as I had always imagined, all about facts. In the end he had been animated by a passion that would not subside. Like Huck and so many other lost souls wandering about the American landscape, he was in fact all heart. My brother, who went to the University of Oklahoma for two semesters, remembered Mike as warm and unusually generous. He reminded me that Mike had been the one who had warned him that the governor of Oklahoma had mounted a court case against him and five other students for interrupting an ROTC drill to protest the Vietnam War. The judge hearing the case had dismissed the trumped-up charges, noting the lack of evidence and commenting that in any case there was more violence at your average campus football game than at the demonstration in question. Of all our many friends, Mike had been the only one to take the trouble to try to find our address in Tehran so that he could warn him about the charges. People who wrote about Mike after his death—friends, family and strangers—all mentioned his kindness and consideration, even if some, like that former OU student, dismissed his radical ideas. He had meant so much to them, they said. But did he know it? Did they ever tell him as much?

I had known many in the movement who had joined because they were lonely and wanted companionship, or because they enjoyed power or felt safer belonging to a group, and also some who were there because they believed in the cause. Mike was among the most selfless: he was there for the cause. It is a tragedy that his passion turned into an obsession, one that, ironically, prevented him from differentiating between fact and gossip, or fact and fantasy.

That sense of loyalty to a cause, that burning passion that might frustrate you to the point of violence, inevitably leaves a trace behind. We find it in so many revolutionaries and idealists, but also in broken spirits damaged by the atrophying of their dream. McCullers explained in her outline that Mick, Jake and Dr. Copeland (especially the last two) were very similar "in spirit" and that despite all the "fettering circumstances . . . the great effort of each of them has been to give and there has been no thought of personal returns." Mike was, like them, motivated by a passion that burned bright and consumed him with a mixture of righteous commitment to the cause and deep hatred. Hatred is a potent force, and every idealist has to grapple with its distorting fury. If, in his arguments, Mike turned out to be more similar to the ideologues and functionaries he so despised, in his actions he remained an idealist, a loner, more similar to the isolated characters of *The Heart Is a Lonely Hunter* than he himself would ever have imagined.

# 19

"What good was it?" This is a question Mick Kelly asks herself as she gets off work, that stays with her at the New York Café while she waits for her chocolate sundae and a nickel glass of draft beer. Mick used to have her dream, her music, her free hours to roam the streets, her inside and outside rooms, and she also had Mr. Singer to confide in. But now this hope and secret pleasure have been taken away from her. What good was it indeed, when she had to spend ten hours a day working on her feet at the ten-cent store to support her family, giving up school and, instead of reflecting on that fellow Motsart, having to worry about the runs in her stockings and whether she would have the money to mend the worn-out bottoms of her shoes? "There were these two things she could never believe. That

Mister Singer had killed himself and was dead. And that she was grown and had to work at Woolworth's."

There is a correlation between Singer's suicide and the end of Mick's childhood. She has had her first sexual experience, accompanied by her first sense of guilt and shame, a secret different from her passion for music. For one thing, she looks different: she is no longer the boyish girl wearing khaki shorts and tennis shoes. Now she wears dresses, even a pair of dangling green earrings and a silver bangle bracelet. She has grown up all right, and how better to prove it than by the fact that, although she was the one who had found Singer dead, she had gone to work as usual: she was no longer considered a child who had to be protected, for whom the secrets of life and death were to remain secret. That very day at work, she "wrapped packages and handed them across the counter and rung the money in the till. She walked when she was supposed to walk and ate when she sat down to the table. Only at first when she went to bed at night she couldn't sleep. But now she slept like she was supposed to." Back when she went to school, she would come home feeling fresh and could focus on her music, but after a day working at Woolworth's she could not return to the music; she was too tired. It seemed as if "the inside room was locked somewhere away from her."

Mick's despair is echoed by Singer's other disciples: the time has come for each of them to grow up and face the world. After Singer's death, Dr. Copeland's disease weakens his body and soul to the point that he can no longer practice or keep up the fight. His children want him to live with his father-in-law, but he does not want to leave his dark and empty home. "This could not truly be the end. Other voices called wordless in his heart. The voice of Jesus and of John Brown. The voice of the great Spinoza and of Karl Marx. The calling voices of all those who had fought and to whom it had been vouchsafed to complete their missions. The grief-bound voices of his people. And also the voice of the dead. Of the mute Singer, who was a righteous white man of understanding." The "mystery" of Singer's suicide "left him baffled and without support. There was neither beginning nor end to this sorrow. Nor understanding."

Where Jake works, meanwhile, there is a murder: a young black boy is killed, and Jake takes off running through the streets. It starts when he gets into the middle of a fight between the black boy and a white boy, which escalates into a full-scale brawl, the crowd joining in with razors and knives. He is knocked out, only to open his eyes and find out that he "lay half on and half beside the body of a young Negro boy." The boy is dead, the police are coming and Jake starts to run. He runs toward the Kellys' boardinghouse, seeking Mr. Singer, only to find out that Singer is dead and cannot comfort him. The news made him not sad but angry. It seems to Jake that with Singer's death, all of the innermost thoughts he had confided in him have also died.

"What good was it?" Not just for Mick but for Jake, for Dr. Copeland and for Biff Brannon? Singer's death marks the end of childhood for Mick—the only real adolescent in the story—but it signals a period of transformation for the three adults as well. It takes immense pain and disillusionment, and a death, to awaken them into consciousness and to rescue them from the acts of violence that loneliness and despair can induce. For the first time they cannot just talk and talk in the hope that this one man will understand them. They have to slow down, to reflect, to take account. Singer's death has in a sense liberated them, forcing them to face reality both on the surface and in their inner lives. They have to do something, to make a move, now that they can no longer go around the circle of their fantasies, repeating them eagerly and longingly to the uncomprehending Singer.

Growth for McCullers has two stages: consciousness of the self, and the will to belong. "The sense of moral isolation is intolerable to us," she writes. With "the first establishment of identity there comes the imperative need to lose this new-found sense of separateness and to belong to something larger and more powerful than the weak, lonely self." We leave adolescence behind when we allow ourselves to change by connecting with others. For McCullers this "primitive grasp of identity develops with constantly shifting emphasis through all our years. Perhaps maturity is simply the history of those mutations that reveal to the individual the relation between himself and the world in which he finds himself."

All the characters in *The Heart Is a Lonely Hunter* are oppressed by their inability to connect, to express the inner urges that consume them. This crippling inability can lead to violence. After Singer's death, every one of the principal characters is shocked and grief-stricken. For each, this shock invites a period of transition, or what McCullers calls "maturation." Of all the characters in the novel, it is Singer—whom everyone in town identifies with, believing that he knows and understands them—who has no real goal or passion beyond connecting with his friend Antonopoulos, who in turn has no understanding of Singer and, unlike Singer, has no real kindness in him.

Singer's death is liberating to each of the characters who have grown to depend on him, because it forces them to confront their true selves, to see their yearnings unfiltered and raw. It is a myth that such liberation can come without pain, that we can read Dale Carnegie or one of those bestselling self-help books and learn how to overcome grief, or take solace in one of those life stories whose descriptions of pain and brutality are like a lollipop you suck on to ease your toothache. The characters themselves might not know it, but we as readers realize that in fact the most childish of them all was Singer. He did not have the passion, the one thing that connects them to the world. Singer's world, his obsession, begins and ends with his friend Antonapoulos, and it is not enough to live through another person. It is only with Singer's death that we discover that the others all have something to live for.

That is why they survive and why they may in the end succeed in obtaining what they are after. To connect, you need something in you that is worth connecting to, some desire to leave the self and become part of something bigger than you. Passion works in mysterious ways—its rewards cannot be counted or saved in the bank—and yet no democracy, no genuine human community, can live without it.

Until Singer's death, Biff, Mick, Jake and Dr. Copeland are not only childlike; they are childish. Their inability not just to know what they want but to articulate it leaves them with a gaping void. If it is not filled, this void or inner anguish can lead to violence—a violence that we find manifested in the novel when Jake beats his head against the wall or Dr. Copeland beats the wife he loves. But perhaps the greatest violence is committed by the gentle Singer when he takes his own life.

Violence is an integral part of so many great works of American fiction. We see it almost unbearably brilliantly portrayed in the works of Flannery O'Connor and Shirley Jackson, who capture the kind of horrendous cruelty that is rooted in life's everyday tedium and repetitiousness. Or in Nathanael West's *The Day of the Locust,* in which people flock to California to escape the boredom of their lives, to be entertained, only to find that the vacancy of their hearts and minds leads them to a scene of mass violence. In *The Heart Is a Lonely Hunter* there is more hope and less brutality, but it is no less disturbing. To me the most tragic act of violence in the novel is Singer's suicide, an act of profound desperation; on the other side of the spectrum is the accidental shooting of Baby, Biff's little niece, when the gun in the hands of Mick's sensitive brother accidentally goes off, turning the lives of both families upside down. Then there is the violence that flares up as a result of repressed anger and frustration, both personal and political, that we see in Jake and Dr. Copeland, whose rage disables him from articulating his emotions and alienates him from his wife and children. The story begins with the personal lives of these isolated small-town characters, but it ultimately links them to the destiny of the whole of humanity as the feeling of menace that only Harry Minowitz, Mick's Jewish friend, felt threatened by closes in. We are left at the end with Biff, who, while offering us a glimmer of hope, also leaves us with a sense of creeping danger as the transatlantic voices he hears on the radio are as yet distant drums, warning us of what is to come. It is the same urge that compelled the gentle "other Mike" to put his beloved dog in a sack and beat him, and it may

stand up and not give in, an innate form of rebellion against submission to any force, be it that of man or destiny, which in this book is best presented through the young girl Mick. Despite their burning need to communicate, not one of Singer's disciples has learned to listen and take notice of the others around him or her. It is only after his death that they become conscious of themselves and their surroundings. No more "I want—I want—I want," but a certain taking into account.

Taking into account is the price that must be paid if we are to transcend our narcissistic preoccupations. In all great works of fiction, including fairy tales, a price must be paid—there will be no glass slipper before scrubbing the floors. No tweeting and texting your pain to the world and getting millions of sympathizers who feel your pain or are amused by it, no downloading of self-help books on your Kindle or iPad, no antianxiety pills, no Dr. Phil or Honey Boo Boo or *Real Housewives* (descendants of the little glamour girl Baby in the novel). Mick and her family will not become stars of a reality show, Jake will not move the masses to demand social justice on YouTube. What will rescue them is good old-fashioned passion, a belief that one can give meaning to an otherwise meaningless life, the desire to create—to face the world, with its pain and grief, and not evade it. That passion enables them to connect; it is something at once evanescent and enduring, a bit like snow. In that passion there is pain and anguish and redemption, even if that redemption is just a firefly glimmer on the dark horizon.

There are no promises of a great and fabulous ending: there will be no concert pianist falling in love with Mick and no gathering of all the workers of the world around Jake, no lessening of the pain for Mady Copeland. But there is that glimmer of hope in the fact that, now Singer is dead, they will have to do more than merely talk—they can no longer lash out in episodic violence as they take refuge in reflection, in building a rudimentary plan. Though their friend is dead, their urges are not, and they will have to find a new and more meaningful way to communicate them.

So this new era without Singer is opaque; there are glimmers of hope in the decisions each character makes. The last we see of Copeland, he is seated in a wagon beside his father-in-law, heading out to the country. "He felt the fire in him and he could not be still. He wanted to sit up and speak in a loud voice—yet when he tried to raise himself he could not find the strength. The words in his heart grew big and they would not be silent. But the old man had ceased to listen and there was no one to hear him."

When Jake discovers that Singer is dead, an urge overcomes him to leave town. Where will he go this time? "The names of cities called to him—Memphis, Wilmington, Gastonia, New Orleans. He would go somewhere. But not out of the South. The old restlessness and hunger were in him again. It was different this time. He did not long for open space and freedom—just the reverse." Only then does Jake think of Dr. Copeland and of a visit he made to Copeland's house when the doctor was very sick and could not leave his bed. Jake had barged in, without paying attention to the people who had come to visit Willie. He had made his way to the sick man's room, where he found Dr. Copeland lying in bed with a high fever, and right away he started in on a long and arduous argument. The two men had fought until they passed out, one from delirium and the other from too much alcohol.

Now Jake remembers the doctor's advice that night: "Do not attempt to stand alone." Jake thinks, "Copeland *knew*. And those who knew were like a handful of naked soldiers before an armed battalion. And what had they done? They had turned to quarrel with each other." He has a sudden urge to go and see Copeland. But Copeland is gone, too, so instead he goes to the New York Café to have a bite to eat. "The emptiness in him hurt. He wanted to look neither backward nor forward." He thinks of Singer and how "now it was up to him to get out of it by himself and make a new start again." He is tired and unmoored, but in the end he does leave town:

> The late afternoon sun was out again. Heat made the steam rise from the wet pavement. Jake walked steadily. As soon as the town was behind a new surge of energy came to him. But was this flight or was it onslaught? Anyway, he was going. All was to begin another time. The road ahead lay to the north and slightly to the west. But he would not go too far away. He would not leave the South. That was one clear thing. There was hope in him, and soon perhaps the outline of his journey would take form.

One by one the characters take charge of their lives and grapple more honestly with themselves. But this does not stop them from holding on to their dreams. Mick, sitting in the New York Café, concludes that "maybe it would be true about the piano and turn out O.K. Maybe she would get a chance soon. Else what the hell good had it all been—the way she felt about music and the plans she had made in the inside room? It had to be some good if anything made sense. And it was too and it was too and it was too and it was too. It was some good."

Biff Brannon is left to puzzle over the enduring mystery of what makes human beings who they are. Biff is alone in the night, thinking that his is the only all-night place, which is what he likes. He thinks of the others, of how things have changed. The menace, the violence, does not exist only in his own backyard, but thousands of miles across the Atlantic, traveling like a deadly virus around the world. The radio is on, and a foreign voice is speaking in German, French or Spanish—he cannot tell, but the voice from across the Atlantic comes to him like a sinister whisper in the dark. To him, "it sounded like doom. It gave him the jitters to listen to it. When he turned it off the silence was deep and unbroken. He felt the night outside. Loneliness gripped him so that his breath quickened."

There is a moment, a brief flash of universal comprehension, in which he is awed by seeing himself as part of the whole of humanity. "The silence in the room was deep as the night itself. Biff stood transfixed, lost in his meditations. Then suddenly he felt a quickening in him. His heart turned and he leaned his back against the counter for support. For in a swift radiance of illumination he saw a glimpse of human struggle and of valor. Of the endless fluid passage of humanity through endless time. And of those who labor and of those who—one word—love. His soul expanded. But for a moment only. For in him he felt a warning, a shaft of terror. Between the two worlds he was suspended. . . . And he was suspended between radiance and darkness. Between bitter irony and faith. Sharply he turned away."

Biff calls for his assistant, but there is no answer. He then tries to calm down and reason away the terror he feels. "Somehow he remembered that the awning had not yet been raised. As he went to the door his walk gained steadiness. And when at last he was inside again he composed himself soberly to await the morning sun."

# 21

The story ends, and no matter how many years go by, it will remain the same: we continue to wait with Biff for the rising sun as a new generation of readers discovers these characters and gives them a new life. What good is it for us, seventy-four years later, in the second decade of the twenty-first century? The realities of our lives have changed a great deal since the publication of *The Heart Is a Lonely Hunter* in 1940, on the eve of America's involvement in a war not of its own making—its last "good" war, followed by Korea, Vietnam, Grenada, Nicaragua, Kuwait, Afghanistan and Iraq. The inarticulate feeling of rage that stalked Dr. Copeland has been articulated, leading to a real march on Washington and many more confrontations before an African American could be elected president of the United States. And yet the poverty and inequality that Jake railed against, the savage daily threats to individual integrity and liberty, still exist and are justified in far more sophisticated ways. The labor movement has moved beyond Jake's dreams, and yet many of the same questions he had then could be asked today. The miniature radios Mick dreamed of that were small enough to fit into your ear have been invented, along with so many other unimaginable gadgets and innovations. And the creative urges that made Mick roam the streets are as potent and neglected today as they were then. My conversations with Mike and Joanna have remained with me all these years, as well as the questions, carrying the seeds of their own answers, and the resolution inviting and implying new questions.

I wonder what I would have done differently had I known how easy it is to lose people, how someone who has been an intense part of your life can suddenly vanish, leaving their traces only in a few selective memories. That is what happened to Joanna. I went away for the summer, and on my return she was not there. A few times, people from my past life have called, e-mailed or appeared out of the blue at a talk or a book signing, saying, "Do you remember me?" This happened most recently during a talk at Trinity University, in San Antonio, Texas, when I ran into my friend Joan Frederick, with whom I had fled into the National Gallery when we were teargassed during a demonstration in Washington. Maybe Joanna will appear similarly unannounced, and we will continue our discussion and she will tell me how wrong I still am. I am not sure I will concede, but I will always be grateful to her for the gift of the southern sun.

Some of the facts have changed, but the South has the same climate, with the same sun shining over its small towns. It has become more prosperous in parts, with its own skyscrapers now home to Fortune 500 companies in cities like Atlanta and Charlotte, Dallas and Birmingham, and yet the hankering of isolated human souls, the urge to articulate, to connect, to belong, still remains. The creative urge has not changed any of the old verities and truths Faulkner wrote about—nor will they fundamentally change for as long as the beating of the human heart remains the same. Some attention must be paid to things that endure.

In "Loneliness . . . An American Malady," McCullers argued that America has been caught in a protracted adolescence, searching for an identity and wanting desperately to belong. In the twenties and thirties, right until it entered the Second World War, America was undergoing a process of questioning and self-questioning, wondering how to define itself and relate to the rest of the world. And like all younger siblings, it seems it will never completely lose the sense of being the youngest, with all its privileges and burdens. Perhaps this is the main reason why McCullers's novel still reads as if it were written yesterday.

But each new generation must discover its own response to its own specific form of loneliness. What we do know is that loneliness, in and of itself, is not a positive attribute. Even the lone cowboy who rides into town needs a few good guys to defend and bad guys to defeat before he can move on to the next town.

What if today we have finally reached the point of technological progress at which we can eliminate solitariness? What if the efficiency that we so worship, rather than paving the way for the actualization of passions, has become a tool for easy escapes, inviting less thinking, less confrontation with real pain and actual impediment? What if in our search for elsewhere, we have managed to destroy this place, this home we live in, pillaging our natural resources and turning all reality into virtual reality? What if, gradually losing our ability to be childlike, we have remained childish and infantile? What if that prized individualism, the one that was worth risking life and property to secure, that found its apotheosis in a kind of universal empathy, is being transformed into a narcissistic self-indulgence or greedy selfishness? The world of McCullers's characters is inherently in opposition to that of Babbitt and his mates, but in the history of America and American fiction, there has been a constant battle between the two mind-sets. Can we afford to let Babbitt win?

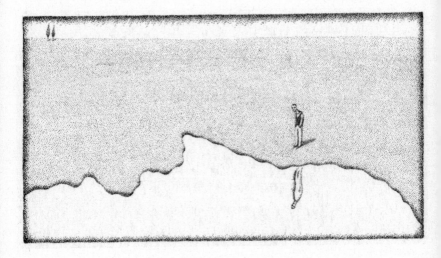

# Epilogue: Baldwin

Last September I gave a talk at the Baltimore Book Festival. I should have stayed at home—I had work to do—but I can seldom avoid the temptation of a book festival, with its transient sense of festivity and community: all those strangers sharing the same interest, if not exactly the same passions. Add to this the fact that I was hosted by one of my favorite independent bookstores, the Ivy, and my university, Johns Hopkins, and the lure was inescapable.

I love the chaos of book festivals, the way different characters, cultures, stories and times all jumble together to the accompaniment of music, food and art, all the good things in life shared with gusto, but not too seriously. It is as if the abundant variety of human existence contained in the thousands of books under consideration spills over onto the sidewalks and streets of the host city. This particular festival was sunny and celebratory. I couldn't help but smile as I made my way through various book pavilions, from mystery tales and romance to "literary" fiction, poetry, science fiction and comic books. From time to time I felt I'd spotted a comic book character walking around or waiting in line at the food vendors, but mostly it was couples holding hands and browsing while their children squealed and fought or found distractions of their own.

Each city lends something of its character to these events.

With Baltimore, home of Omar Little and at one point Edgar Allan Poe, its grittiness gives it an edge, different from the more formal arrangements of the National Book Festival, in Washington, which was held on the National Mall and attended by well over a hundred thousand people until 2014, when it was exiled to the ungainly convention center—a move that was more a reflection of the city's "guardians" than of its citizens. Baltimore's festival had a feel of the mass gatherings of the sixties and seventies, where people doing their own thing were tuned in to one another and appeared to be conspicuously enjoying themselves, a conspiracy of smiles that seemed to be a sort of protest against the harsh reality of the city. But of course the resemblance was, on some level, skin-deep: here the dominant attitude was one of giving in and having fun, rather than protesting and having fun.

I had about an hour and a half to spare before my talk. I like to walk or roam around a place as I fashion my thoughts. Browsing in the sun, I tried to focus on my topic that day. I carried two quotes with me, one by F. Scott Fitzgerald and the other by James Baldwin, and wondered if I should insert one or both into my speech. It wasn't that they were necessary, but I liked them, having come across them the day before while thinking of what I had taken to calling "my Baldwin chapter," though my editor would only say, "Let's see."

I strolled in a state of mind I would define as "alert absent-mindedness," taking in the sights and sounds while busily weaving ideas into words. These times of aimless wandering are some of my most lucid moments, before the painful process of combining and shaping the exuberant jumble of thought into a coherent form and structure begins. Thoughts flowed freely as I earnestly poured out words to my imaginary interlocutors; I was seemingly as oblivious of the world around me as it was of me. That's the thing about books, I thought. They're like children: enthralling, exasperating and not quite so predictable as you might have imagined. You believe you are in control, but a serious give-and-take is really in operation, and in some mysterious way they are equally in charge of you, dragging you to new places, bringing strangers into your house and questioning your ways and habits. So there I was, having initially wanted to write about twenty-four books but now focusing on three, wanting to concentrate on the text but constantly being pulled away by the facts of life and the world around me. Unlikely places, events and people kept tempting me with new revelations, flashing like fireflies and demanding my attention. In the Metro, in the middle of a conversation, even while watching a film, I would take out my pen and paper and jot down notes, some of which I could not decipher when I turned to them later at home.

When I started writing this book all too many years ago, I knew I wanted to begin with Mark Twain and end with James Baldwin. What was it that made me see Baldwin as Twain's literary kith and kin? He himself never made such a claim; in fact, he largely ignored Twain, preferring that other, altogether more patrician great realist, Henry James. Baldwin liked to cite an uncharacteristically rousing quote from the Master: "We work in the dark—we do what we can—we give what we have. Our doubt is our passion and our passion is our task. The rest is the madness of art." To this he would add, in "As Much Truth As One Can Bear," one of his best essays on literature, "This madness, thank heaven, is still at work among us. . . . It will bring, inexorably, to the light at last the truth about our despairing young, our bewildered lovers, our defeated junkies, our demoralized young executives, our psychiatrists and politicians, cities, towns, suburbs, and interracial housing projects." Baldwin genuinely believed that literature had a vital role to play as a sort of social glue. He felt there was, as he put it, "a thread . . . which unites every one of us" and saw a deep-rooted and necessary affinity between our everyday lives, anxieties, joys and sorrows and the act of writing.

Writers are truth tellers, and that can sometimes put them in conflict with the state. "Patriotism is supporting your country all the time, and your government when it deserves it," Twain once said in a searing critique of complacent jingoism. "The gospel of monarchical patriotism is: 'The King can do no wrong.' We have adopted it with all its servility, with an unimportant change in the wording: 'Our country, right or wrong!' We have thrown away the most valuable asset we had: —the individual's right to oppose both flag and country when he (just *he*, by himself) believed them to be in the wrong. We have thrown it away; and with it all that was really respectable about that grotesque and laughable word, Patriotism." If Twain abhorred the smug bombast of self-proclaimed patriots, it was not because he did not love his country. He held it up to a higher standard, that of the ultimate code of honor, courage and decency: the standard of the writer. The writer questions social norms and homes in on uncomfortable truths. He (or she) forces us to admit impulses and yearnings we would prefer to ignore or deny, and to acknowledge the yawning gap between what is and what should be. The American writer does so with a special mandate, Twain suggests, because in a democratic society, far more so than in a monarchical or totalitarian one, the writer speaks for the individual and not for the state. America has always conceived of herself as a country that exalts the individual, and it is not incidental that she has nurtured such exceptional and varied writers. But she has not always made her writers feel altogether at home.

"I was forced to recognize that I was a kind of bastard of the West," Baldwin wrote in *Notes of a Native Son*. Time and again in his essays, talks and interviews, he tried to describe what it meant to live as the grandson of a slave, born illegitimate and living in dire poverty. "It comes as a great shock around the age of five or six or seven," he said, "to discover that the flag to which you have pledged allegiance, along with everybody else, has not pledged allegiance to you. It comes as a great shock to discover that Gary Cooper killing off the Indians, when you were rooting for Gary Cooper, that the Indians were you. It comes as a great shock to discover that the country which is your birthplace, and to which you owe your life and your identity, has not in its whole system of reality evolved any place for you."

There is such generosity of spirit in Baldwin, despite all the hatred and humiliation piled on him. He recognized in each of us the potential for the best and the worst. "I love America more than any other country in the world," he said, "and, exactly for this reason, I insist on the right to criticize her perpetually. I think all theories are suspect, that the finest principles may have to be modified, or may even be pulverized by the demands of life, and that one must find, therefore, one's own moral center and move through the world hoping that this center will guide one aright. I consider that I have many responsibilities, but none greater than this: to last, as Hemingway says, and get my work done. I want to be an honest man and a good writer."

When he was told by Bobby Kennedy that someday, in thirty years' time, he could be president, Baldwin said, "What really exercises my mind is not this hypothetical day on which some other Negro 'first' will become the first Negro President. What I am really curious about is just what kind of country he'll be President of." I suggest he would nevertheless have celebrated in his own fashion when America elected Barack Obama; I wish I could have seen that Baldwin smile, half of which would be on his lips and the other half somewhere deep within, reacting to the news. And yet I suggest he would be as anxious now as he was then about the state of his country. Certain victories have been won, major victories, but new problems have arisen, and some of the old ones have resurfaced in new garb. He said, back in 1961, "I still believe that we can do with this country something that has not been done. We are misled here because we think of numbers. You don't need numbers; you need passion. And this is proven by the history of the world."

As I meandered among the stalls, I returned to the unexpected similarities between Twain and Baldwin, in particular their idea of patriotism, a topic I was going to talk about that day—loyalty to country, or to the act of writing and what many writers call "truth." Why was it that after the Islamic revolution, when I wanted to make sense of things and examine how much of what our new rulers (or old ones, for that matter) said about Iran was true, I had turned not to political theorists or historians but to writers and poets? And why was I doing the same thing now in America? "Societies are never able to examine, to overhaul themselves," Baldwin once said. To him, "this effort must be made by that yeast which every society cunningly and unfailingly secretes. This ferment, this disturbance, is the responsibility, and the necessity, of writers."

I stopped at the tent set up by Red Emma's bookstore, named after Emma Goldman, the legendary radical anarchist. A little farther, lo and behold, there was the H. L. Mencken Society, a tribute to the brilliant, grouchy inventor of the term "Booboisie," a very famous critic in the first few decades of the last century whom few people read today. I was sure that many of today's young would enjoy these eccentric and exceptional characters, committed and utterly unconventional, if only they would be given a chance to discover them. For some reason I found myself imagining a comic book version of their lives— what fun would a comic book Mencken have today, bombarding us with his word inventions! Just imagine what he would have to say of some of our political leaders. He'd give Jon Stewart and Stephen Colbert a run for their money.

Baldwin was born fourteen years after Mark Twain's death, and yet despite their different backgrounds (just being black and white was enough to create a chasm between them), they had both in their own ways experienced the worst that human beings can do to one another. It is enough to read Twain's "United States of Lyncherdom" or "Only a Nigger" to understand his rage and his shame. What he was reticent to write about was his own personal life. "You cannot lay bare your private soul and look at it," he said, in an effort to explain why he was having such a hard time writing his memoirs. "You are too much ashamed of yourself. It is too disgusting." But that is exactly what James Baldwin did: he laid bare his private soul and did not shy away from the shame and the guilt. One of his greatest artistic achievements was to seamlessly weave together the private and the public, the personal and the political and the social. Yet his life as a writer was dedicated to the proposition that one should not be defined by one's biography. His highest achievement was to transcend, rather than succumb to, the limitations imposed on him by the circumstances of his life. "Now, when you were starting out as a writer, you were black, impoverished, homosexual," said an interviewer in a clip. "You must have said to yourself, 'Gee, how disadvantaged can I get?'"

And there is Baldwin, with his huge, bulging eyes, looking roguishly both at and beyond his interlocutor, saying, "No, I thought I'd hit the jackpot!" And then, to the accompaniment of the audience's laughter, he rejoins, "It was so outrageous, you could not go any further. So you had to find a way to use it." And use it he did.

Baldwin was the grandson of a slave, and he never knew his biological father. He spent his childhood and adolescence in Harlem, the stepson of an abusive preacher whom all his life he called father and whom he loved and hated in equal measure ("righteous in the pulpit and a monster in the house," he would later say). He would abandon him and his mother along with Harlem, greater New York City, and America and move thousands of miles away across the Atlantic to Paris in order to write, and through his writing he discovered something essential about his stepfather, his race, his city, his people and his country. Perhaps most crucially of all, he discovered James Baldwin, and rescued him from the clutches of racism, poverty and abuse to rewrite his life story all over again. For much of his life he was an outsider even to himself: in one interview he spoke of "all those strangers called Jimmy Baldwin."

Other writers have left America to find themselves and their worldview—Henry James, Edith Wharton, Gertrude Stein, and later Hemingway, Fitzgerald, Bowles and Richard Wright, who was at one time his mentor, having taken him under his wing. But Paris was a different experience for each of them, and Baldwin's Paris was not Hemingway's *Moveable Feast*. It was the bleak and seedy Paris of *Giovanni's Room*, usually gray and raining or about to rain. Baldwin said he went to Paris not because it was Paris—it could have been any other place—but because he had to leave New York. In a film made of him by Sedat Pakay in 1970, Baldwin says, "One sees [one's country] better from a distance . . . from another place, from another country." David in *Giovanni's Room* articulates his creator's viewpoint when he says, "Perhaps home is not a place but simply an irrevocable condition."

In 1946, Eugene Worth, a close friend with whom Baldwin was in love but never had a physical relationship, threw himself off the George Washington Bridge. Worth was the model for Rufus, who, in *Another Country*, commits suicide in the same manner and whose death is the central event that links the other characters and becomes a source of revelation for them. Baldwin later said that the same fate would have awaited him had he stayed in New York and not become a writer. *In Another Country,* after Rufus's suicide, Cass, a young white woman, says, "Perhaps such secrets, the secrets of everyone, were only expressed when the person laboriously dragged them into the light of the world, imposed them on the world, and made them a part of the world's experience. Without this effort, the secret place was merely a dungeon in which the person perished; without this effort, indeed, the entire world would be an un-inhabitable darkness." Baldwin went to Paris to cleanse himself of his secrets, and to learn to write not out of rage but for the ages.

"All art," Baldwin said, "is a kind of confession, more or less oblique. All artists, if they are to survive, are forced, at last, to tell the whole story, to vomit the anguish up." His participation in the civil rights movement, his sympathy for the Algerians' suffering in France, were acts of witnessing, but it was only in his writing—his fiction and his essays—that he became the true witness. "I have never seen myself as a spokesman. I am a witness." And this was what distinguished him from many other progressive writers at the time.

One of the confounding things about writing about great literature is that there is really nothing to say: everything is already there in the work itself. It is a little like trying to describe the act of falling unconditionally in love. But still we need to talk about the experience, actual and imagined; we need to share something of the anguish and the joy of having experienced something unique and universal. In this manner, the act of reading and responding is in itself an act of witnessing.

In one of the first classes I taught at SAIS in the late nineties (I think it was called Politics and Culture), I printed two articles for my students. The first was by the great Peruvian writer Mario Vargas Llosa; it was the title essay in his book *Making Waves,* on the importance of literature in a global world. The other was a report published in *The Washington Post* on why J. D. Salinger was increasingly being removed from high school curriculums. My interest in the article principally had to do with the arguments voiced by several of the teachers who supported dropping *The Catcher in the Rye,* and their students' responses. The teachers pointed out that since Holden Caulfield, the protagonist, was a privileged white male, minority students in their classes would not relate to him. While the students conceded that Holden Caulfield was indeed not at all like them, they went on to say that this was exactly why they wanted to read the book. They were curious about this other world and enjoyed the glimpse the novel offered into his thoughts and anxieties.

These students were instinctively expressing a point some teachers and academic theoreticians have altogether missed; namely, that literature is in essence an investigation of the "other," a term used in such a stale and rigid manner, it has lost its original meaning and is no longer about actual difference so much as identifying subcultures and ethnicities and placing people within increasingly confining categories. Even when we put aside the current stultifying obsession with political correctness, a doctrine of comfortable questions and easy, ready-made answers, the fact remains that for most people it is simply boring to constantly read, write and talk about themselves. Shouldn't the point of books be not to affirm our views and prejudices but to question and confront them? Why read about things you already know? I asked my students. While it is fine and good to discover our differences and accept them—and at times celebrate them—the real surprise comes from the discovery of how alike we are, how much we all have in common. No great work of art or literature would survive the test of time if it were not in some deep sense universal.

My students at SAIS, who came from such vastly different countries and backgrounds, mostly welcomed this notion. A majority of them were not English literature majors; the course was an elective, and thus they were there because they wanted to be. I remember one student, a German as I recall, who wrote in her journal something to the effect that she found exhilarating the thought of so many strangers like Holden Caulfield, Gatsby and even Daisy and Tom residing within her. I remember that word, "exhilarating," so breathless, so full of possibilities.

Salinger published his first novel, *The Catcher in the Rye,* in 1951, Baldwin's first novel, *Go Tell It on the Mountain*, followed two years later. Baldwin's novel won much acclaim, but Salinger's trumped his and was welcomed as the latest kid in the Great American Novel's hall of fame, a testament to the newly articulated angst of the American teenager. If by "Great American Novel" we mean one that is representative of its era and sheds light on certain essential aspects of American life, then I think Baldwin's novel should be right up there with Salinger's. *Go Tell It on the Mountain* is a different kind of coming-of-age story, that of a young African American boy, and as such it complements *The Catcher in the Rye*. John Grimes is as American as Holden Caulfield and their mutual ancestor Huckleberry Finn. Both Caulfield and Grimes are "bothered" about the meaning of life; what differentiates them is their deeply contrasting experiences and attitudes. It is as if they come from another country—in fact, another world.

The seventeen-year-old Holden, like so many other American protagonists, is trying to escape the suffocating conformity and hypocrisy of his life, and despite his charm he is a bit irritating at times. In the course of one day, Holden, who a few days before Christmas has been expelled from his posh prep school in Pennsylvania but does not want to go home to New York before the holidays, lest his parents find out, checks into a hotel in another part of the city and moves from place to place searching for some way to appease and nourish his vague dissatisfaction with the state of things, complaining about his conformist school, where he is "surrounded by phonies;" his encounter with girls who are dumb and have nothing intelligent to say; his lousy sex life or absence thereof; his older brother, a sellout to Hollywood; the prostitute he meets over the course of his wanderings, with whom he is unable to have sex and who, although he pays her, returns with her pimp and forces more money out of him; and the overall mess that he believes has become his life. He likes his old schoolteacher, Spencer, who seems not to have much to live for but at the same time gets a "big bang" out of buying an old Navajo blanket. It is a beautifully written book and constantly veers toward cynicism, but in the end there is a glimmer of hope because Holden has a heart, and that heart beats for his ten-year-old sister, Phoebe. His decision to leave home is set aside because Phoebe wants to go with him and he knows he can't take her. Instead he takes her to a ride on her favorite carousel, although it is winter, and while they are there "it began to rain like a bastard. In *buckets*." But unlike others, he doesn't take refuge under the roof of the carousel, preferring to get soaked because he feels "damn happy all of a sudden, the way old Phoebe kept going around and around. I was damn near bawling, I felt so damn happy. . . . I don't know why. It was just that she looked so damn nice, the way she kept going around and around, in her blue coat and all. God, I wish you could've been there."

Holden tells us that at one point he hears a kid singing, "If a body catch a body comin' through the rye," which in reality is a poem by the eighteenth-century Scottish poet Robert Burns. But he mistakes its meaning: "'Anyway, I keep picturing all these little kids playing some game in this big field of rye and all. Thousands of little kids, and nobody's around—nobody big, I mean—except me. And I'm standing on the edge of some crazy cliff. What I have to do, I have to catch everybody if they start to go over the cliff—I mean if they're running and they don't look where they're going I have to come out from somewhere and *catch* them. That's all I'd do all day. I'd just be the catcher in the rye, and all. I know it's crazy, but that's the only thing I'd really like to be.'"

Near the end of the story, when Holden finds graffiti in various places (on two of his school staircases, and on a mummy tomb in a museum) saying simply "Fuck you," it makes him sick and angry. "That's the whole trouble," he informs us. "You can't ever find a place that's nice and peaceful, because there isn't any." You might think you have a peaceful place, but then "somebody'll sneak up and write 'Fuck you' right under your nose."

Holden is driven crazy by this and wants to kill the person who wrote it, because Phoebe or some other child might see the graffiti and wonder about its meaning and then "finally some dirty kid would tell them—all cockeyed, naturally—what it meant, and how they'd all *think* about it and maybe even *worry* about it for a couple of days." So we can conclude that Holden, who seems unable to sustain meaningful relationships with adults, even kids his own age, connects only to children, whose innocence he is eager to protect. Their differing attitude toward innocence is in fact what sets John Grimes, Baldwin's protagonist, apart from Holden Caulfield.

*Go Tell It on the Mountain* is a semi-autobiographical novel that focuses on the coming of age of a young African American boy while narrating his emotions, reflections and reminiscences over the course of twenty-four hours, from the morning of his fourteenth birthday to the next morning, and his spiritual rebirth on the threshing floor of his community's storefront church. Between those two mornings, we follow John's movements—at home, around the city and finally at his church—and discover stories about him, his family and his community; each one becomes part of the puzzle that is John. Holden Caulfield might have felt the past and his personal background are "all that David Copperfield kind of crap." Not for John. "Go back to where you started," James Baldwin advised his nephew, "or as far back as you can, examine all of it, travel your road again and tell the truth about it. Sing or shout or testify or keep it to yourself: but know whence you came."

The similarities between John Grimes's life and Baldwin's are quite obvious. Both were illegitimate. In John's case, he is the only character in the book who is a child born of love. His parents have eloped to New York City, where his father, Richard, would commit suicide after a brutal and humiliating incarceration on a trumped-up charge. Richard is a self-made man. When Elizabeth, John's mother, discovering he has barely had any schooling, asks him, "'Then how come you got to be so smart? How come you got to know so much?'" Richard tells her, "'I just decided me one day that I was going to get to know everything them white bastards knew.'" Then he adds, "'I was going to get to know it better than them, so could no white son-of-a-bitch *nowhere* never talk *me* down, and never make me feel like *I* was dirt.'" The irony, of course, is that he commits suicide because those sons of bitches, by framing him, make him feel like dirt. All his books and learning could do nothing to protect him from that pervasive sense of shame. John's mother then marries a fanatical and abusive preacher who promises to take care of her son like their own and whom John calls father, but instead he self-righteously attempts to humiliate and destroy the boy. Gabriel, John's stepfather, says he is going "'to beat the sin out of him.'" A reformed womanizer, he is a reminder of Baldwin's claim that "nobody is more dangerous than he who imagines himself pure in heart; for his purity, by definition, is unassailable."

Baldwin and John Grimes share something that goes beyond the facts of their lives: their stories begin with a fundamental crisis of faith. "It happened, as many things do, imperceptibly, in many ways at once," Baldwin wrote. "I date it—the slow crumbling of my faith, the pulverization of my fortress—from the time, about a year after I had begun to preach, when I began to read again. I justified this desire by the fact that I was still in school, and I began, fatally, with Dostoyevsky." *Go Tell It on the Mountain* is a meditation on John Grimes's "crumbling of faith" and all the forces of authority that have held him back, that have kept him in darkness: racism, religious fanaticism, blind faith. "John's heart was hardened against the Lord. His father was God's minister, the ambassador of the King of Heaven, and John could not bow before the throne of grace without first kneeling to his father." He promises himself that "he would not be like his father, or his father's fathers. He would have another life." That new life would offer him a new spirituality, no longer tethered to a rejection of his own body and his body's desire for love.

Sensuality, as Baldwin saw it, was the essence of life; to be deprived of it would mean missing out on living. "To be sensual, I think, is to respect and rejoice in the force of life, of life itself, and to be *present* in all that one does, from the effort of loving to the breaking of bread." For Baldwin this was a serious matter, one that he would make the main topic of his second book, *Giovanni's Room*. Anyone who has lived like I did for eighteen years under fundamentalist rule, or in a secular totalitarian state like the Soviet Union, can testify to the truth of a statement he made in an interview with the *Village Voice* late in life: that "terror of the flesh . . . is a doctrine which has led to untold horrors."

When I reread *Go Tell It on the Mountain* after almost thirty years, I was surprised by how much I had missed: its cadences that capture the rhythms of Negro spirituals, moving with such physical and emotional force, its light and dark imagery and its theme of death and rebirth. John Grimes, like Huck, obeys the dictates of his heart, turning away from the false gods, and is reborn on the threshing floor of the very church that had suffocated him with its unforgiving rigidity. What could be closer to the cherished ideal of American individualism than to stand up to obstacles regardless of the consequences, to say no to stifling authority and face the darkness with no safety net, mastering one's fear?

To be reborn, John Grimes must rid himself of the very thing Holden Caulfield wishes to preserve and protect: his innocence. "It is not permissible that the authors of devastation should also be innocent," Baldwin wrote in *The Fire Next Time*. "It is the innocence which constitutes the crime." Innocence protects us from knowledge, but knowledge leads to the truth. Shedding your innocence, facing the truth, is thus the first step toward becoming a responsible individual. Of course, it is easier said than done.

"I am a preacher's son," James Baldwin informs us in "As Much Truth As One Can Bear." "I beg you to remember the proper name of that troubling tree in Eden: it is 'the tree of the knowledge of good and evil.'" Curiosity was man's first sin, the urge that motivated him to risk being thrown out of Paradise, and this perhaps is the great human paradox: with the urge to know comes the desire to live in safety, to remain innocent. We have heard the story so many times that we might be forgiven for forgetting how very frightening it is to be thrown out of the security of heaven, into the unknown void, into darkness.

Do we really want to be free? Is not the desire to be free different from choosing freedom? Eric, the protagonist in Baldwin's third novel, *Another Country,* can embrace freedom because he "did not believe in the vast, gray sleep which was called security . . . and this meant that he had to create his standards . . . as he went along." Americans think of themselves as champions of freedom, but that does not mean that, at a deep personal level, they are ready to be free. "I have met only a very few people—and most of these were not Americans—who had any real desire to be free," Baldwin wrote. He then added, "Freedom is hard to bear. It can be objected that I am speaking of political freedom in spiritual terms, but the political institutions of any nation are always menaced and are ultimately controlled by the spiritual state of that nation. We are controlled here by our confusion, far more than we know, and the American dream has therefore become something much more closely resembling a nightmare, on the private, domestic, and international levels."

All writers must take risks; all must tread into the void and darkness; all do so passionately, embracing the agony of freedom and the unknown—that is the price of the ticket, as Baldwin would have said. "Any real change implies the breakup of the world as one has always known it, the loss of all that gave one an identity, the end of safety. And at such a moment, unable to see and not daring to imagine what the future will now bring forth, one clings to what one knew, or dreamed that one possessed. Yet, it is only when a man is able, without bitterness or self-pity, to surrender a dream he has long cherished or a privilege he has long possessed that he is set free—he has set himself free—for higher dreams, for greater privileges."

With *Go Tell It on the Mountain*, Baldwin made his name as a brilliant "Negro" writer. Everyone seemed to be happy with that: his publisher, agent and readers—everyone, that is, but him. "I have not written about being a Negro at such length because I expect that to be my only subject," he wrote in 1958, "but only because it was the gate I had to unlock before I could hope to write about anything else."

He had no fear of being thrown out of one paradise after another. So he went on to write a book about a young white male and his homosexual love affair. A writer's job, he said, was to disturb the peace, and he was doing a good job of that. Needless to say, this book made his agent, Helen Strauss, panic. Her motherly advice to the young author was that, rather than risk a bright future, he should simply burn the book. Baldwin reported that his publisher, Alfred Knopf, had informed him that as a Negro writer he had reached a certain audience. "You cannot afford to alienate that audience," he told him. "This new book will ruin your career." Baldwin's response was short and to the point: "I told them, 'Fuck you.'" Then he went to England and sold his book there, before selling it in America. He was not about to compromise his freedom as a writer in order to market his book. For the benefit of those who would now categorize him as a homosexual writer, he said *Giovanni's Room* "is not about homosexual love, it's about what happens to you if you're afraid to love anybody." Later in life he would say that the novel was for him a "declaration of independence." After which he added, "And then I was in some sense, if not free, clear."

I read an article recently in the *New York Times* about how the teaching of Baldwin was on the decline in public schools. He is too complex, or too controversial, it was suggested, and besides, there are now other great African American writers to choose from. All his life, Baldwin struggled to be a writer, not a Negro writer, but with the best of intentions we have put him back into the box he was so desperate to escape. Nowadays we treat our writers and artists like fashion accessories: once a new trend is set, the old one is relegated to the dustbin. (Baldwin and Twain, incidentally, are not on the Common Core reading list.)

Baldwin is becoming old-fashioned not because of his writing but because of his race—otherwise why focus only, as the article did, on African American students and other African American writers? Don't other students need to read him, too? Should we interview young white male students to find out if they are reading Saul Bellow or John Cheever, or decide that those older white males don't matter so much anymore because there are now other white male writers to choose from? Surely any writer wants to be known simply as a writer, acknowledging that his or her work is rooted in particular circumstances but hoping that it manages to vault beyond those narrow constraints. This attitude is particularly disturbing when applied to Baldwin, who believed that race was a political construct used to enslave people: "As long as you think you're white," he once said, "I'm forced to think I'm black." Literature was to his mind a vehicle for escape. He was promiscuous when it came to literary influences and felt that all literature belonged to him: "When one begins looking for influences one finds them by the score," he wrote. "I haven't thought much about my own, not enough anyway; I hazard that the King James Bible, the rhetoric of the store-front church, something ironic and violent and perpetually understated in Negro speech—and something of Dickens' love for bravura—have something to do with me today; but I wouldn't stake my life on it." On another occasion he said, "What the writer is always trying to do is utilize the particular in order to reveal something much larger and heavier than any particular can be."

Baldwin called the simplification of complex issues—this categorization of human beings by race, gender, religion and ethnicity—"the death of the paradox." As long as we each remain in our separate categories and are outraged only when something is said about us, as long as we read only about ourselves and go around only with other people like us, we will never grow or learn. "Our passion for categorization, life neatly fitted into pegs, has led to an unforeseen, paradoxical distress; confusion, a breakdown of meaning," he wrote in "Everybody's

Protest Novel." "Those categories which were meant to define and control the world for us have boomeranged us into chaos."

Baldwin's independence of mind won him many friends and quite a few enemies, black and white. He retained this independence all through the course of his involvement in the civil rights movement, taking sides with Martin Luther King Jr. while appreciating and admiring Malcolm X and always remaining wary of Elijah Muhammad. He feared being defined by whites. Like Zora Neale Hurston, a black writer was not what he wanted to be: he wanted to be defined simply as a writer, even if a bad one. "You read something which you thought only happened to you," he said in an interview, "and you discover it happened a hundred years ago to Dostoyevsky. This is a very great liberation for the suffering, struggling person, who always thinks that he is alone." Then he added, "This is why art is important. Art would not be important if life were not important, and life *is* important."

When, in 1937, Zora Neale Hurston published *Their Eyes Were Watching God,* the story of a young black woman's search for freedom, she was reproached by many prominent black intellectuals and writers, such as Ralph Ellison and Richard Wright, for having written a novel that was not about race. Wright dismissed it as a "minstrel" novel. *Their Eyes Were Watching God* is in fact about freedom on several levels: freedom from slavery is the first step that leads to other forms of freedom—individual freedom and the freedom to control your own body and mind. I always felt it should be taught alongside *Pride and Prejudice,* as both center on a woman's right to choose. Hurston's heroine, Janie, defends her right to choose her own lover, a man seventeen years her junior, remaining true first to the demands of love. Because that notion was preposterously new and threatening and insufficiently political for men who wanted more pointed considerations of injustice, it was scoffed at.

In *Notes of a Native Son,* Baldwin describes how he and a friend once went to a diner in New York and were refused service. "We don't serve Negroes here," they were told. Back outside on the street, he was so angry, so overwhelmed, that he walked ahead of his friend into a fashionable restaurant and sat down. When approached by the "frightened waitress" and told again, "We don't serve Negroes here," he became so enraged that he threw a glass of water at the waitress, shattering the mirror behind the bar. He got away, but it made him reflect not simply on the fact that he could have been murdered for what he had done but on how he himself, in that instant, had been ready to commit murder. "My life, my *real* life, was in danger," he writes, "and not from anything other people might do but from the hatred I carried in my own heart." He believed the greatest danger for African Americans was not hatred of what had been done to them, but the risk of surrendering to that hatred. For as Baldwin so poignantly wrote in one of his later essays, "The object of one's hatred is never, alas, conveniently outside but is seated in one's lap, stirring in one's bowels—and dictating the beat of one's heart. And if one does not know this, one risks becoming an imitation—and, therefore, a continuation—of principles one imagines oneself to despise."

All his life, Baldwin was afraid of becoming like his

narrative traditions culled from the Bible with his own favorite writers, like Henry James and James Joyce. In his essay "Why I Stopped Hating Shakespeare," he explains how at first he was "dubious about Othello" and "bitter about Caliban," just as "some Jews bitterly and mistakenly resent Shylock." He attributed this to being a victim of "that loveless education which causes so many schoolboys to detest Shakespeare." He rediscovered Shakespeare when he read him again in France, where he came to peace with the English language, having earlier rejected it because he felt it reflected none of his experience. In France he came to see that the "greatest poet in the English language found his poetry where poetry is found: in the lives of the people. He could have done this only through love—by knowing, which is not the same thing as understanding, that whatever was happening to anyone was happening to him."

"There is no reason for you to try to become like white people and there is no basis whatever for their impertinent assumption that *they* must accept *you*," Baldwin wrote to his nephew James in *The Fire Next Time*. Then he added, "The really terrible thing, old buddy, is that *you* must accept *them*. . . . You must accept them and accept them with love." This recommendation did not stem from weakness or a sense of inferiority, but from strength. In *The Fire Next Time,* he tells his nephew, "It will be hard, James," he says, "but you come from sturdy peasant stock, men who picked cotton and dammed rivers and built railroads, and, in the teeth of the most terrifying odds, achieved an unassailable and monumental dignity. You come from a long line of great poets, some of the greatest poets since Homer. One of them said, 'The very time I thought I was lost, my dungeon shook and my chains fell off.' . . . You know, and I know, that the country is celebrating one hundred years of freedom one hundred years too soon."

When his friend William Styron decided that he wanted to write about Nat Turner, the rebel slave leader, Baldwin celebrated his courage and applauded the desire to get under his skin, however flawed the attempt might be. He praised Styron for writing their "common history." Some objected to this: a white southern man writing a history of a black slave's rebellion. But how could the history of the slave be separate from that of the slave owner? The oppressor and the oppressed of necessity share the same history—but they have very different stories to tell, and each one's story must be told.

Baldwin disliked the safety and security of generalizations. He refused to give his readers a safety net. To read him, as with any great writer, is to go to dark places. After *Go Tell It on the Mountain,* instead of writing another "Negro novel," he wrote an essay denouncing his mentor, Richard Wright, and Wright's most famous novel, *Native Son.* In "Everybody's Protest Novel," he argued that Wright's portrayal of Bigger Thomas as a violent man whose violence is justified by what has been done to him is fundamentally flawed. Bigger Thomas is a preconceived and prepackaged image of the African American; he is not a character but a type. "Our humanity is our burden, our life," Baldwin writes. "We need not battle for it; we need only do what is infinitely more difficult—that is, accept it. The failure of the protest novel lies in its rejection of life, the human being, the denial of his beauty, dread, power, in its insistence that it is his categorization alone which is real and which cannot be transcended."

Ideology eliminates paradox and seeks to destroy contradiction and ambiguity. While it is generally ruthless to outsiders, it can be consoling when you are in the group that always wears the white hat no matter what. Hatred and ideology, contrary to all appearances, are comforting and safe for those who practice them. They tend to be accompanied by an odious self-righteousness. You don't need to think—the party has already thought things out for you. This is true whether the ideology in question is of the right or of the left. It does not matter what your ideology is; what matters is that you are ideological. Fox News is a beautiful manifestation of this, but so are the politically correct who seek to put us all in our stultifying box. And even if we dislike the ideology in question, our reaction to it is also sort of comforting, for we already know what they will say and how we will respond. In essence, we need our nemesis—we are codependent.

Baldwin was attacked by many, including a new wave of African Americans, disgusted with the violence that did not seem to abate and impatient with the nonviolent strategy of Martin Luther King Jr. Most notoriously, Eldridge Cleaver claimed in *Soul on Ice* (a book that mixed some brilliance and poignancy with much rant) that Baldwin's work includes the "most grueling, agonizing, total hatred of blacks, particularly of himself." Cleaver went on to say that there was in his writing also a "most shameful, fanatical, fawning, sycophantic love of the whites that one can find in the writings of any black

American writer of note in our time." He claimed, as was the fashion then among the Black Panthers, that homosexuality was a "sickness" and that the "white man" had deprived Baldwin of his "masculinity." After years of living abroad, including in Cuba (and, while abroad, appealing to Baldwin for money, which he, generous as ever, provided), Cleaver returned to America and was deeply involved in various religious groups, including the Mormon church, and in the end he became a conservative Republican. Throughout this time, Baldwin remained Baldwin.

A piece that ran recently in the *New York Times* set me thinking again about Ramin. The article, entitled "Warning: The Literary Canon Could Make Students Squirm," begins by asking, "Should students about to read 'The Great Gatsby' be forewarned about 'a variety of scenes that reference gory, abusive and misogynistic violence,' as one Rutgers student proposed?" It goes on to ask whether *Huckleberry Finn* and *Things Fall Apart* should come with a "note of caution" because they address racism. The rest of the article enumerates how students from different colleges have requested that classic works of fiction be labeled with warnings to prevent the students from being traumatized by the books' painful content. The most chilling part of this terrible story is a draft guide for these new warnings, circulated on the website of Oberlin College: "The guide said they should flag anything that might 'disrupt a student's learning' and 'cause trauma.' . . . Be aware of racism, classism, sexism, heterosexism, cissexism, ableism, and other issues of privilege and oppression. Realize that all forms of violence are traumatic, and that your students have lives before and outside your classroom, experiences you may not expect or understand." The guide was removed because of several faculty protests, "pending a more thorough review by a faculty-and-student task force."

I find it amazing that concepts like race, class and gender, once so incendiary, have now been reduced to these empty but menacing words that explain nothing, whose main function is censorship, justified like all acts of censorship by the self-righteous pretense of combatting oppression. Is this really what they want? Perhaps those at Oberlin and other universities who have caved in to this nonsense should take another look at the world and this country before redefining "privilege" and "oppression"—or simply take another look at how much they charge students to enroll in their institutions. To find this non-sense at universities—whose basis for existence is a mandate to encourage us to question, to think, to imagine and of course to learn. I would like to take the hand of that young man or woman who wants to be warned before reading *The Great Gatsby* or *The Merchant of Venice* (another one of those traumatizing books) and remind him/her of what the Haitian American writer Edwidge Danticat, herself a witness to many horrors and much anguish, wrote: "No one will love you more than you love your pain."

A few years ago, in an interview with Scott Simon at the Holocaust Memorial Museum, Sir Ben Kingsley lamented the fact that we are shielding our young people from pain, and teaching them to avoid tragedy. This attempt to eliminate all that strikes us as unpleasant is the real danger to our expunge all pain from the classroom. No one has ever been comforted by knowledge, but numerous individuals throughout the ages have found purpose and passion, been strengthened—in short, have gained the ability to accept life, or the desire to change it—from books. Not sugarcoated stories with happy endings, but challenging, difficult, sometimes traumatic and inspiring stories. But now we on the one hand celebrate phony trauma every day on our reality TV shows (even the so-called news on some channels has become a form of reality TV), and every day our young people are exposed on the Internet or television to sex and violence, but these are mere facsimiles: it has become difficult for us to face real trauma, to face life.

I keep thinking of those classical fairy tales, so full of fear and hatred and pain, each of which had to be experienced before confidence, love and joy could be offered up as a reward for ingenuity under pressure and for surviving hardships big and small. Those tales about eating the poison apple, being swallowed by the whale or being abandoned and left to die in the dark forest. Think of Hansel and Gretel being seduced by the evil witch's beautiful house made of candy and chocolate, lured by the illusion of sweetness and safety, only to find out that the witch wants to burn them in her oven. Hansel and Gretel had to leave the security of home and face the darkness; they had to learn to recognize the dangers of illusion and discover how to fight back if they wanted to return home with the treasure. Children learn through these stories, as they do now through Harry Potter's adventures, to be brave, to recognize false conjurers and to fight them. What will happen to our young people if they lose the will to fear and learn? Why do they need to be so protected from pain and offense? Why are they so easily offended, and why, for that matter, are we? How will young people fend for themselves in a world where the Big Bad Wolf comes in so many guises? Baldwin warned his readers that they should beware of fiction, because it was the path to truth. But there was no getting there without pain: "If one can live with one's own pain, then one respects the pain of others, and so, briefly, but transcendentally, we can release each other from pain."

Time and again, I have wondered if our current assault on literature, which so many like to think of as useless and irrelevant, is not a reflection of the desire to remove from the equation anything that is painful or distasteful to us, anything that does not fit our norms or make life easy and fall within our sphere of power and control. In one sense, to deny literature is to deny pain and the dilemma that is called life. Blindness comes in all forms. We seem to feel that through sheer willpower married to technology we can live in eternal bliss, refusing to age, avoiding pain, burying ourselves in self-help and how-to books that foster an illusion of eternal possibility, making us believe, despite all evidence to the contrary, that happiness is within easy reach if only we tried harder, and that security will be ours if we simply follow these five simple steps. We are constantly reaching out for aspirin for our souls—happy pills, similar to what the great Polish poet Czeslaw Milosz mentions in *The Captive Mind*. Citing a dystopian novel by another Polish writer, Stanislaw Ignacy Witkiewicz, Milosz describes a decadent society somewhere in Europe that is cleverly invaded by an all-powerful Sino Mongolian army by spreading into the market Murti-Bing pills, which transform individuals into a state of serene indifference, "impervious to any metaphysical concerns," such as art, which appeases their "spiritual hunger." Such things become "outmoded stupidities" for them. In a society like ours, it is the Murti-Bing or happy pills that kill our desire to face life. Every now and then I find myself thinking of something my daughter told me when she was in medical school: one sign that a patient is dying is that she feels no pain.

We should be teaching our students that they need to have their peace disturbed, that there is a difference between individualism that encourages self-confidence and independence, and narcissism, in which everything and everyone becomes a reflection of ourselves, preventing us from growing, and that so long as they are afraid of trauma, they will remain its victim: their oppressor will once again win. For eighteen years I experienced a revolution, a war, murder and the persecution of people close to me. Even then, in the midst of the sirens and the bombs, we turned to books, because we wanted to make sense of this senseless brutality. We read Primo Levi's memories of a concentration camp, Anna Akhmatova and Osip Mandelstam, whose poetry chronicles the darkest hours of the Soviet Union, Frederick Douglass and Toni Morrison, Sylvia Plath and Philip Roth, and we read about ordinary people who showed extraordinary courage in the face of unimaginable pain. Through this we learned how to acknowledge the pain and the horror but also to know that we were not alone—that in the face of all that horror, what you have to do is live, live to the fullest. As Henry James put it, the best way to resist the horror of war is to "feel for all you're worth, and even if it half kills you, for that is the only way to live."

America's elite are worried that the country is falling behind China in mathematics, but they should start worrying that it is falling behind in a more fundamental way, in something that was always considered America's strength: namely, the ability to stand up to any challenge, no matter how difficult or daunting. In Pakistan, a girl called Malala was willing to give her life to be able to learn to read and write. What would it take to rekindle that hunger here? That many of our children are illiterate when it comes to history and literature is a much lamented fact known to all, but do they know what they are missing?

If colleges were genuinely interested in fighting "oppression and privilege," they would not only teach children the great works of fiction, they would make them aware that a real and serious fight against racism and oppression is being fought in impoverished neighborhoods all around the country. They would encourage their students to get to know the facts of life, beginning with a simple one: according to UCLA's Civil Rights Project, the number of "doubly segregated" schools has grown in the last twenty-five years. Shouldn't we be curious as to why we have regressed since the 1980s?

I don't really blame those young students who want to tack warnings on books and films on our college campuses. I disagree with them, but I don't blame them. But I do blame my own generation. Where did we go wrong? Is this what we were fighting for when we came into the streets and demanded freedom? I blame my generation for having neglected to teach our children that in life there are no safe places, that safety is an illusion. "Most of us, no matter what we say, are walking in the dark, whistling in the dark," Baldwin said in an interview in 1961. "Nobody knows what is going to happen to him from one moment to the next, or how one will bear it. This is irreducible. And it's true of everybody. Now, it is true that the nature of society is to create, among its citizens, an illusion of safety; but it is also absolutely true that the safety is always necessarily an illusion. Artists are here to disturb the peace."

At the end of my talk that day at the Baltimore Book Festival, two friends, Kurt and Cindy, came up to say hello, and then two young girls came up and joined us. One of the girls, who was almost breathless, told me she had always liked books, that she would find secret places to read them and she underlined and "made a mess" of her favorite books. "Who's your favorite?" she asked. I was about to tell her what I usually say—that when it comes to books I am promiscuous—but somehow I didn't want to say that to her—there was such glow and glitter in her eyes, and she was just a book lover, wanting in on a treasure. She surprised me when she told me that one of her "finds" was Jean Rhys, the author of *Wide Sargasso Sea*. "My God," I said. "I used to love her. A friend sent me all of her novels when I was living in Tehran, and for a long time I kept going back to her. I didn't know anyone here would read her still." She said, "I do. Isn't it awesome?" And I could not help but think that, yes, it was awesome.

So I didn't dismiss her question. Instead I said, "My favorite right now, because I am reading and thinking about him, is James Baldwin, but there are so many others." She told me she had not read Baldwin, but she had a good friend who was crazy about him and had read everything he could get his hands on. Her friend had told her that there was a James Baldwin Society in Baltimore. We talked a little more about Baldwin, and I mentioned Zora Neale Hurston, whom she in fact had read in high school. At first she found it hard to understand because of the language, and then, yes, she had liked it very much.

She and her friend went their way after that, and I followed my sponsor to the car, talking about books and festivals and the fate of our much beleaguered bookstores. I still had in my pocket the quote from James Baldwin. I had been meaning to mention it at the end of my talk, but instead I had spoken about Mark Twain. I unfolded the piece of paper in the car on my way home and read the quote again: "For, while the tale of how we suffer, and how we are delighted, and how we may triumph is never new, it always must be heard. There isn't any other tale to tell, it's the only light we've got in all this darkness." Can there be joy without peril? Light without darkness?

Those days, for me everything was Baldwin, as it had been with Twain, Nabokov, Lawrence Sterne, the Brontë sisters, Flaubert, Svevo, Austen and Gogol, and as it will be with the younger writers I am still discovering: David Foster Wallace, Gary Shteyngart, Ann Patchett, Jeffrey Eugenides. . . . Was I choosing them or were they choosing me? For thirty years, Baldwin had been waiting patiently in a corner of my mind, or heart, waiting for me finally to hear his voice. And I had come back to him, here in America—not by way of any of the writers he was generally affiliated with but by way of my interest in Mark Twain.

That is the way it is with stories: they hinge on unexpected connections and mysterious coincidences. It is funny how writers, no matter where they come from or from what age or era, all acknowledge the darkness before the light, the risks and rewards of fiction and of life. I thought of Edwidge Danticat, whose book I had recently read and who herself was deeply moved by Camus. When I got home from Baltimore, the first thing I did was try to find her book, but I had misplaced it. I did find the quote I was after in my diary, right under the words "Call Sunny," with a circle around it. I typed up the quote before I could lose it again: "Create dangerously, for people who read dangerously . . . knowing in part that no matter how trivial your words may seem, someday, somewhere, someone may risk his or her life to read them."

A vague kind of happiness bubbled slowly to the surface, something I am not sure how to define. I felt a bit like Alice when she first saw the White Rabbit and started to run after him and jumped down that hole. Alice! Another book I want to write about. The true lure of a great book is not that sugarcoated candy house offered by the witch but the mysterious whisper that beckons, saying, as F. Scott Fitzgerald once did, "Draw up your chair to the edge of the precipice and I'll tell you a story."

# Acknowledgments

The first word that came to my mind when I started thinking about writing the acknowledgements for this book was "patience," for which, first and foremost, I thank my husband, mate and first critic, Bijan Naderi. I thank him also for his love, support and sense of humor. Our children, Negar and Dara, were a constant source of inspiration; along with their partners, Jason Guedenis and Kelli Colman, they provided me with new insights gleaned over long discussions and debates about being young in America and about the role of imagination and culture in their lives. Bryce Nafisi Naderi has once again been my silent and gentle companion through the most painful as well as the most joyous hours of writing this book.

My brother, Mohammad Nafisi, as always, supported me and worried about my work. I am grateful for his insights and endless curiosity and for introducing me to his beloved Robert Bellah (*Habits of the Heart: Individualism and Commitment in American Life*). My thanks also to my niece, Sanam, and nephew, Sina, and my beloved friend Shahran (Shasha) Tabari.

I have always been fascinated by my close childhood friend Farah Ebrahimi's story and even tried unsuccessfully to integrate it into my last two books. Farah used to tease me about this. Neither one of us could have known, as we spent hours talking about our fascination with literature and the challenges we faced in life, that she would finally appear in this book, along with our favorite American hero, Huck Finn.

I would like to thank Farah's family, all of them storytellers in their own right, beginning with her wonderful children, Neda and Nema Semnani. (It was Neda's e-mail and my long phone conversation with her about her mother's shared fascination with Huck that convinced me to include Farah in this book.) Hamid, Farah's brother, generously offered his time and his own stories, at times more fantastic than the fictional works he and I both loved. And my friend Mahnaz Afkhami, Farah's sister and most trusted friend, was an enthusiastic supporter throughout the writing of this book. Despite having to resurrect at times painful memories, she generously gave a great deal of her time and allowed me to quote from her book *Women in Exile*. I am grateful for her careful and perceptive reading of the Huck chapter, for providing me with missing details and information and for her insights into Farah and her life. Mahnaz and I got into the habit of talking for hours on the phone, just as we both used to talk with Farah all those years ago about our passion for literature, our frustration with politics and our anxieties and love for our two homes, Iran and America. I also want to acknowledge other members of Farah's circle: her sisters-in-law Roshanak Semnani and Niloofar Ziaie Ebrahimi; Jaleh Behroozi, her friend, mate and comrade; Habib Lajevardi, her beloved second husband and Gholam Reza Afkhami, her good friend and brother-in-law.

Friends and family who suffered and supported me, inspired me and offered their company and comments: Ladan Boroumand and Abdi Nafisi, for many, many reasons (we will have a work-free vacation one of these days); Massumeh Farhad (hours of conversation on art and imagination) and Stanley Staniski (opening my eyes to southern art and photography); Roya Boroumand; Parvin, for her friendship, encouragement and unconditional love; Joanne Leedom-Ackerman; Sophie Benini Pietromarchi, my magical friend and collaborator on our children's book; and Valerie Miles, Jeff Brown and Gail Sinclair of Rollins College. I would also like to thank Michael Feldman, for his commitment to the Republic of Imagination; Carl Gershman, for introducing me to Bayard Rustin; and Amy Matthusen, for being a source of inspiration and for her classes at the Bronx Academy.

A conversation with Rose Styron at Dublin's Art for Amnesty event led to my almost obsessive interest in the relationship between William Styron and James Baldwin. I would like to thank Rose for igniting that spark and for generously offering her time and thoughts on the relationship between these two extraordinary writers and their work. Although this book ultimately could not do justice to that theme, conversations with Rose and my reading of Styron helped shape my thoughts on Baldwin, and I hope to return to this obsession later.

The School of Advanced International Studies at Johns Hopkins University has been my intellectual and academic home since I first moved to Washington, D.C., in 1997. I would like to thank the Foreign Policy Institute at SAIS and its director, Carla Freeman, for supporting my work and providing me with the space to write my books and pursue my passions; and Jessica Einhorn, the former dean of SAIS, and Vali Nasr, the current dean, for his friendship, unconditional support of my book and patience while I wrote it. My associate Leila Austin helped make the whole process of writing go smoother.

Especial thanks and gratitude go to my editor and friend Joy de Menil, who also edited *Reading Lolita in Tehran*. Joy believed in this book even when I doubted it. She showed admirable patience and understanding over a protracted period of time when I refused to hand in the manuscript and then again when I made constant changes, a trend that continues even as I write these lines. I am thankful for Joy's meticulous editing, her third eye of the imagination, her attention to the "divine details" that provide the secret ingredients books are made of and her dedication to doing everything right, all the way down to choosing the right font for the jacket—the kind of focus that comes only with passion and vision.

I would also like to thank Clare Ferraro, my publisher, and others at Viking and Penguin for their enthusiasm and their creative ways of helping this book come into the world: Paul Slovak, Kathryn Court, Nancy Sheppard, Carolyn Coleburn, Lindsay Prevette (my ever vigilant and thoughtful publicist), Kristin Matzen, the ever creative and supportive Winnie de Moya, Elda Rotor, Fred Huber and Alan Walker. I look forward to continuing our collaboration. My thanks to the ever understanding and meticulous Christopher Russell, Joy's associate editor, who helped in countless ways, finding files I had given up all hope of recovering and gently but persistently reminding me of broken deadlines and missing pieces, bringing calm and order to panic-stricken moments. In Veronica Windholz, my production editor at Viking, with whom I connected when writing *Reading Lolita in Tehran*, I found a passionate reader and dedicated guardian. My thanks also to Veronica's team for their meticulous reading and helpful comments: Will Palmer, whose copyediting sharpened and improved the book; Christopher Ross, Gabriel Cohen DeVries and Debbie Weiss Geline.

My thanks once more to Andrew Wylie and the Wylie Agency, especially to my agent, Sarah Chalfant, for her friendship, grace, patience, advice and fierce support of her authors. And to Jin Auh, Charles Buchan and Rebecca Nagel for their help and understanding.

Steven Barclay, my lecture agent and my good and trusted friend, I thank for his tender and subtle ways of supporting me during the difficult period of writing, for his honesty as a critic and for introducing me to Philippe Jaroussky, whose voice, along with those of Nina Simone, Bessie Smith and Janis Joplin, was my constant companion throughout the writing of this book. I also want to thank his colleagues at the agency, especially Sara Bixler, Kathryn Barcos and Eliza Fischer, for making life much easier during a difficult period.

From the moment I saw Peter Sís's magnificent adaptation of the Persian mystic poet Attar's *The Conference of the Birds* I wishfully hoped he would design the jacket for this book. I never dreamed that Peter would be generous enough to further grace the book with his illustrations. Despite a very busy schedule, including the creation of a tapestry in memory of the great poet Seamus Heaney for the Dublin airport and the publication of his own wonderful new book on Antoine de Saint-Exupéry, he spent an enormous amount of time, emotional energy and imagination in providing us with art for this book. I now cannot imagine this book without Peter's images, flying messengers that link our earthbound existence to the skies. He has given physical form to our Republic of Imagination. I would also like to thank Bill Shipsey, the founder of Arts for Amnesty and a passionate citizen of the Republic of Imagination, for introducing me to Peter and for his own infectious commitment and vision, which embodies both human rights and art.

My thanks to the Mason Library at Johns Hopkins University; the Gelman Library at George Washington University; the D.C. Public Library, especially my local West End branch and its wonderful librarian, William Turner; Bridge Street Books' Philip Levy and the rest of the team; and the Politics and Prose bookstore.

During the course of writing this book, I have benefited a great deal from a number of PBS programs, especially *American Masters, PBS NewsHour*'s reports on education and its series with Jeffrey Brown and former poet laureate Natasha Trethewey on the role of poetry in schools, and many fine documentaries on the civil rights movement and other aspects of American history.

I have also greatly benefited from various blog posts and articles on education and other matters, some of which I mention in the book. I started with *The Chronicle of Higher Education* and the insightful essays in *Declining by Degrees: Higher Education at Risk,* edited by Richard H. Hersh and John Merrow, and I read widely on the state of public schools and education in general. Diane Ravitch's always intriguing views, expressed in her blog and her latest book, *Reign of Error,* have helped a great deal in guiding my understanding of some of the challenges in educational policy.

The underlying concept for this book was first articulated

in a lecture at the Rome International Literary Festival in 2004, published in the festival catalog as "Loitering with Intent: The Subversive Power of Literature." A slightly different and more condensed version of this talk appeared in the Book World section of the December 5, 2004, *Washington Post,* entitled "The Republic of the Imagination," and I have been building on this concept ever since. A version of the story of my becoming an American, in chapter 1, was published in *The New Yorker*'s April 18, 2011, issue, under the title "Vagabond Nation."

## Note on Sources

This book is not a scholarly work of literary criticism. I had my eye on a certain destination, but rather than focus strictly on that destination, like Dorothy in the Land of Oz, I roamed and deviated from my course, meeting with unexpected allies and foes. I wandered from one field to another, intrigued by the associations between works of fiction and science, politics, technology, education, history and biography. Although for several years I had orgies of reading, both fiction and nonfiction, the books I depended on most were mainly biography and history; the rest helped me re-create the texture and feel of the times and events. Here I would like to acknowledge the biographies and works of history I have specifically relied on.

For Mark Twain, in addition to his own voluminous autobiographies, I relied on Susy Clemens, *Papa: An Intimate Biography of Mark Twain by His Thirteen-year-old Daughter Susy;* William Dean Howells, *My Mark Twain;* Lewis Lapham, "Mark

Twain and the Loss of American Courage," *Harper's*, April 2011; Fred Kaplan, *The Singular Mark Twain;* Justin Kaplan, *Mr. Clemens and Mark Twain: A Biography;* Toni Morrison's introduction to the Oxford edition of *Huckleberry Finn;* Roy Morris Jr., *Lighting Out for the Territory;* Ron Powers, *Mark Twain: A Life;* and Michael Shelden, *Mark Twain: Man in White: The Grand Adventure of His Final Years.*

For Sinclair Lewis: Grace Hegger Lewis, *With Love from Gracie;* Richard Lingeman, *Sinclair Lewis: Rebel from Main Street;* Mark Schorer, *Sinclair Lewis: An American Life;* James M. Hutchinson, *The Rise of Sinclair Lewis, 1920–1930;* Gore Vidal, "The Romance of Sinclair Lewis," *The New York Review of Books,* October 8, 1992; John Updike, "No Brakes," *The New Yorker,* February 4, 2002; and the *Selected Letters of Sinclair Lewis,* edited by John J. Koblas and Dave Page.

For Carson McCullers: Virginia Spencer Carr, *A Lonely Hunter: A Biography of Carson McCullers;* Josyane Savigneau, *Carson McCullers: A Life;* McCullers's *The Mortgaged Heart,* edited by Margarita G. Smith, and her *Illumination and Night Glare: The Unfinished Autobiography of Carson McCullers,* edited by Carlos L. Dews; Margaret B. McDowell, *Carson McCullers;* and Brooke Allen, "Emotional Vampire," *The New Criterion,* January 2000.

James Baldwin's books of essays (*Notes of a Native Son, The Fire Next Time, The Cross of Redemption, The Price of the Ticket*) were the most helpful guides to his life and fiction. In addition, I relied on the following as my main biographical sources: James Campbell, *Talking at the Gates: A Life of James Baldwin;* David Leeming, *James Baldwin: A Biography;* Douglas Field, *James Baldwin; Conversations with James Baldwin,* edited by Fred L. Standley and Louis H. Pratt; Magdalena J. Zaborowska, *James Baldwin's Turkish Decade: Erotics of Exile*; and Henry Louis Gates Jr. "The Fire Last Time," *The New Republic*, June 1, 1992.

On American history, apart from original documents and books, I have relied mainly on the works of Joseph J. Ellis and Gordon S. Wood on the American Revolution and the founding fathers. I am also indebted to Horace M. Kallen, *Culture and Democracy in the United States of America* (with thanks to Leon Wieseltier); David McCullough, *The Greater Journey: Americans in Paris;* Ronald C. White Jr., *A. Lincoln: A Biography;* Drew Gilpin Faust, *This Republic of Suffering: Death and the American Civil War;* and James McPherson, *Battle Cry of Freedom*. On literary America at the beginning of the twentieth century, I have used, among others, Malcolm Cowley's *Exile's Return: A Literary Odyssey of the 1920s;* Frederick J. Hoffman, *The 20's: American Writing in the Postwar Decade;* and *H. L. Mencken's* Smart Set *Criticism,* edited by William H. Nolte.

Finally, I would like to acknowledge my present hometown of Washington, D.C. Although the city is defined mainly by its politics and the presence of its most temporary residents, the policy makers, I have come to appreciate it for very different reasons, ones that have been essential to the writing of this book. The three National Endowments—for Democracy, the Arts and the Humanities—to my mind embody the real spirit of D.C. I have enjoyed tracing American history through the city's historical monuments and observing how they blend in with and complement the great cultural, civic, and scientific institutions: the Library of Congress, the Folger Theatre and Folger Shakespeare Library, the Smithsonian museums, the

Shakespeare Theatre Company, and the Kennedy Center— all enduring monuments to a different kind of civic patriotism, testaments to a love and appreciation not just of American history and culture but of the irreversible way it is linked to the rest of the world.